S0-ENV-708

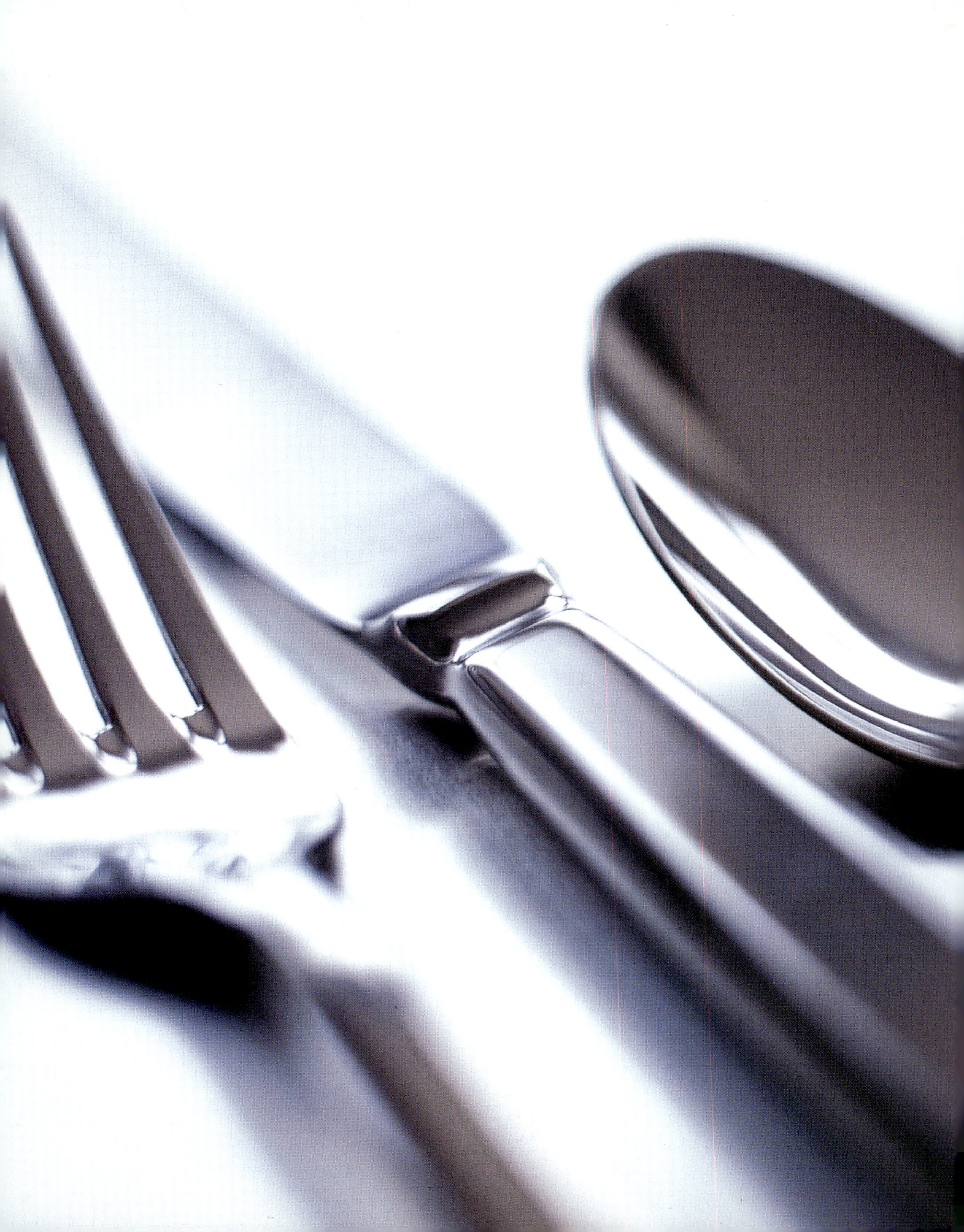

A COOKBOOK CREATED IN
THE HOMES OF CELEBRITIES

RECIPES AND TEXT DEVELOPED BY

HARRY SCHWARTZ

STAR GRAZING

Based Upon The TV Show Chef Harry & Friends

EDITED BY

DEBORA DEMAREST

jsa
communications

Star Grazing Created by **HARRY SCHWARTZ**
Recipes and Text Developed by **HARRY SCHWARTZ**

Editor: DEBORA DEMAREST

Associate Editor: MARTY JEFFCOCK

Creative Director: HOWARD MAAT

Book Designer: AMPARO DEL RIO

Book Layout and Production: amparodesign.com

Additional Design: LINDA BIRCH, LEAH MARKOS AND REBECCA ROGERS

Chef Harry Cover Photography: RONI RAMOS

Food Photography: LORI EANES

Food Photography Assistant: PAT MAZZERA

Food Stylist: ANDREA LUCICH

Food Stylist Assistant: EDWIGE GAMACHE

Still Photography: EDDIE GARCIA

Recipe Testing: SASHA MARTINUS

Recipe Tasting: The Celebrities and TV Viewers!

Chef Harry's Publicist: JOHN BLANCHETTE

PUBLISHER:

JSA Communications

www.jsacom.com

925.283.5525

Chief Executive Officer: JEFF STERN

President: BARRY FREILICHER

ISBN 0-9700989-0-1

Printed in: Hong Kong through GLOBAL INTERPRINT, INC.

©2000 JSA Communications

DEDICATION

THE MOST IMPORTANT

element in anything that I have been able
and lucky enough to accomplish is faith. My faith in
God, and the reassurance and spiritual calm I get from my faith
allowed me to reach this far in life and has yielded countless blessings.
Thank you, God, for all of the greatness in my life.

FOR MY FAMILY

My mother is a woman of the heart. She loves, teaches, nurtures, encourages, and shares with me with every breath she takes. I owe her everything. ■ My wife of 20 years, Laurie, is the ultimate soul mate. I did not know how much being loved by a woman could mean until she loved me. She gave me the courage to accomplish my goals. I marvel at her ability as a mother, which has allowed me to focus on my career. My days and nights would be empty without Laurie. And she gave me my precious daughter. ■ Alexa has taught me the true meaning of love. She inspires me to be the best that I can be and amazes me with her existence. I love her more than words could ever express. She makes everything matter. To the three most important people in my life: thank you for your love! ■ My father taught me a lot about business. The most important thing I learned from him is that anything worth having takes a lot of hard work. I thank him for showing me what it really takes. ■ And thank you to Harry Galinsky, a wonderful father to me in his own gentle and generous way.

FOR MY COLLEAGUES

I am lucky to be doing what I love to do. It is not an easy road and I could never have traveled it without a great deal of "roadside assistance." My publicist, John Blanchette, follows me like a shadow. He guides me, cares for me, and repairs the crashes. He has helped me realize my dream. ■ My production and culinary associate, Sasha Martinus, is invaluable. We share the vision. Thank you to her wonderful family, Vikki, Jimmy, Jeanie Rose, and Seth, for sharing her with me. When I get on camera and make it look easy, it is because Sasha has done the hard part. She puts up with me and is a tireless and immeasurable help.

Thank You All!

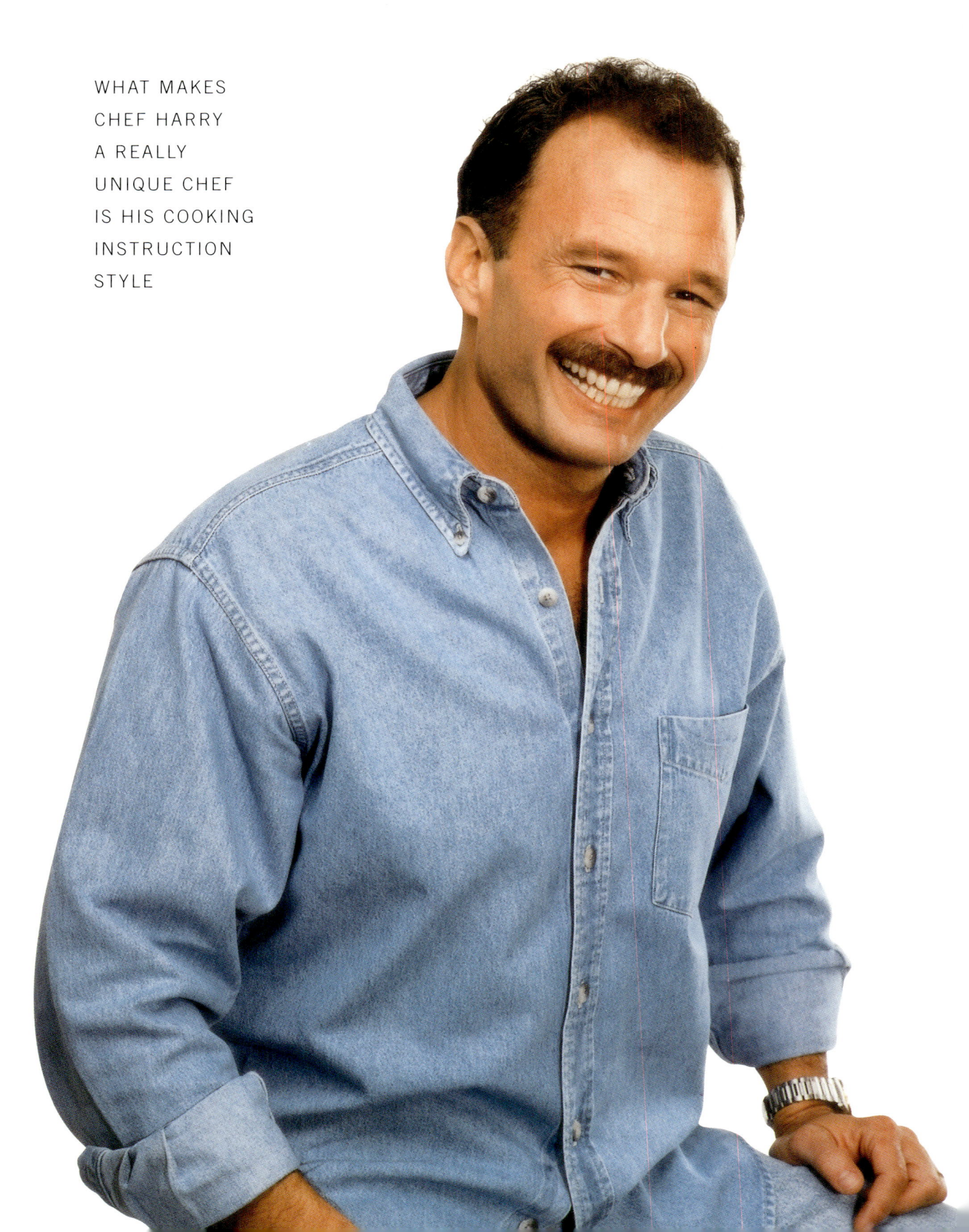

WHAT MAKES
CHEF HARRY
A REALLY
UNIQUE CHEF
IS HIS COOKING
INSTRUCTION
STYLE

MEET CHEF HARRY

Can you believe Chef Harry began his professional life far from the kitchen? Hailing from Iowa, Harry Schwartz found that his Grinnell College and Harvard Business School education were excellent preparation for an entrepreneurial career. After becoming CEO of a Tulsa-based scrap metal company, Harry quickly learned that while he was great at business, his true home and heart were in the kitchen, cooking for family and friends.

Harry's passion for food inspired Back Bay Gourmet, an eclectic Tulsa restaurant and catering business, which he and his wife Laurie founded in 1986. Next up in Harry's culinary life was his first cookbook, *Easygoing Entertaining, The Harry's Wild about You Cookbook*. Publication of that cookbook was quickly followed by an appearance on the *Today Show*. Harry's casual cooking style and sense of humor proved a hit, and he became a *Today Show* regular, demonstrating his unique cooking techniques and easy-to-make recipes.

Shortly after his first *Today Show* appearance, Harry started his popular Public Television Show, *Chef Harry & Friends*, on PBS. Today—in his spare time—Harry is also a regular on CBS Los Angeles, where he is known as the "Food Guru," writes syndicated newspaper features for Copley News Service, and serves as a culinary spokesperson for many corporations.

The inspiration behind *Star Grazing* is Harry's Public Television Show *Chef Harry & Friends*. He is excited to share with his viewers and cooking enthusiasts this collection of recipes developed especially for his celebrity guests and their friends. Harry's recipes emphasize the fun of cooking and a fabulous variety of tastes—perfect for today's Renaissance person, who often has little time to cook but likes to eat a variety of dishes.

For more Chef Harry recipes, we invite you to visit his web site: www.chefharry.com. Log on—he loves visitors!

STAR GRAZING, the companion cookbook to the popular *Chef Harry & Friends* PBS series, offers the best from his one-of-a-kind cooking show. You're treated to a front-row seat as Harry chats with fascinating celebrities and then goes into their kitchens to cook up a meal they've specially requested. Also on the menu is an up-close and personal "cook's tour" of their beautiful homes. The imaginative recipes in *Star Grazing* are adapted from Chef Harry's show and other special celebrity events. Each chapter is based on a different theme. Flip through this book and you'll find recipes from Italy, Asia, and the Deep American South, as well as inspired ideas for vegetarian meals—and even lazy lunches! Each recipe reflects Harry's personal cooking style—easy-to-cook and tasty meals your family and friends will love. Chef Harry designed this cookbook so all these recipes mix and match—it's as easy to put together an enticing buffet as a quick family supper. *Star Grazing* also introduces a new feature from Chef Harry—Kitchen Klips—short-cut cooking and kitchen ideas. So go for it—let *Star Grazing* add a little spice to your cooking life!

A COOKBOOK CREATED IN THE HOMES OF CELEBRITIES

CONTENTS

QUICK MISO SOUP GINGERED CRAB PUFFS CHICKEN SESAME LETTUCE WRAPS SHIITAKE MUSHROOM BOXES COOLIO'S SPECIAL SATAY TUSCAN BREAD SALAD MARINATED ARTICHOKES BRUSCHETTA SICILIAN EGGPLANT BRUSCHETTA PORTUGUESE MUSSEL POT ROSEMARY GRILLED LAMB CHOPS GARLIC CRUSTED TROUT PASTA CARBONALFREDO BAYOU GREENS AND DIJON VINAIGRETTE SALAD MEDLEY POACHED SCALLOP SEVICHE CAJUN DRIED SHRIMP OYSTERS FLORENTINE SOUTHERN STYLE CRAB CAKES WINTER SQUASH SOUP WHITE RADISH SALAD LENTIL AND CORN CHUTNEY TOFU LASAGNA ROSEMARY ROASTED WINTER VEGETABLES TORTILLA SOUP YELLOW TOMATO SALSA MUY PICANTE SALSA TOMATILLO SALSA PAPAYA SALSA QUESO FUNDIDO SHREDDED BEEF AND BRIE TOSTADAS BORDEAUX OLIVE PÂTÉ DUNGENESS CRAB SUMMER ROLLS COBB SALAD SMOKED SALMON CAKES PEPPER

EASY food to prepare

CHAPTER 1
ASIAN INFLUENCE

Quick Miso Soup 18

Gingered Crab Puffs 18

Chicken Sesame Lettuce Wraps 20

Shiitake Mushroom Boxes 21

Coolio's Special Satay 23

Peanut Coconut Dipping Sauce 23

Lemongrass Beef 24

Oyster Mushroom Duck with Jasmine Tea Pancakes 25

Coconut Crusted Snapper 26

Tzatziki 26

Smoked Chicken with Rice Noodles and Spicy Peanut Sauce 27

Rickshaw Duck Fried Rice 28

Pineapple Glazed Spareribs 29

Pepper Dusted Shrimp Tempura 30

Sesame Scallion Sauce 30

Pineapple Yam Cakes 31

Japanese Cucumber Salad 31

Mandarin Orange Angel Cake Pudding with Caramel Sauce 32

Fruits over Vanilla Bean Ice Cream 32

CHAPTER 2
MEDITERRANEAN MELLOW

Grilled Artichoke Antipasto 38

Tuscan Bread Salad 39

Marinated Artichoke Bruschetta 39

Sicilian Eggplant Bruschetta 40

Portuguese Mussel Pot 40

Rosemary Grilled Lamb Chops with Mediterranean Salsa 42

Garlic Crusted Trout 44

Pasta Carbonalfredo 44

Basil Shrimp Scampi 45

Benevenuto Swordfish and Brown Rice 45

Basil Cheese Stuffed Manicotti 46

Garlic Crusted Pork Chops with Apricot Chutney 47

Lemon Cake with Strawberry Sauce 49

Citrus Sorbet 50

Venetian Coffees: Café Chocolate, Brandied Coffee 51

CHAPTER 3
SOUTHERN STYLE

Bayou Greens and Dijon Vinaigrette 56

Salad Medley with Warm Pecan Dressing 56

Poached Scallop Seviche 59

Cajun Dipped Shrimp 59

Oysters Florentine with White Truffles 60

Southern Style Crab Cakes 60

Tennessee Whiskey Chicken Cutlets 61

Red Currant Barbecued Ribs 62

Shellfish Gumbo 63

Hazelnut Grouper 65

Southern Comfort Chicken 66

Caramelized Greens and Onions 67

Blue Grass Pasta 68

Black-Eyed Peas and Beans 69

Orange Sesame Yam Pudding 69

Quick Ginger Pecan Pie Crust 70

Coconut Custard Pie 71

Sweet Potato Pie 71

CHAPTER 4
VERY VEGETARIAN

Winter Squash Soup 76

Pumpkin Soup in Pumpkin Bowls 76

White Radish Salad 77

Thrice Cooked Artichokes 78

Lentil and Corn Chutney 79

Quick Tofu Lasagna 80

Rosemary Roasted Winter Vegetables 80

Vegetable Egg Foo Young 81

Fettuccine with Toasted Walnut Sauce 83

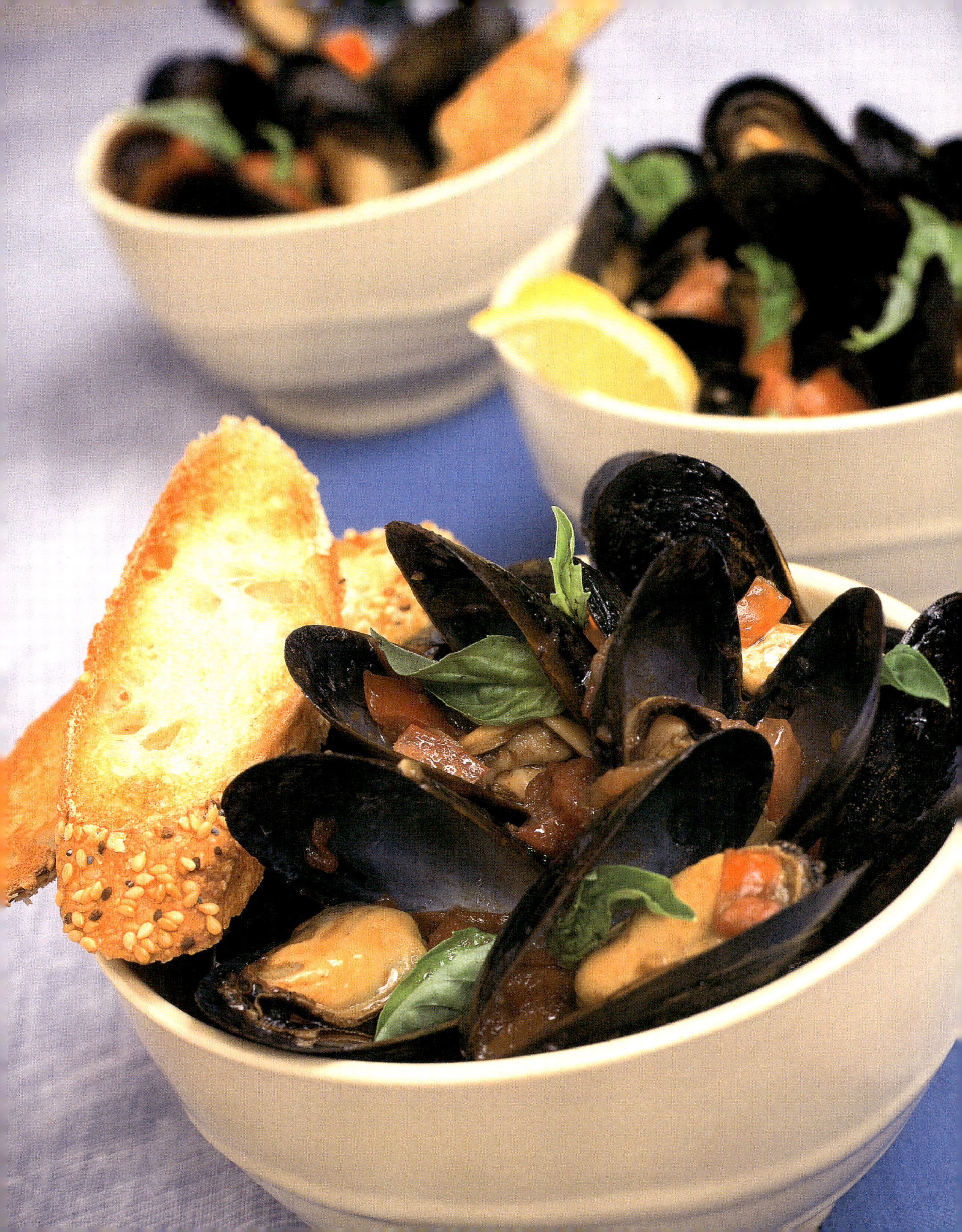

Easy Soy Burger 83

Balsamic Grilled Veggies 84

Pasta à la Melanzane 84

Grilled Eggplant 86

Toasted Tofu and Friends 86

Caramelized Brussels Sprouts 87

Mom's Kasha 87

Cashew Brown Rice 88

Cream Cheese Brownies and Raspberry Sauce 88

Tequila Drenched Fruit 90

Ginger Baked Apples 90

Quick Warm Caramel Sauce 91

Date Granola Shake 91

CHAPTER 5

LATIN LOVERS

Tortilla Soup 96

Muy Picante Salsa 98

Yellow Tomato Salsa 98

Harry's Salsas: Tomatillo Salsa, Papaya Salsa 99

Quick and Cheesy Jalapeño Roll-Ups 100

Crab Firecrackers 101

Shooter Shrimp 101

Queso Fundido 103

Shredded Beef and Brie Tostadas 104

Cha-Cha Carrot Mango Salad 105

Baked Stuffed Langosta 107

South-of-the-Border Posole 108

Chilaquiles 109

Jumping Refried Beans 110

Brown Rice Latin Style 110

Chocolate Cheese Flan 111

Patricia's Chocolate Ecstasy 112

Chef Harry's Frozen Margaritas: Plain, Watermelon, Raspberry 113

CHAPTER 6

LAZY LUNCHES

Jesse James Soup 118

Bordeaux Olive Pâté and Herb Toasts 119

Dungeness Crab Summer Rolls 121

Curried New Potatoes with Caviar 122

Chopped Cobb Salad 123

Smoked Salmon Cakes with Caviar Cucumber Chutney 124

Citrus Scallop Salad 125

Corned Beef and Cabbage Reuben 126

Thousand Island Dressing 126

Elegant Chicken Salad 127

Fettuccine with Roasted Vegetables 128

Egg Salad "90265" 129

Red and White New Potato Salad 131

Poached Salmon with Ginger Garlic Chutney 132

Grapefruit Cake with Pineapple Frosting 133

Ginger Lemon Tarts 134

CHAPTER 7

COMFORT CUISINE

Farmer's Cottage Cheese 140

Yatze Schmear 140

Brooklyn Potato Latkes 141

Loaded Potato Skins 142

Grilled Pepper Steak 143

50s Meatloaf and Toasted Scallion Mashed Potatoes 144

Traditional Turkey 146

Garlic and Chive Mashed Potatoes 146

Grandma's Corn Bread Dressing 147

Cranberry Citrus Relish 147

Veggie Egg White Omelet 148

Roasted Chicken Potato Pie 149

Roasted Rosemary Chicken 149

Cheese Soufflé in a Pan 150

Quick Pickled French Green Beans 150

Pecan Garlic Spinach Sauté 152

Black Bottomed Lemon Meringue Pie 153

Berry Peach Crumble 154

Brown Rice Custard 156

Barry's Irish Coffee 156

Spiced Citrus Cider 157

CHAPTER 8

SIMPLY SCANDINAVIAN

Bergen Shellfish Soup 162

Alderwood Smoked Salmon Salad 162

Chopped Herring 163

Crawfish and Wild Rice Salad 163

Potato Pea Soup 164

Salad of Pickled Beets 167

Cabbage, Apple, and Onion Salad 167

Fjord's Fish and Chips with Dilled Tartar Sauce 168

Sweet and Sour Swedish Meatball Stew 169

Country Meatloaf in Sour Cream Pastry 170

Danish Pancakes 173

Apple Almond Orange Loaf 173

Fruit Confit 174

Peach Ginger Muffins 174

Orange Almond Danish 175

CHAPTER 9

PARTY CENTRAL

Jazzy Cheddar Spread 180

Three Cheese Pâté with Toasted Leek 180

Peachy Salad in Poppy Seed Vinaigrette 181

Purple Asparagus Salad 181

Caesar Salad with Rosemary Croutons 183

Blue Cheese Wheat Tart with Caramelized Onions 184

Shrimp Toasts 186

Brie Topped with Peaches in Phyllo Pastry 186

Roasted Pepper Lasagna 187

Scalloped Potatoes with Pork Sausage 188

Maple Barbecued Pork 189

Seasoned Chicken Strips 190

Party Peanut Brittle 192

La Bohème Meringues 192

PARTY food

CHAPTER 1

ASIAN INFLUENCE

"IT'S A SMALL WORLD" IS A POPULAR SAYING. **And now this adage has become a part of all our lives, as global communication becomes even more of a way of life. The blending of culture and cuisine is one important result of our emerging global village. East has truly met West, and the demand for Asian food is on the upswing. Depending upon the country of origin, an Asian recipe might be created to emphasize contrasting food flavors, a spiritual influence, or even herbal ingredients to revitalize your Yin and Yang. Most Asian cultures believe that all your senses should partake in a meal—particularly your sense of touch. That's why there are so many finger foods (wraps, satays, pancake roll-ups). Until recently, most Americans thought that going to a restaurant for Asian food was the only way to experience this cuisine. After all, for a start, where do you buy the ingredients? And what exactly is miso, what is hoisin sauce, and so on? Well, get out your wok and see just how easy and fun it is to cook an Asian meal, especially following the recipes of the stars!**

> EAST HAS TRULY MET WEST, AND THE DEMAND FOR ASIAN FOOD IS ON THE UPSWING.

Now On to The
STARS

PERHAPS THE MOST UNIQUE and intriguing aspect of my TV show *Chef Harry and Friends* is that I really do cook in the kitchens of celebrities, not on a set. Coolio, one of today's hottest Rap vocalists, loves Thai food. He asked me to teach him how to prepare dishes with a Thai twist. And in another of my shows featuring Asian cuisine, I interviewed and cooked with the popular actress Julie Benz and her husband, actor John Kassir. ■ When I arrived at Coolio's home it was apparent that he's become a big hit. His expansive gated estate captures an exquisite panoramic view of Los Angeles. When you enter Coolio's house you can tell that it is a child-friendly home. Coolio has seven beautiful children. His wife, Josefa, a native Mexican, has tastefully decorated their home. A fountain based on the principle of Feng Shui reflects the couple's appreciation for the serenity of Asia. ■ Their commercially equipped kitchen is a perfect place to cook. Josefa explains, "As any wife and mom I spend a lot of time in the kitchen." Coolio adds, "Josefa makes awesome Mexican dishes. And even I make killer enchiladas." We cooked up some delicious Asian

We cooked up some delicious Asian dishes, and Coolio and Josefa informally served them to guests, among them family friend Ed McMahon.

ASIAN INFLUENCE 16

dishes, and Coolio and Josefa informally served them to guests, among them family friend Ed McMahon.

NEWLYWEDS' JULIE BENZ AND JOHN KASSIR'S love-nest offers a contrast to Coolio's family-style home. Julie starred in *Jawbreakers* and is best known for her role in *Buffy the Vampire Slayer*. Her husband John is the voice of the Crypt Keeper and is currently starring in the stage play *Reefer Madness*. He is slated to play the role of Shemp in the new Three Stooges film. ■ Julie and John's house radiates rustic warmth. Well-appointed with wood and cut stone, it is heated by two river-rock fireplaces and cooled by pacific breezes. Their roomy, fully equipped kitchen makes cooking a joy. ■ "We cook together a lot when we manage to get home at the same time," John comments. Julie adds, "One of our favorite kinds of foods to eat—and cook—is Asian." So we cooked up some easy-to-make Asian recipes. One of the best parts of my visit to Julie and John's home was eating in their two-story dining atrium, surrounded by vibrant gardens and rugged stone walls. The setting and Asian food both revitalized the spirit and nourished the body.

ASIAN INFLUENCE **17**

Quick MISO SOUP

Bring water to a simmer over heat. Place miso in a heat-proof cup and stir in just enough hot water to make a thin paste. Stir the miso paste and ginger into the water. Keep soup hot, but do not let boil.

Five minutes prior to serving the soup, place bean thread noodles in a strainer and run under hot water for 1 minute. Add noodles, spinach, basil, chives, and sesame seeds to soup and cook for 2 minutes. Place bean sprouts in bottom of presentation bowl(s) and ladle soup over sprouts. Serve with sesame hot oil if desired.

SERVES 6 TO 8

INGREDIENTS

- 6 to 8 cups water
- ½ cup dark miso
- 2 tablespoons minced fresh ginger
- 2 bundles of bean threads or rice noodles (about 2 ounces)
- 2 cups baby spinach
- 1 cup fresh basil
- ¼ cup chives, chopped finely
- ½ cup toasted sesame seeds
- 2 cups bean sprouts

Gingered CRAB PUFFS

INGREDIENTS

- 1 pound Dungeness, or similar, fresh crab meat
- ½ cup plain breadcrumbs
- 2 eggs, slightly beaten
- 2 tablespoons minced fresh garlic
- 1 tablespoon minced fresh ginger
- ¼ cup chives, chopped
- ⅛ cup minced fresh dill
- Salt and pepper to taste
- Butter for browning

Rinse and pick over crabmeat to remove any remaining shell. Drain well. Combine crab, breadcrumbs, and eggs. Add garlic, ginger, chives, dill, and salt and pepper. Mix thoroughly but gently.

Butter a heavy, nonstick skillet or griddle and heat over medium heat. When butter begins to turn golden, drop small spoonfuls of the crab mixture onto the pan and brown on both sides, turning gently.

MAKES ABOUT 24 CRAB PUFFS

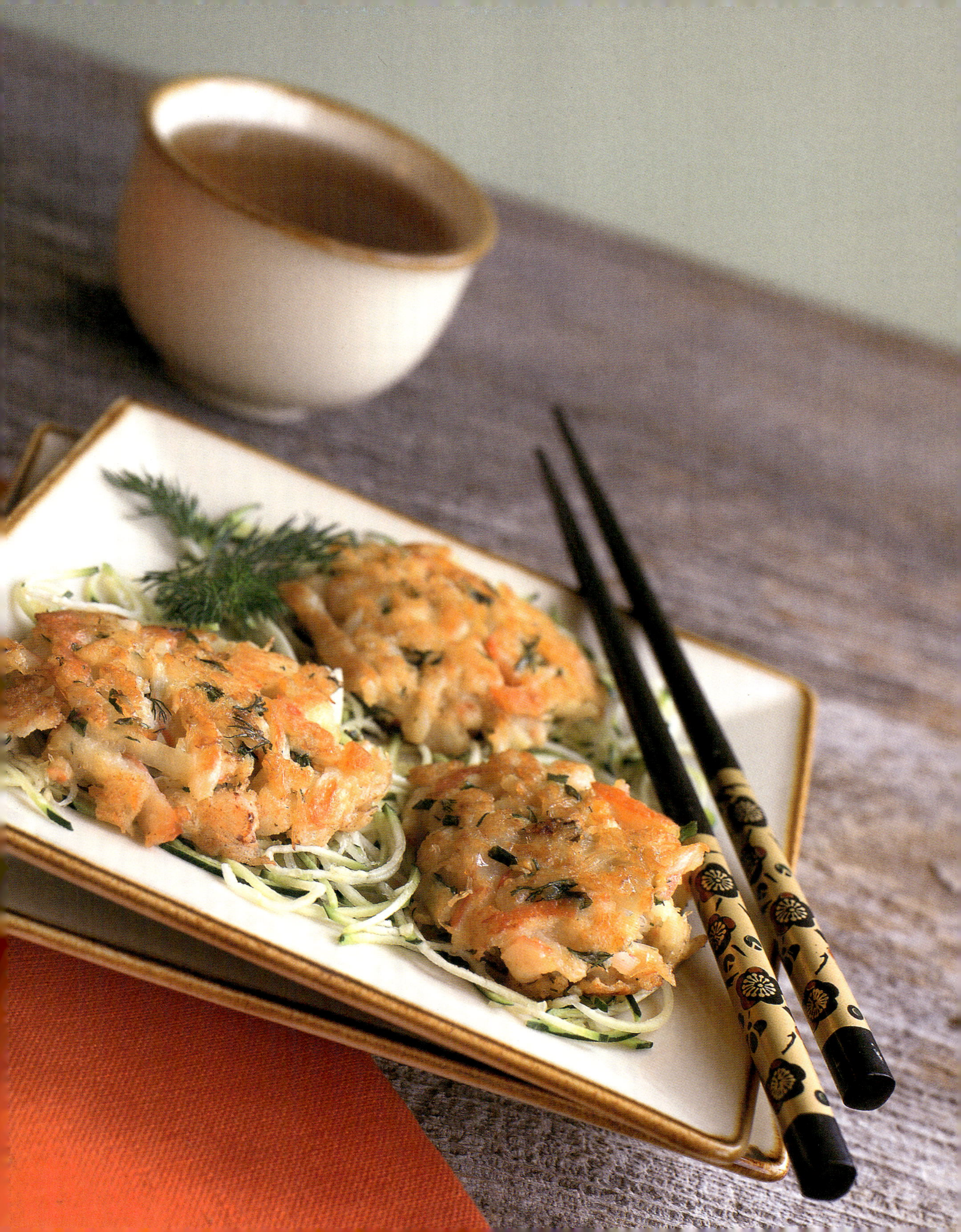

Chicken Sesame LETTUCE WRAPS

Sauté, while constantly stirring, the ground chicken in a nonstick wok or sauté pan over high heat until the meat is lightly browned. Add garlic and ginger and cook for 2 minutes.

Stir in pine nuts and sesame seeds, mixing until the pine nuts are lightly toasted. Remove cooking pan with the chicken and nut mixture from heat, and stir in soy, hoisin sauce, sesame oil, and scallions.

Either endive leaves or butter lettuce will serve as a base for this dish. If you're using butter lettuce, you can spoon in chicken mixture and then roll the leaf up for a wrap effect. If you use endive, scoop a tablespoon of the chicken on the leaf and pat down onto leaf. Both types of leaves make a great appetizer.

This dish can be served at room temperature, hot or cold.

SERVES 8 TO 10 AS AN APPETIZER;
4 IF YOU SERVE ON NOODLES AS A MAIN DISH

INGREDIENTS

- 1 pound ground chicken
- 3 tablespoons minced fresh garlic
- 3 tablespoons minced fresh ginger
- ¾ cup pine nuts
- ½ cup toasted sesame seeds
- 1 tablespoon soy sauce
- 8 ounces hoisin sauce
- ½ teaspoon sesame oil
- 1 cup finely minced scallions
- 18 to 24 endive leaves or butter lettuce leaves, rinsed and patted dry

Shiitake
MUSHROOM BOXES

Remove and discard the stems from the mushrooms. Rinse the mushroom caps quickly and pat dry. Chop coarsely. Heat the 1/8 cup butter in a large, heavy, nonstick sauté pan over medium high heat and stir in the garlic and shallots. Sauté 5 minutes. Reduce heat to medium and stir in mushrooms.

Sprinkle vermouth and soy sauce over the mushrooms and cook 2 minutes. Sprinkle flour over pan and stir while cooking for 90 seconds. Stir in heavy cream and sour cream and bring to a simmer. Stir in breadcrumbs and remove pan from heat.

Preheat oven to 350°.

Place one sheet phyllo pastry on worktop with long side facing you. Paint with melted butter and top with a second phyllo sheet. Paint the top of the second sheet.

When following the folding technique below, think of it as rolling up a burrito with a rectangular tortilla.

Place 1/10 of the mushroom filling in the middle of the short end of the pastry. Fold one-third of the length of the pastry lengthwise over the center. Paint the newly exposed third side with butter, and fold the top third of the pastry over that side. Paint with butter.

Roll the now enclosed rectangle of filling over and over to the end, creating a large, rectangular shape. Place in buttered nonstick jellyroll pan and repeat with the remaining ingredients, creating 10 "boxes." Paint the top of each box with butter. At this point, they may be refrigerated for up to 24 hours.

Bake in preheated 350° oven until puffed, crisp, and golden, about 25 minutes. Makes 10 boxes.

SERVES 8 TO 10 AS AN APPETIZER;
4 IF YOU SERVE ON NOODLES AS A MAIN DISH

INGREDIENTS

- 1 lb. shiitake mushrooms
- 1/8 cup butter
- 1 clove minced garlic
- 3 shallots, minced
- 1/3 cup extra dry vermouth
- 1 tablespoon soy sauce
- 1 teaspoon flour
- 1 cup heavy cream
- 1 cup sour cream
- 1 cup plain breadcrumbs (just buy them ready-made)
- 20 sheets phyllo pastry
- 1 stick butter, melted

KITCHEN KLIPS

Before you begin an Asian feast, consider sharpening your knives and organizing your counters to create lots of workspace. The more prepared you are before you begin, the more fun you will have in preparations!

ASIAN INFLUENCE

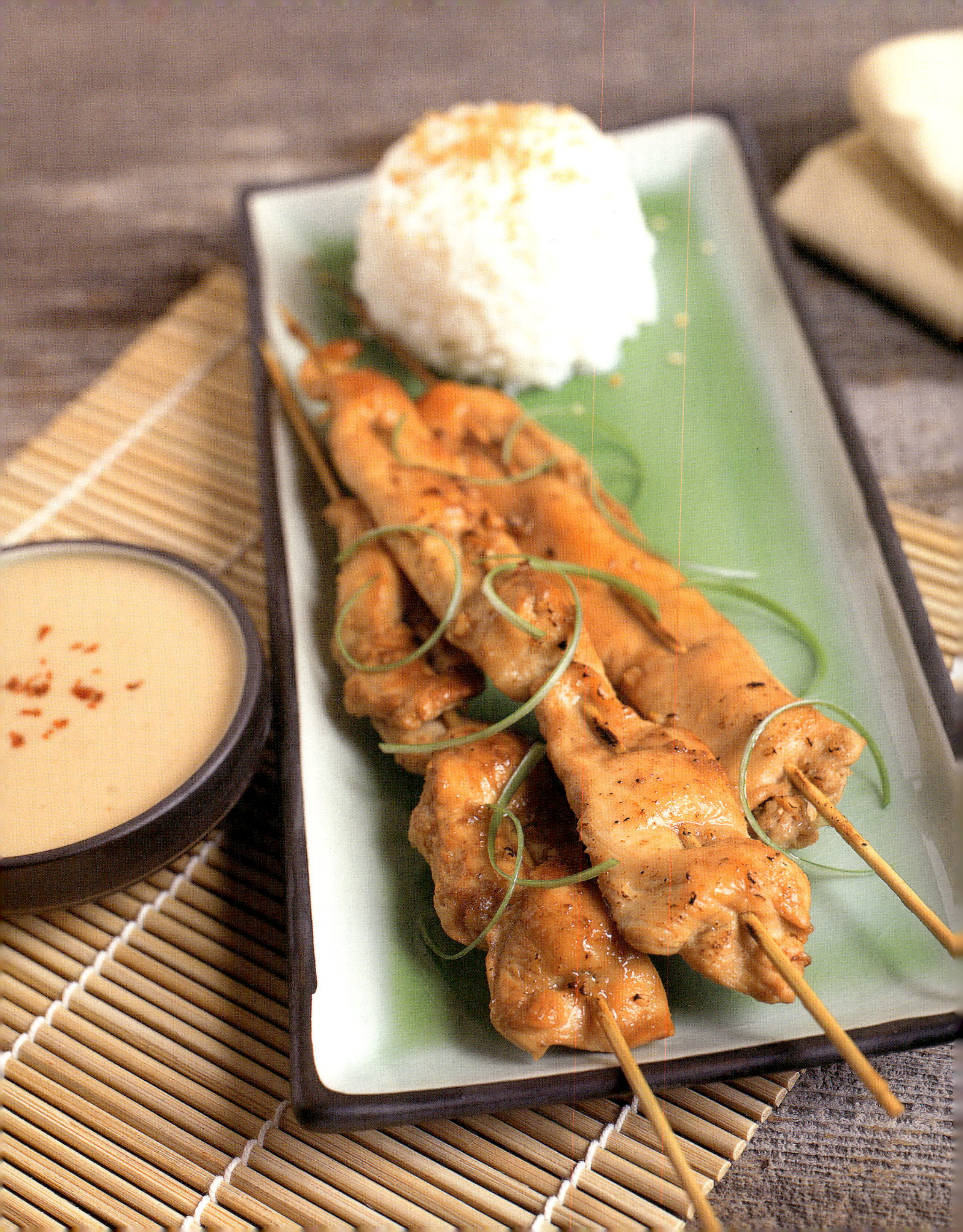

Coolio's Special SATAY

Cut the chicken into long strips. With a whisk, mix in a bowl soy sauce, garlic, ginger, cumin, curry, and lime juice. Pour this mixture over the chicken and toss well. Marinate several hours in refrigerator.

Skewer chicken, lengthwise, on bamboo skewers and place on a baking tray.

Drizzle coconut milk over chicken. Allow the chicken to absorb the milk, about 10 minutes.

Grill chicken skewers over hot coals, about 3-4 minutes per side, or broil in oven. Serve hot with Peanut Coconut dipping sauce. Makes about 16 satay sticks.

SERVES 8 TO 10 AS AN APPETIZER

INGREDIENTS

2 skinless boneless chicken breasts, slit down center into 4 halves

½ cup light soy sauce

1 tablespoon minced fresh garlic

1 tablespoon minced fresh ginger

1 tablespoon ground cumin

1 teaspoon, or to taste, of a mild curry powder

Juice from 2 limes

1 cup unsweetened coconut milk

Peanut Coconut DIPPING SAUCE

Stir coconut milk into peanut butter a little at a time until a smooth paste is formed.

Stir in remaining ingredients. Serve as a dipping sauce for Coolio's Special Satay or with any skewered food. Makes about 2 cups.

The rich and flavorful Peanut Butter Coconut Dipping Sauce is wonderful on almost anything coming off the grill!

INGREDIENTS

1 cup coconut milk

⅔ cup chunky peanut butter

1 tablespoon minced garlic

1 tablespoon minced ginger

⅛ cup soy sauce

1 tablespoon sesame oil

1 tablespoon Cognac

ASIAN INFLUENCE

Lemongrass BEEF

Preheat oven to 275°. Arrange onions in the bottom of a high-sided roasting pan that will accommodate brisket. Rinse brisket and lay on top of onions, fat side up. Pour water into pan and place bay leaves in water. Arrange garlic over the top and sprinkle with salt and pepper. Seal pan tightly with foil, and roast overnight (8-10 hours) in a 275° oven.

In the morning, cool roast and uncover. Remove meat and trim away remaining fat. Refrigerate until fully chilled.

Preheat grill to medium-high. Grill brisket for about 7 or 8 minutes per side, until meat is crisp and beginning to char on both sides. Meat should be on the dry side and falling apart.

Preheat oven to 250°. Cool beef for 10 minutes. Cut into 1-inch thick pieces, sliced across the grain to help beef to fall into shreds. Place beef in an ovenproof pan or casserole dish and toss with carrots and scallions. Keep beef casserole warm in a 250° oven while preparing glaze.

In a small saucepan over medium heat, gently stir together sugar, soy sauce, and water until sugar is dissolved. Bring mixture to a gentle boil, and reduce heat to maintain gentle boil. Cook for 10 minutes. Stir in ginger, garlic, and lemongrass. Cook for 2 additional minutes. Pour glaze over warm shredded beef and toss to evenly coat beef, carrots, and scallions. Serve hot over rice.

SERVES 6 TO 8

INGREDIENTS

2 large onions thickly sliced

1 5-7 pound beef brisket

4 cups water

2 bay leaves

2 cloves fresh garlic, sliced

1 tablespoon kosher salt

1 tablespoon fresh cracked pepper

2 cups shredded carrots

2 cups chopped scallions

2 cups sugar

$1/3$ cup soy sauce

$1/3$ cup water

$1/4$ cup minced fresh ginger

$1/4$ cup minced fresh garlic

1 tablespoon dried, shredded lemongrass

KITCHEN KLIPS

Check around local farmers' markets for veggies and fruit. They are usually a fresh produce bonanza for a bargain!

Oyster Mushroom **DUCK** with **JASMINE** Tea **PANCAKES**

The Filling

Cool the roasted duck until you can comfortably remove the meat from the bones. Remove meat from the duck. Shred duck meat by pulling it apart with 2 forks.

Heat peanut oil in a wok and stir-fry the scallions until browned. Stir in garlic, ginger, and soy sauce. Add 2 tablespoons of butter and the mushrooms. Stir-fry for 1 minute and add duck to pan, mixing well.

Fill Jasmine Tea Pancakes with duck mixture. Serve with sprouts and hoisin sauce.

The Pancakes

Whisk eggs and cream together. Slowly add a little of this mixture to the flour while stirring to create a smooth paste. Stir in the remaining cream and eggs, mixing well with the flour. Whisk in the tea.

Using the melted butter and a pastry brush, lightly butter a hot small crepe or sauté pan. Spoon in enough batter to coat the bottom of the pan, pouring any excess batter back into the bowl. Cook the pancake over medium-high heat, browning on one side.

Remove to a kitchen towel to cool. Repeat this process to create 12 to 16 thin pancakes.

Pancakes may be made in advance. Wrap each pancake separately in a sheet of plastic wrap, keeping flat. Freeze or refrigerate until ready to use. To warm for use, microwave or heat in tinfoil in warm oven.

SERVES 6 TO 8

The Roast Duck

Preheat oven to 300°. Place duck in a roasting pan. Drizzle about 3 tablespoons of olive oil over the bird and rub salt and pepper into skin. Place 3 whole peeled garlic cloves inside the cavity. Bake in a preheated 300° oven for 3 hours or until done and juices from duck run clear.

INGREDIENTS

THE FILLING

1 roasted duck (see below)

2 tablespoons peanut oil

1 bunch of scallions, trimmed and rinsed, cut into 2-inch lengths

2 tablespoons minced fresh garlic

1 tablespoon minced fresh ginger

1 tablespoon soy sauce

2 tablespoons butter

½ cup oyster mushrooms or mushrooms of your choice

Bean sprouts and hoisin sauce for garnish

THE PANCAKES

1 cup unbleached all purpose flour

2 eggs

½ cup heavy whipping cream

½ cup Jasmine tea (strongly brewed)

Melted butter

KITCHEN KLIPS

Whole or cut-up Peking duck from your favorite Chinese restaurant is a perfect way to simplify any recipe requiring roasted duck.

Coconut **CRUSTED SNAPPER**

Rinse and pat the snapper filets dry. Mix together egg, ginger, and soy. Soak the fish in this mixture for 15 minutes. Coat each piece with the coconut. Fry in butter in nonstick skillet over medium-high heat, turning pieces once, about 4 minutes per side. Fish is done when white throughout and coconut is toasted.

Serve with Tzatziki.

SERVES 6

INGREDIENTS

- 6 6-8 ounces fresh snapper filets
- 3 eggs, slightly beaten
- 2 tablespoons fresh minced ginger
- 1 teaspoon light soy sauce
- 2 cups unsweetened thread coconut (available at health food stores)
- 4 tablespoons butter (or margarine) for frying

TZATZIKI

Mix together sour cream, goat cheese, and yogurt until smooth. Stir in herbs, onion, cucumber, and lemon juice. Season with salt and pepper. Makes about 3 cups, serving 6 to 8 as a side dish or 12 as a refreshing dip with pita bread.

[*Leftover Tzatziki can be stuffed into a pita pocket with fresh greens for a wonderful lunch the next day!*]

INGREDIENTS

- 1 cup sour cream
- 6-8 ounces fresh goat cheese
- 1 cup plain yogurt
- ½ cup chopped fresh basil
- ½ cup chopped fresh parsley
- 2 tablespoons chopped fresh mint
- 1 tablespoon minced fresh tarragon
- ¼ cup minced white onion
- 1 cup chopped, seeded, and peeled fresh cucumber
- Juice from 2 lemons
- Salt and pepper to taste

Smoked **CHICKEN** with **RICE NOODLES** and Spicy **PEANUT SAUCE**

The Spicy Peanut Sauce

In a blender, mix the peanut butter, hoisin, soy, garlic, ginger, rice vinegar, and sesame and canola oils together until smooth and creamy. Combine cilantro leaves with the dressing and toss in the pasta to coat well.

Just before serving, toss with cooked and chilled smoked chicken breasts, fresh bean sprouts, and chopped peanuts.

SERVES 6 TO 8

The Smoked Chicken Breasts

Place all the ingredients (except wood chips) in a zip-lock bag and toss to marinate. Refrigerate up to 24 hours, turning the bag several times.

Heat up grill. Just before placing chicken on the grill, place soaked wood chips in a hot corner of the grill or in a wood chip box in the bottom of the grill. Cover and grill chicken over medium-hot coals until juices run clear, about 4 minutes per side.

Refrigerate chicken until cool. Slice thinly across the grain of the meat and then slice the thin slices again lengthwise as if to julienne. This will cause the chicken to fall into shreds.

INGREDIENTS

THE PEANUT SAUCE

2/3 cup smooth peanut butter

1 cup hoisin sauce

3 tablespoons soy sauce

2 tablespoons minced fresh garlic

2 tablespoons minced fresh ginger

1/4 cup seasoned rice vinegar

2 tablespoons sesame oil

1/4 cup canola oil

1/4 cup chopped cilantro leaves

1 pound cooked and cooled rice noodles, tossed in 1 tablespoon canola oil

2 smoked chicken breasts, shredded (see below)

4 ounces fresh bean sprouts, rinsed and drained

1 cup finely chopped salted peanuts

THE SMOKED CHICKEN

2 skinless, boneless chicken breasts

1/3 cup light soy sauce

1/3 cup extra virgin olive oil

1 tablespoon minced fresh garlic

1 tablespoon minced fresh ginger

1 pound sweet wood chips, such as apple, cherry, and/or sugar maple (soaked for at least one hour in water)

KITCHEN KLIPS

You can serve a stir fry of Chinese vegetables—bok choy, scallions, Napa cabbage—to balance the meal.

Rickshaw **DUCK FRIED RICE**

Preheat oven to 350°.

Heat peanut oil in a large wok or pan over high heat. Sauté onion and garlic for 3 minutes, and stir in cooked rice. Stir-fry to coat rice with oil for about 5 minutes. Add ginger and soy sauce to the wok.

Place the rice mixture in a lightly oiled roasting pan. Bake at 350° for 1 hour, stirring occasionally to toast rice.

Stir in remaining ingredients and serve hot.

SERVES 8 TO 12

INGREDIENTS

- 3 tablespoons peanut oil
- 1 large chopped white onion
- 2 tablespoons minced garlic
- 8 cups cooked brown or Jasmine rice
- 1 tablespoon minced ginger
- 1/8 cup soy sauce
- 1 tablespoon dried, shredded lemongrass
- 2/3 cup chopped fresh basil
- 1/2 cup chopped fresh mint
- 2 red bell peppers, finely chopped
- 1 cup chopped scallions
- 1 roast duck, meat and skin chopped (see page 25 for technique)
- 2 cups chunky pineapple pieces

Pineapple GLAZED SPARERIBS

The Ribs

Place ribs in a large pot of water and bring to a boil. Boil gently for about 40 minutes or until meat is cooked and tender but not falling away from the bone. Drain and cool. Mix together soy sauce, pineapple juice, garlic, and ginger. Marinate boiled ribs in mixture overnight.

Preheat oven to 275°.

Grill the ribs over medium coals until crisp and slightly dry, or smoke them in sweet wood smoke until brown and slightly dry. Remove ribs from grill or smoker and sprinkle with fresh cracked pepper as desired. Cool ribs and cut into individual ribs. Place ribs in uncovered roasting pan in preheated 275° oven uncovered while making glaze.

The Glaze

Heat sugar, lemon juice, and soy sauce in heavy saucepan over medium-high heat until mixture begins to simmer. Boil gently for 10 minutes. Stir in garlic and ginger, and simmer 2 minutes more. Stir in lemongrass and lemon zest. Remove from heat.

To Finish and Serve

Immediately pour glaze over ribs and toss to coat. Sprinkle with sesame seeds, if desired, and serve.

SERVES 8 AS AN APPETIZER OR 4 FOR DINNER

INGREDIENTS

THE RIBS

3 racks spareribs

¼ cup soy sauce

2 cups pineapple juice

¼ cup minced fresh garlic

¼ cup minced fresh ginger

Fresh cracked pepper to taste

THE GLAZE

2 cups granulated sugar

Juice from 2 lemons

⅛ cup soy sauce

¼ cup minced fresh garlic

¼ cup minced fresh ginger

1 tablespoon dried shredded lemongrass

1 tablespoon grated fresh lemon zest

Toasted sesame seeds for garnish, if desired

KITCHEN KLIPS

Asian dishes will have that wonderful crunch only if you use the freshest of produce. Don't use frozen or old vegetables. Substitute ingredients before you compromise quality!

Pepper Dusted SHRIMP TEMPURA

Make several superficial cuts lengthwise along the belly side of the shrimp so they will lay flat. Rinse and drain well.

To make the Tempura batter, mix together the flour and starch. In a separate bowl, slightly beat the egg and mix with the water. Quickly stir into the flour/starch mixture and set bowl into another larger bowl of ice to keep the batter cold. Batter should still be lumpy.

Mix together paprika and pepper in a separate bowl. Place oil in a wok or Dutch oven (about 4" deep). Heat oil to 350°.

Working with 4 or 5 shrimp at a time, dip them first into the paprika/pepper mixture for a quick dusting and then into the batter. Fry in oil about 2 minutes or until brown and crisp. Drain on paper towel and keep warm while frying the remainder. Serve with Sesame Scallion Sauce below. Eat as soon as possible!

SERVES 3 OR 4 AS AN ENTRÉE AND 6 AS AN APPETIZER

INGREDIENTS

- 1 pound large shrimp, shelled and deveined with tails on
- 1 cup unbleached, all-purpose flour
- 1/4 cup corn starch
- 1 egg
- 1 cup ice cold water
- 1/2 cup paprika
- 1 tablespoon ground white pepper or to taste
- peanut oil for frying

Sesame SCALLION SAUCE

Mix together ingredients and place in jar with tight fitting lid. Refrigerate until ready to use.

Shake before serving. Makes about 1 cup.

INGREDIENTS

- 1/2 cup seasoned rice vinegar (must be seasoned "sushi style" vinegar)
- 1/8 cup light soy sauce
- 1/4 cup toasted sesame seeds
- 1/8 cup minced fresh ginger
- 1 tablespoon minced fresh garlic
- 1/4 cup minced scallions

Pineapple YAM CAKES

Place the shredded yam, pineapple, and sesame seeds in a mixing bowl. Lightly beat the eggs and pour into the bowl with the yam mixture. Toss to mix well. With fork, mix in garlic, ginger, and soy sauce.

Heat a ½-inch thick layer of oil in the bottom of a large, heavy, nonstick sauté pan over medium-high heat. Using a tablespoon, drop small dollops of the mixture into the hot oil, flattening each one to create a 3-inch cake. When cakes appear brown and crisp on the bottom (about 5 minutes) and mostly cooked, turn the cake over to brown the other side, about 3-4 more minutes.

When each cake is completed, remove to paper towel-lined tray to drain. Place prepared cakes in warm oven until all pancakes are fried. Makes 12-16 small cakes.

SERVES 6 TO 8 AS A SIDE DISH

INGREDIENTS

- 1 large yam, peeled and grated, or shredded in food processor
- 1 15-ounce can crushed pineapple, drained and squeezed dry in a towel
- 2 tablespoons toasted sesame seeds
- 2 eggs
- 1 tablespoon minced fresh garlic
- 1 tablespoon minced fresh ginger
- 1 tablespoon soy sauce
- Peanut oil for frying

Japanese CUCUMBER SALAD

Peel the cucumbers and slice in half lengthwise. Run a spoon down the center to remove the seeds and slice cucumbers into thin "half-moon" shapes.

Combine the soy sauce, rice vinegar, sesame seeds, pepper, minced ginger, and sesame oil.

Pour over cucumbers. Let the cucumber salad marinate an hour or two.

SERVES 6 TO 8 AS A SIDE DISH

INGREDIENTS

- 2 English cucumbers
- 1 tablespoon soy sauce
- 1 cup seasoned rice vinegar
- ⅓ cup toasted sesame seeds
- Pepper to taste
- 1 tablespoon minced fresh ginger
- 1 teaspoon sesame oil

Mandarin Orange **ANGEL CAKE PUDDING** with Caramel Sauce

The Pudding

Preheat oven to 350°.

Put sugar, butter, and cream in a small, heavy saucepan over medium heat. Stir until butter and sugar melt and the mixture begins to simmer. Simmer 5 minutes, stir in vanilla, and pour sauce into the bottom of a deep 10"x14" (lasagna-sized) baking dish. Arrange cake pieces on top of sauce and sprinkle orange sections among the cake pieces.

Beat together the eggs, milk, and almond extract and pour over the cake. Press cake down gently to help it absorb the liquid. Bake in preheated 350° oven until set and browned on top. Cool on rack while making the sauce.

The Caramel Sauce

Put sugar, butter, and cream into a small, heavy saucepan over medium heat. Stir until the butter and sugar melt and the mixture begins to simmer. Simmer 10 minutes and stir in Amaretto liqueur. Remove from heat.

To Serve

Scoop out warm servings of pudding and drizzle with Amaretto sauce.

INGREDIENTS

THE PUDDING

2 cups brown sugar

1 stick butter, cut into chunks

$^2/_3$ cup heavy whipping cream

1 teaspoon vanilla extract

1 angel food cake, torn into bite-sized pieces

2 cups mandarin orange sections, drained

4 eggs

2 cups milk

1 teaspoon almond extract

THE SAUCE

2 cups brown sugar

1 stick butter, cut into chunks

$^2/_3$ cup heavy whipping cream

$^1/_8$ cup Amaretto liqueur

Fruits over **VANILLA BEAN** Ice Cream

Mix ingredients together in a heavy saucepan and bring to a simmer over medium-high heat. Reduce heat just to maintain simmer. Simmer until fruits appear tender. Cool to warm and serve over vanilla bean ice cream. Sauce keeps up to 5 days in the refrigerator.

SERVES 6 TO 8

INGREDIENTS

1 pineapple, cut up into small chunks

1 cup dried apricots

1 cup dried mango

1 cup dried cherries

1 cup orange juice

1 cup sugar

1 cup sweet vermouth

Vanilla ice cream

ASIAN INFLUENCE

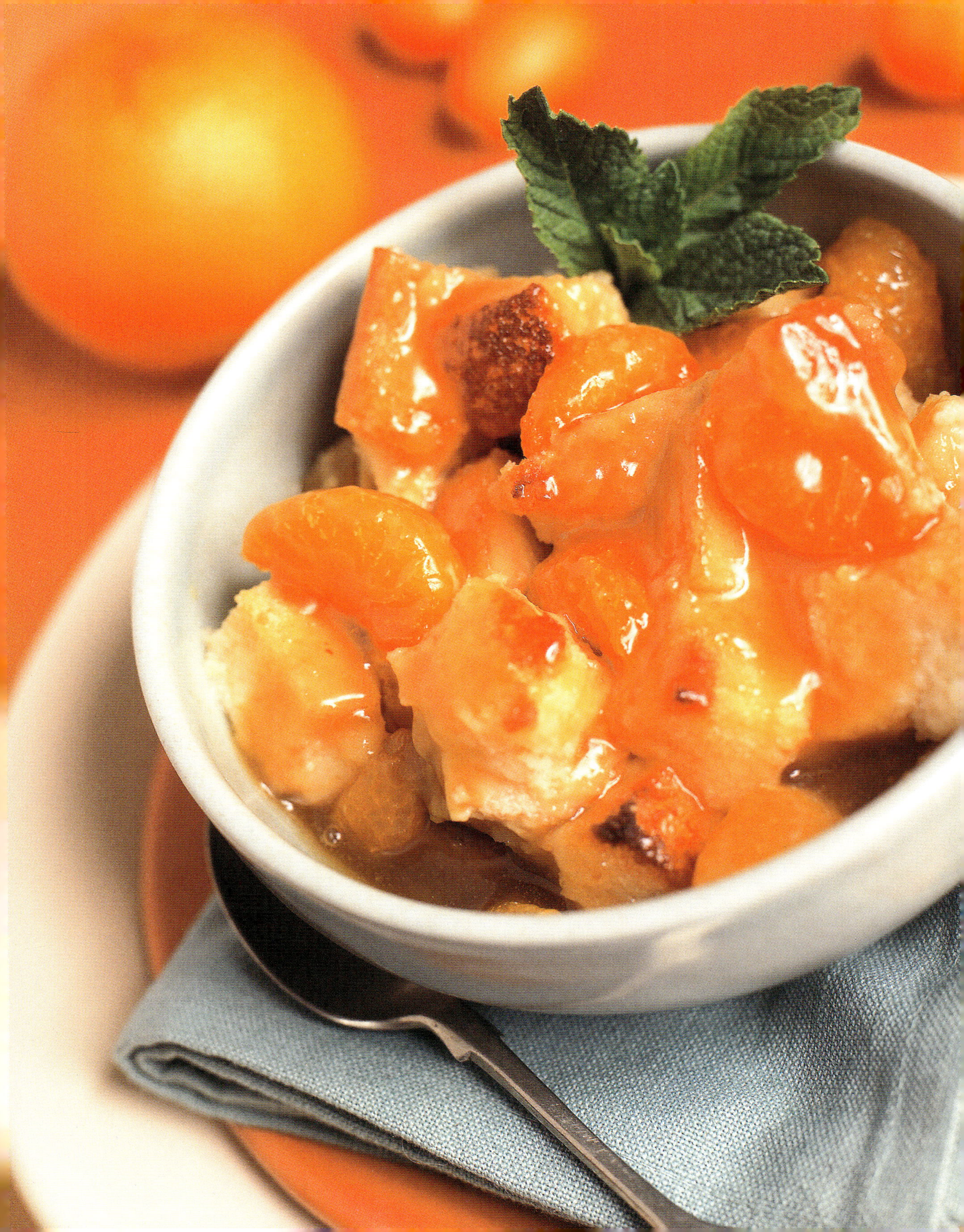

CHAPTER 2

MEDITERRANEAN
MELLOW

ONE OF MY FAVORITES IS MEDITERRANEAN CUISINE—I love the aromas when you cook with olive oil and garlic, the flavors that melt in your mouth, and the crunch of really good Italian bread dipped into a succulent sauce. Partaking of a Mediterranean meal is like tasting a bit of heaven. The Mediterranean is vast, its waters touching countries ranging from Spain, Italy, France, and Greece all the way to Israel, Lebanon, Tunisia, and Morocco. The history and evolution of Mediterranean cuisine is as diverse as its people. They relied on what the land offered them to prepare their meals. For example, the limited amount of pastureland in the Southern Mediterranean made it impossible to raise larger animals, such as cows, for meat. Thus smaller animals—pigs, sheep, and goats—became the primary meat sources. The Northern regions were a contrast, offering rich grazing land for herds of cattle, which in turn yielded milk, butter, and creamy cheeses. And in all the Mediterranean countries greens, wild mushrooms, fish, and game were bountiful, providing the stock ingredients for a variety of dishes. While each of these regions has developed a unique cuisine, they all offer simple, delectable food that embraces the wonder of the land and the sea and the warmth of the people. To capture the true character of a Mediterranean recipe, try to cook with the regional olive oils and squeeze a fresh lemon or lime for added zest. Also, remember that fresh is best: whenever possible, use fresh garlic, basil, and parsley. And bear in mind that this is food to be savored—you never rush a meal while dining in the Mediterranean. Your host will say to you, "Please sit, take a little wine, eat—enjoy your meal. Buon appetito!

> **PARTAKING OF A MEDITERRANEAN MEAL IS LIKE TASTING A BIT OF HEAVEN.**

Now On to The
STARS

WHEN I LEARNED THAT I would have the opportunity to interview film and TV star Linda Hamilton for *Chef Harry & Friends*, I immediately chose Mediterranean cuisine because Linda loves fresh seafood and mushrooms. Soon after, actor David Leisure was slated to appear on my show. Now, he truly is a star who likes Italian! ■ Not only is Linda a well-known and respected actress (the *Terminator* movies, *Dante's Peak*, TV's *Beauty and the Beast*), but she is a dear and treasured family friend. Linda is also a very private person and doesn't usually do promotional media. She was clearly hesitant about bringing "show business" into her home, but after some thought, she agreed to open her kitchen to us. ■ "My home is where I put on my favorite and oldest sweatshirt, and don't worry about makeup," Linda explains. "But, Harry, since I am helpless in the kitchen, I will look at this experience as a private "Mediterranean 101" cooking class in my kitchen!" ■ Linda's home is a reflection of her persona—beautiful, warm, and appealing. Her Mediterranean ranch house is large and very comfortable, with little Hollywood glitz. You want to sink right into the heavenly soft pillows resting on her overstuffed sofas. ■ Her kitchen offers rich golden wood cabinetry, large refrigeration units, a center workstation and a peninsula gas cooktop with four burners and a large gas grill. The commercial stainless steel hood over the stove is decorated with her children's notes and drawings, a very homey touch. Nearby is a comfortable eating area that opens onto a Mediterranean-style courtyard. ■ As the cameras started to roll, Linda appeared in the kitchen.

Linda's home is a reflection of her persona—beautiful, warm, and appealing.

MEDITERRANEAN MELLOW

She came off just as she is: charming, funny, talented, and a genuinely wonderful person.

DAVID LEISURE WAS MY NEXT CELEBRITY CRAVING A taste of Mediterranean cooking. David, perhaps best known for his role as the wacky neighbor on "Empty Nest," has a very different home than you'd expect. His wife Patty and daughter Madison have filled their contemporary Mediterranean house with family mementos. Photos of parents, grandparents, and great-grandparents complement an antique heirloom sofa and chair. ■ The Leisures' kitchen, with marble floors and warm maple cabinets, opens onto a wonderful family room. Beyond its French doors is a stunning backyard. ■ "This was just rough land when I bought this house. I couldn't wait to get dirty hands and create an imprint on my land," David comments. ■ Cooking with David was a blast. He is funny, charming, and warm all at the same time. He may enjoy joking around, but most of all he believes, "It's family that matters."

MEDITERRANEAN MELLOW **37**

Grilled ARTICHOKE Antipasto

To Boil the Artichokes

Trim stems from artichokes so that they are about 3/4 of an inch long. Squeeze the lemon juice into the water and drop in the lemon halves and artichokes. Boil until they are tender. (A good way to judge is if you can easily insert the tip of a knife an inch or two into the stem.) Remove artichokes from boiling water and rinse under cold water. Cut artichokes in half through the stem and remove hairy chokes from center by scraping out with a teaspoon.

To Grill the Artichokes

Mix together the olive oil, garlic, and soy and season with pepper. Toss with artichoke halves and grill over medium-hot coals until they are very tender and tips are slightly charred. Sprinkle with fresh cracked pepper as they come off the grill.

To Grill the Marinated Peppers

Mix together the olive oil, garlic, and soy and season with pepper. Toss with peppers and grill over medium-hot coals until tender and skin blisters, about 2 minutes per side.

To Toast the Pine Nuts

In a sauté pan over medium-high heat, heat the oil and in it sauté the garlic and pine nuts until pine nuts begin to toast and turn golden brown. Remove from heat immediately and cool. Pine nuts burn quickly!

To Assemble the Antipasto

Arrange artichokes on a serving platter with salami and peppers. Arrange cheese over the top. Dot with olives and sprinkle with pine nuts. Drizzle balsamic vinegar over the top as a finishing touch. Serve with crusty bread or herbed flat bread.

SERVES 8 AS AN APPETIZER

INGREDIENTS

- 4 large artichokes or 8 baby ones, boiled, split, and grilled (see below)
- 8 ounces thinly sliced Genoa salami
- 4 grilled and marinated red peppers (see below), sliced
- 8 ounces thinly shaved Parmesan cheese
- 1 cup pitted Greek olives
- 1 cup garlic toasted pine nuts (see below)
- ¼ cup balsamic vinegar

TO BOIL THE ARTICHOKES

- 3 lemons, cut in half
- A large stock pot of boiling salted water

TO GRILL THE ARTICHOKES

- ⅓ cup extra virgin olive oil
- 1 tablespoon minced fresh garlic
- ⅓ cup soy sauce
- Fresh cracked pepper to taste

TO GRILL THE PEPPERS

- 4 red bell peppers, seeded and trimmed, quartered
- ¼ cup extra virgin olive oil
- 1 tablespoon minced fresh garlic
- ¼ cup soy sauce
- Fresh cracked pepper to taste

TO TOAST THE PINE NUTS

- 1 tablespoon olive oil
- 1 teaspoon minced fresh garlic
- 1 cup pine nuts

Tuscan Bread SALAD

Cut the bread into small (½ inch) squares. Chop the anchovies and mix with garlic, olive oil, vinegar, Italian herb blend, and honey. Stir well. Pour dressing over bread cubes and toss well. Toss in oregano, basil, capers, and tomatoes to mix well. Season with salt and pepper. Allow mixture to sit for 30 minutes for flavors to infuse. Serve over arugula.

SERVES 6 TO 8

INGREDIENTS

1 medium-to-large loaf crusty Rosemary bread, or soft herbed focaccia

12 anchovy filets

1 heaping tablespoon minced fresh garlic

⅛ cup virgin olive oil

2 tablespoon red wine vinegar

1 teaspoon dried Italian herb blend

1 teaspoon honey

1 teaspoon minced fresh oregano leaves

½ cup chopped fresh basil

¼ cup capers, drained and rinsed

2 tomatoes, seeded and chopped

Salt and pepper to taste

4 to 6 ounces fresh baby arugula (a type of salad green)

Marinated Artichoke BRUSCHETTA

Place artichokes, basil, pitted Mediterranean olives, garlic, and roasted peppers in food processor fitted with steel blade. Pulse until chopped into small chunks. Add oil and vinegar. Remove to bowl.

Add tomatoes and toss with artichoke mixture. Season with salt and pepper.

Serve on toasted pieces of Italian bread.

SERVES 6 TO 8 AS A FIRST COURSE OR 12 AS COCKTAIL APPETIZERS

INGREDIENTS

2 cups marinated artichoke hearts, drained (you can buy them ready-made, in jars)

½ cup chopped fresh basil leaf

1 cup pitted Mediterranean style black olives

1 teaspoon minced fresh garlic

½ cup marinated roasted red peppers or pimentos (also available in jars)

2 tablespoons extra virgin olive oil

2 tablespoons balsamic vinegar

3 ripe Roma tomatoes, seeded and chopped

Salt and pepper to taste

Sicilian EGGPLANT BRUSCHETTA

Trim the stem end off the eggplant and discard. Split the eggplants in half, lengthwise. Cover eggplant with lemon juice. Mix together 1 tablespoon of the minced garlic, soy sauce, and the canola or safflower oil. Pour over eggplant and toss to coat. Marinate about 1 hour.

Grill over medium-hot coals (or under broiler) until tender, about 3 minutes per side, depending on the eggplant's thickness. (Center should be tender but firm.) Remove to cool.

Cut into chunks and place in food processor fitted with steel blade along with basil, olive oil, and vinegar. Pulse until chopped into small chunks. Remove to a bowl. Add tomatoes and toss with eggplant mixture. Season with salt and pepper. Serve on toasted pieces of Italian bread.

SERVES 6 AS A FIRST COURSE, OR 12 AS APPETIZER FOR COCKTAILS

INGREDIENTS

- 8 baby eggplant
- Juice from 2 lemons
- 1 tablespoon plus 1 teaspoon minced fresh garlic
- 1/3 cup light soy sauce
- 1/8 cup canola or safflower oil
- 1/2 cup chopped fresh basil
- 2 tablespoons extra virgin olive oil
- 2 tablespoons balsamic vinegar
- 3 firm, Roma tomatoes, seeded and chopped
- Salt and pepper to taste

Portuguese MUSSEL POT

Remove fuzz from the outside of the mussels' shells and rinse under cool water. Heat olive oil in a pot that will accommodate mussels (one with a tight fitting lid), over medium to high heat. Sauté the garlic for 2 or 3 minutes and add tomatoes. Sauté 2 minutes more and then add the mussels, basil, and vinegar. Cover tightly and steam for 5 to 8 minutes. Mussels should open wide. Discard any mussels that do not open.

SERVES 8

INGREDIENTS

- 48 small to medium live mussels
- 2 tablespoons extra virgin olive oil
- 1 teaspoon minced fresh garlic
- 3 ripe tomatoes, seeded and chopped
- 1 cup fresh basil leaves
- 1/2 cup balsamic vinegar

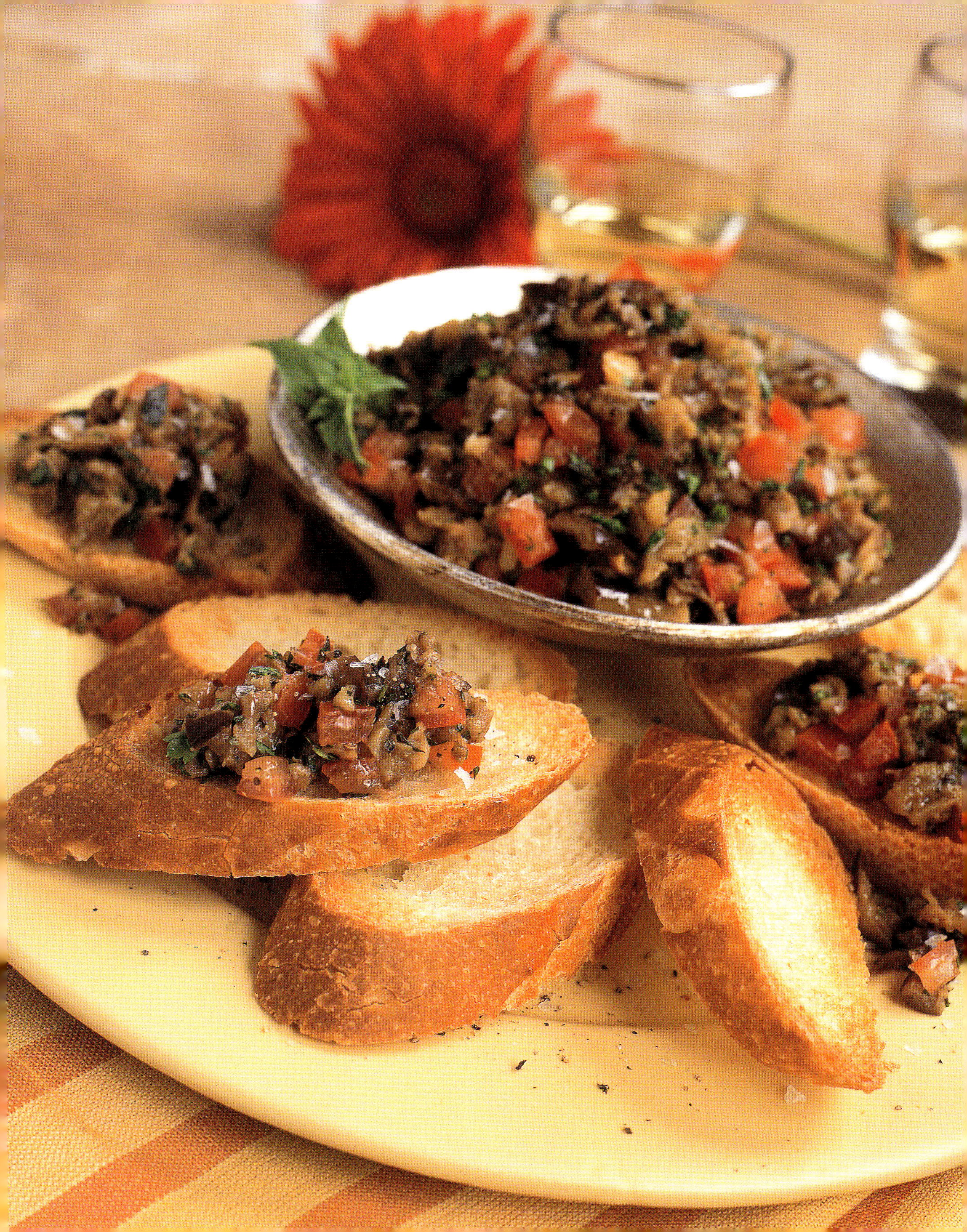

Rosemary Grilled LAMB CHOPS with Mediterranean SALSA

The Lamb Chops

Rinse chops. Mix together soy sauce, olive oil, and garlic. Place in a zip-lock bag and toss to marinate. Refrigerate up to 12 hours turning the bag several times.

Heat grill until coals are medium-hot then carefully place rosemary bundle on coals, then chops on the grill and cover the grill.

Grill on one side about 3 minutes. Sprinkle with pepper, turn chops, sprinkle with pepper again, and replace cover to grill.

For well-done chops, about 4 more minutes on the grill is fine; 3 minutes for medium and about 2 minutes for medium rare.

SERVES 4 TO 6

The Mediterranean Salsa

Mix ingredients together, cover, and refrigerate for 2 hours to overnight.

Makes about 1 1/2 cups.

To serve: Divide the salsa among the plates in an even layer. Place two chops on top of the salsa.

SERVES 4 TO 6

INGREDIENTS

THE LAMB COPS

8 to 12 lamb chops, 3/4 inches thick

1/4 cup soy sauce

2 tablespoons extra virgin olive oil

2 tablespoons minced fresh garlic

1 generous bundle of fresh rosemary tied with cotton twine

fresh ground black pepper to taste

THE SALSA

1 cup finely chopped, seeded tomato

1/8 cup minced fresh garlic

1/4 cup minced fresh basil

1/4 cup minced fresh parsley

2 tablespoons extra virgin olive oil

1 tablespoon balsamic vinegar

Salt and pepper to taste

Harry first met Linda Hamilton while standing in line to register their kids for school.

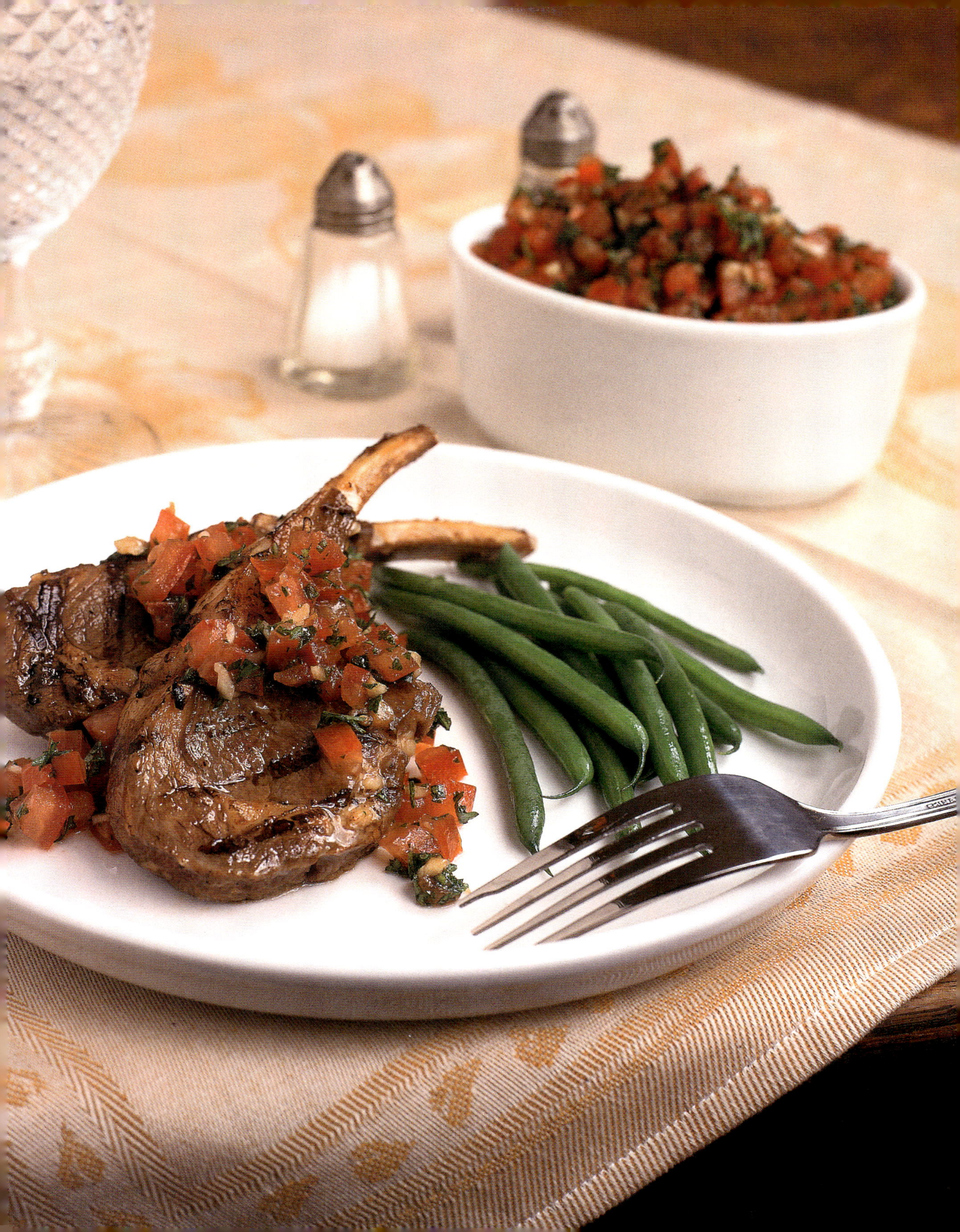

Garlic Crusted TROUT

Place the filets in a shallow dish and pour the milk over them. Allow filets to stand about 10 minutes. Drain the filets.

Mix together the breadcrumbs, herbs, salt, and pepper. Dredge filets in the bread crumb mixture to coat. Heat about a 1/2 inch layer of oil in a large skillet until hot. Quickly stir in half of the garlic and rosemary. Place 3 filets, skin side up, in oil and sauté for 2 minutes. Turn and sauté 2 minutes more. Fish should be fully cooked. Repeat with remaining filets, garlic, and rosemary.

SERVES 6

INGREDIENTS

- 6 trout filets
- 2 cups milk
- 2 cups fine breadcrumbs
- 1 teaspoon dried Italian herb blend
- 1 teaspoon each salt and pepper
- Extra virgin olive oil for frying
- 1 teaspoon minced fresh garlic
- 2 tablespoons fresh rosemary leaves, stemmed

PASTA Carbonalfredo

In a large, heavy, nonstick sauté pan over medium-high heat, cook bacon until almost crisp and brown, about 15 minutes. Drain off all but 1 teaspoonful of bacon fat, and add onion and garlic to pan.

Sauté until golden. Melt butter and sprinkle flour onto contents. Sauté, stirring constantly, for 2 to 3 minutes.

Add basil. Stir in cream in a slow stream. Add cheese and pasta. Bring to a simmer. Serve hot!

SERVES 4 TO 6

INGREDIENTS

- 1 pound bacon, cut into bits
- 1 chopped red or white onion
- 1 tablespoon minced fresh garlic
- 4 tablespoons butter
- 1 tablespoon unbleached all purpose flour
- 1/2 cup chopped fresh basil
- 2 cups heavy whipping cream
- 1 pound Parmesan cheese, shredded
- 1 pound fettucini or pasta of choice, cooked

Basil SHRIMP Scampi

Heat the butter in a large, heavy nonstick sauté pan over medium high heat and stir in the garlic. Sauté until garlic is slightly golden. Stir in shrimp and drizzle with vermouth. Sauté until shrimp is no longer pink and quickly stir in basil leaves. Serve warm.

SERVES 6 TO 10

INGREDIENTS

2 sticks unsalted butter

4 cloves thinly sliced fresh garlic

2 to 3 pounds large shrimp, pealed, deveined, and tails removed

2 tablespoons dry vermouth

2 cups whole fresh basil leaves

Benevenuto SWORDFISH and Brown Rice

Melt the butter in a heavy saucepan with tight fitting lid over medium high heat. Sauté the garlic and onion until golden.

Add the vegetable stock and bring to boil. Stir in rice and cover. Reduce heat to allow for simmer, and simmer 40 minutes or until rice is tender and liquid is absorbed.

Remove from heat and fluff with fork. Cool rice. (You may substitute quick-cooking brown rice.) Stir parsley into rice.

Preheat oven to 350°.

Place rice in the bottom of a baking pan or dish that will accommodate the fish in an even layer. Rinse swordfish steaks.

Place the swordfish steaks on top of the cooked rice. Squeeze lemon juice over the fish and rice. Core and slice tomatoes and arrange neatly over fish filets. Scatter basil leaves over tomatoes. Sprinkle with scallions and drizzle with olive oil. Bake, uncovered, in preheated 350° oven until fish is cooked, about 20 to 25 minutes. Sprinkle with toasted pine nuts before serving, if desired.

SERVES 8

INGREDIENTS

4 ounces unsalted butter

1 tablespoon minced fresh garlic

1 onion, chopped

4 cups vegetable stock

2 cups brown rice

½ cup minced fresh parsley

6 1-inch thick, 8 to 10 ounce, swordfish steaks

3 lemons cut into halves

2 yellow and 2 red tomatoes (or 4 red tomatoes)

1 cup whole fresh basil leaves

½ cup chopped fresh scallions

2 tablespoons extra virgin olive oil

(Use toasted pine nuts for garnish—see page 38)

Basil CHEESE Stuffed MANICOTTI

Heat oil in a heavy saucepan over medium-high heat and stir in shallots and garlic. Sauté until golden, about 5 minutes. Reduce heat to low and stir in wine.

Stir in tomato puree and heat while stirring, until sauce is just about to simmer. Add sugar and season with salt and pepper. Stir in cream until smooth and remove from heat.

Boil noodles in salted water until cooked but still firm. Drain and rinse under cold water to stop cooking.

Preheat oven to 350°.

Mix together the ricotta cheese with basil, and season with salt and pepper. Place ricotta mixture in a pastry bag fitted with a large, round tip and fill manicotti noodles with cheese.

Place about 1/3 of the tomato sauce in the bottom of a baking dish that will accommodate the manicotti. Arrange stuffed manicotti on top of sauce and pour balance of sauce over manicotti.

Sprinkle shredded fontina and mozzarella over the top. Bake in preheated 350° oven until bubbly and browned, about 30 minutes. Garnish with fresh basil leaves. Serve hot.

SERVES 6 TO 8

INGREDIENTS

- 2 tablespoons extra virgin olive oil
- 4 shallots, minced
- 2 garlic cloves, minced
- 1/2 cup red wine
- 30 ounces tomato puree
- 1 tablespoon sugar
- Salt and pepper to taste
- 1 cup heavy cream
- 12 manicotti noodles
- 16 ounces ricotta cheese
- 1/2 cup chopped fresh basil leaves
- 1/2 cup shredded Fontina cheese
- 2 cups shredded mozzarella cheese
- large, fresh basil leaves, for garnish

KITCHEN KLIPS

For a Mediterranean flavored garnish, toast pine nuts with a little garlic and oil in a sauté pan. Sprinkle on anything Italian!

Garlic Crusted **PORK CHOPS** with Apricot Chutney

The Pork Chops

Rinse the chops in water, pat dry and place each one between a sheet of waxed paper.

Using a meat mallet, gently pound the meat portion of each chop until it is half as thick as its original size.

Remove chops from paper and place in a bowl with beaten eggs. Toss to coat and allow to sit for 10 minutes. Meanwhile, mix the breadcrumbs with the oregano, basil, salt, and pepper. Dredge chops in breadcrumbs to coat.

Heat 1/4-inch deep layer of oil in a heavy, nonstick sauté pan over medium-high heat. Fry chops until golden.

Add garlic to pan. Turn chops and fry until golden on the other side and until chops are fully cooked; about 3 or 4 minutes per side.

Drain on paper towels and hold in warm oven until ready to serve, up to 20 minutes. Top with apricot chutney.

SERVES 6 TO 8

The Apricot Chutney

In a heavy saucepan over medium-high heat, heat oil and stir in shallots.

Sauté until shallots begin to brown. Reduce heat to low, stir in soy sauce, apricots, vermouth, and preserves. Bring to a simmer. Simmer gently until apricot chunks are tender. Use to top pork chops, or remove to glass bowl, cover and refrigerate up to 3 days until ready to use. Makes 2 1/2 cups.

SERVES 6 TO 8

INGREDIENTS

THE PORK CHOPS

6 to 8 pork loin chops, bone in

3 eggs, lightly beaten

2 cups bread crumbs

1 tablespoon dried oregano

2 tablespoons dried basil

2 tablespoons salt

1 tablespoon fresh cracked pepper

Canola or safflower oil for frying

1/8 cup minced fresh garlic

THE CHUTNEY

1 tablespoon extra virgin olive oil

1/2 cup chopped fresh shallots

1/4 cup soy sauce

8 ounces dried apricots, cut into chunks

1/4 cup extra dry vermouth

20 ounces apricot preserves

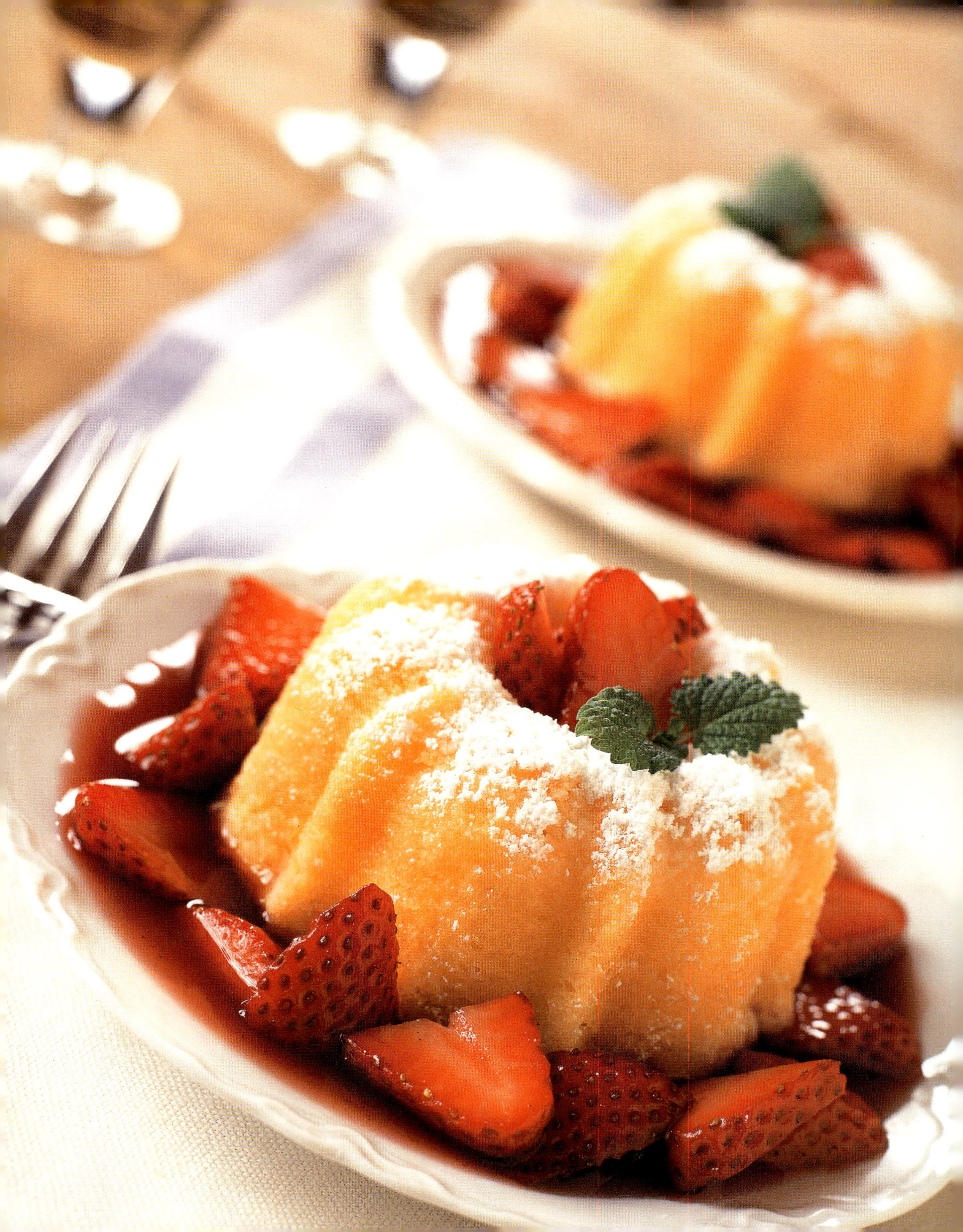

LEMON CAKE with Strawberry Sauce

The Cake

Prepare the cake in a Bundt pan according to the box's directions, but replace 1⅓ cup of the water with ⅓ cup lemon juice.

The Drizzle

Make the drizzle by mixing together ⅓ cup lemon juice, ½ cup water, 1 cup granulated sugar, and lemon zest in a small saucepan over medium heat. Bring to a simmer, stirring the mixture until sugar dissolves. Remove from heat to cool until cake is finished baking.

When cake comes out of oven, allow it to stand 10 minutes. Pierce with a toothpick or skewer in a square grid design with 1-inch spaces. Slowly pour the warm drizzle over the cake in a stream following the grid design.

Over the next 2 hours, while the cake cools, repeatedly sprinkle the top of the cake with powdered sugar, stopping when the cake stays powdered with sugar and the sugar does not turn to liquid.

The Strawberry Sauce

Toss the strawberries, cinnamon, and powdered sugar together. Pour the Chianti over the berries and toss until sugar dissolves. Allow to stand an hour or two before serving. To serve, spoon over lemon cake.

KITCHEN KLIPS

For a decorative looking dessert, put powdered sugar in a small sieve (strainer) and use the back of a spoon to press the sugar through to create an even layer.

INGREDIENTS

THE CAKE

1 packaged yellow cake mix plus necessary ingredients to complete mix

⅓ cup fresh lemon juice

THE DRIZZLE

⅓ cup lemon juice

½ cup water

1 cup granulated sugar

2 tablespoons finely grated lemon zest

2 cups powdered sugar

THE SAUCE

32 ounces whole fresh strawberries, rinsed and hulled

1 teaspoon cinnamon

1 cup powdered sugar

1 cup Chianti

Citrus **SORBET**

Process the orange and grapefruit in a food processor until pureed. Pulse in lime and lemon juice and sugar. Add enough water to make 6 cups total. Freeze in sorbet or ice cream maker according to manufacturer's directions.

To serve place petite biscotti in sorbet.

SERVES 8

INGREDIENTS

4 seedless oranges, peeled

1 grapefruit, seeded and peeled

Juice from 2 limes

Juice from 2 lemons

1 to 2 cups sugar

Petite biscotti, if desired

Venetian COFFEES

Cafe Chocolate

In a medium-sized saucepan over medium heat, stir together the sugar and cocoa with the water until smooth and mixture begins to boil. Simmer gently for a minute or two and stir in vanilla and hot coffee. Serve immediately.

SERVES 4

Brandied Coffee

Mix the brandy and the sugar until the sugar dissolves. Divide among 4 coffee cups. Pour in coffee. Whisk together cream, powdered sugar, and vanilla until soft peaks form. Top coffee with cream as desired.

SERVES 4

INGREDIENTS

THE CAFE CHOCOLATE

- 4 tablespoons granulated sugar
- ¼ cup Dutch process cocoa
- ½ cup water
- 1 teaspoon vanilla extract
- 4 cups freshly brewed coffee

BRANDIED COFFEE

- ½ cup brandy
- 3 tablespoons sugar
- 4 cups freshly brewed coffee
- 1 cup heavy whipping cream
- 3 tablespoons powdered sugar
- 1 teaspoon vanilla extract

"But, Harry, since I am helpless in the kitchen, I will look at this experience as a private "Mediterranean 101" cooking class in my kitchen!"

CHAPTER 3

SOUTHERN STYLE

SOUTHERN COOKING TO ME MEANS gracious Southern hospitality and soul-warming food. Many of the celebrities I interviewed in my show *Chef Harry & Friends* loved Southern food. Southern food is as varied as the South's many states. In Louisiana's bayous, the aromas of Cajun spices whet your appetite for simmering gumbo and other zesty seafood dishes. Or in Arkansas, you just might sit down to mouth-watering fried chicken, cornbread, and black-eyed peas and beans. Besides great food, when I conjure up an image of the deep South it always includes a Blues bar, where the Blues truly began. Many recipes cooked in the back kitchens of these Blues bars would be passed down from generation to generation as traditional Southern dishes. So cook up some tasty Southern dishes, invite over lots of people, put some Blues on the stereo. Most importantly, relax, kick-back and enjoy yourself—like the stars on my show did!

> IN LOUISIANA'S BAYOUS, THE AROMAS OF CAJUN SPICES WHET YOUR APPETITE FOR SIMMERING GUMBO AND OTHER ZESTY SEAFOOD DISHES.

Now On to The **STARS**

I ALWAYS ENJOY INTERVIEWING Hollywood stars to find out what they really like to eat when they're "kicking-back" at home. When *Chef Harry & Friends* decided to do a Southern cuisine theme, I first got together with country singer and songwriter Suzy Bogguss and then General Hospital's Brad Maule. They each welcomed me into their homes with a touch of traditional Southern hospitality and gave me an interesting glimpse of what they like to eat and how they rose to stardom. ■ The contemporary colonial home of Suzy Bogguss in Nashville, Tennessee reflects her love of the Southwest countryside as well as her love of family. It's comfortable with a touch of elegance. ■ Suzy and her husband, songwriter Doug Crider, work from a home office to be near their son, Ben. "Except when we are on tour I love to come back here and be a mom and write my music. I like to cook and have friends over, too. It makes me happy to feed people!" Suzy comments. ■ Her kitchen is truly gorgeous. Maple glass front cabinets, earth-toned granite counters, and

> They welcomed me into their homes with a touch of traditional Southern hospitality and gave me an interesting glimpse of what they like to eat and how they rose to stardom.

SOUTHERN STYLE **54**

oak wood floors make it as warm and inviting as Suzy is herself. Her center-island cooktop and double ovens make cooking a breeze. "I like everything that's bad for you, so bring it on," she told me. "I'll exercise two hours tomorrow if I have to, but I am going to cook and eat with you like there will be no more eating!" Then Suzy took out her guitar and played a short song. That was enough incentive to get me cooking!

BRAD MAULE, A "GENERAL HOSPITAL" STAR FOR over fifteen years, also requested a taste of the South. Brad, his wife Laverne, and their daughter live in a quiet Los Angeles neighborhood. Their Mediterranean house is styled with a barrel tile roof and stucco finish. Inside, its open main floor is dotted with Southwestern accents. Earth-toned stuffed couches and chairs are generously mixed with antiques. ■ The kitchen is the center of Brad and Laverne's home. It is highly functional, with white tile floors and glass front cupboards. A butcher-block island and some hand-painted tiles make it warm and inviting. "I love to cook but we keep it kind of casual," Brad notes, adding, "Laverne is a great cook, too. And we both love Cajun food, so we are anxious to get cooking!" ■ While Brad and I began the prep work, Laverne set their beautiful antique pine table. Surrounded by non-matching benches and chairs, the table offered a charming and comfortable gathering place to enjoy this wonderful meal.

SOUTHERN STYLE 55

Bayou GREENS and DIJON Vinaigrette

Whisk together mustard, vinegar, sugar, and dried Italian herbs until sugar dissolves.

Add in the olive oil in a slow stream until oil is incorporated and vinaigrette dressing is slightly thickened.

Whisk in the parsley and pimento, and season with salt and pepper. Just before serving, toss with onion and lettuce.

SERVES 8 AS A SIDE SALAD

INGREDIENTS

- 1 tablespoon Dijon mustard
- 1/3 cup balsamic vinegar
- 1 teaspoon sugar
- 1 teaspoon dried Italian herb blend
- 1/2 cup extra virgin olive oil
- 1/4 cup minced fresh parsley leaf
- 1 tablespoon finely minced pimento
- Salt and pepper, to taste
- 1 small, purple onion, sliced thinly
- 6 to 8 ounces organic baby lettuce blend, rinsed and dried

INGREDIENTS

- 2 tablespoons extra virgin olive oil
- 1 clove garlic, thinly sliced (more to taste)
- 1 bunch green scallions
- 1 cup chopped pecans
- 1 cup balsamic vinegar
- 1/2 cup chopped fresh bay leaf
- 1 teaspoon minced fresh oregano leaf
- 2 teaspoons honey
- 1/2 cup shredded arugula
- 1/2 cup shredded endive
- 1/2 cup shredded radicchio
- 6- to 8-ounces fresh mozzarella cheese, sliced in strips
- Salt and pepper to taste

SALAD MEDLEY with Warm Pecan Dressing

Sauté garlic, scallions, and pecans in olive oil until nuts are toasted. Remove from heat.

Stir in balsamic vinegar, bay leaf, oregano leaf, and honey. While still hot, pour over shredded greens.

Add cheese, and salt and pepper to taste.

SERVES 8 AS SIDE SALAD OR 4 AS AN ENTRÉE

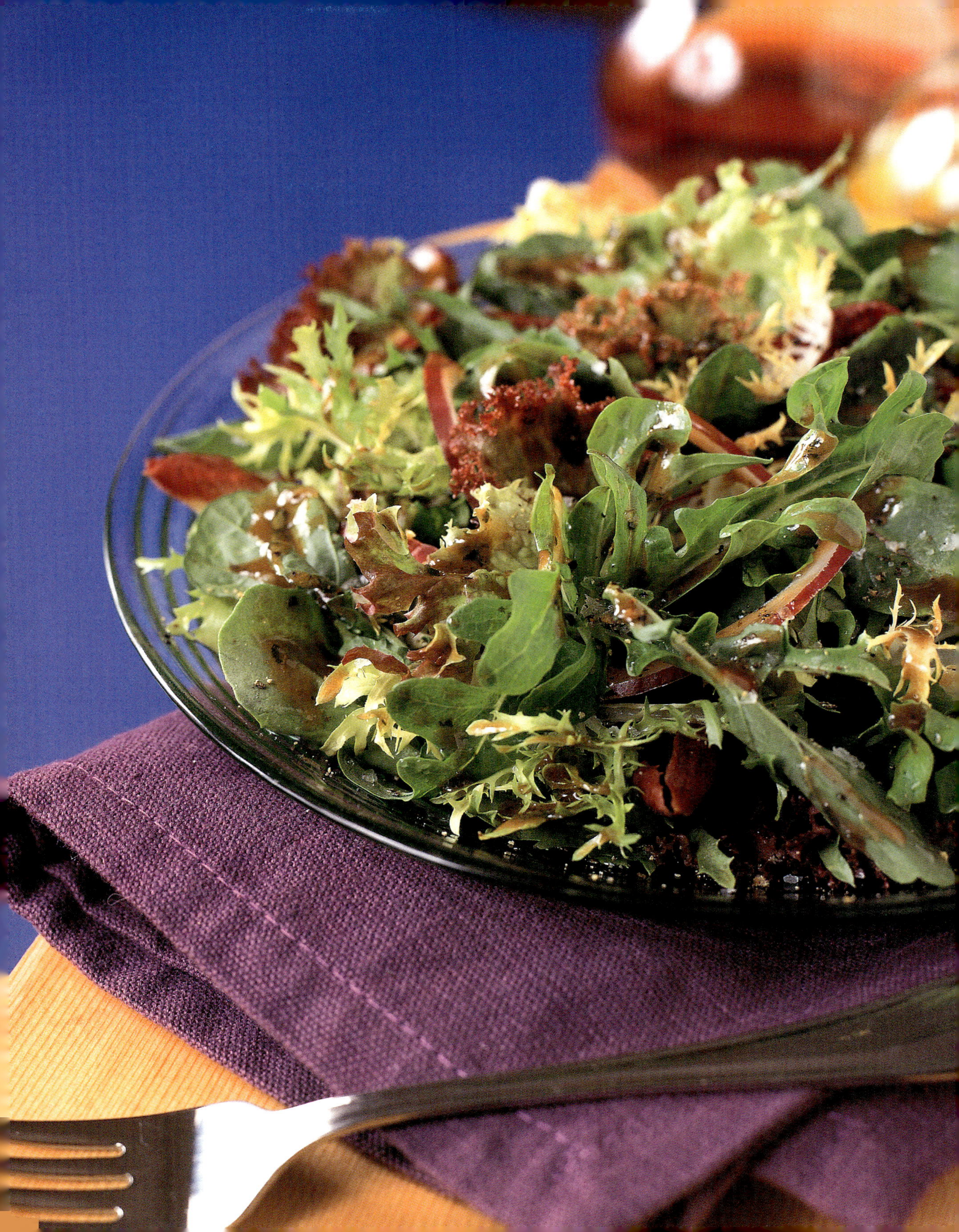

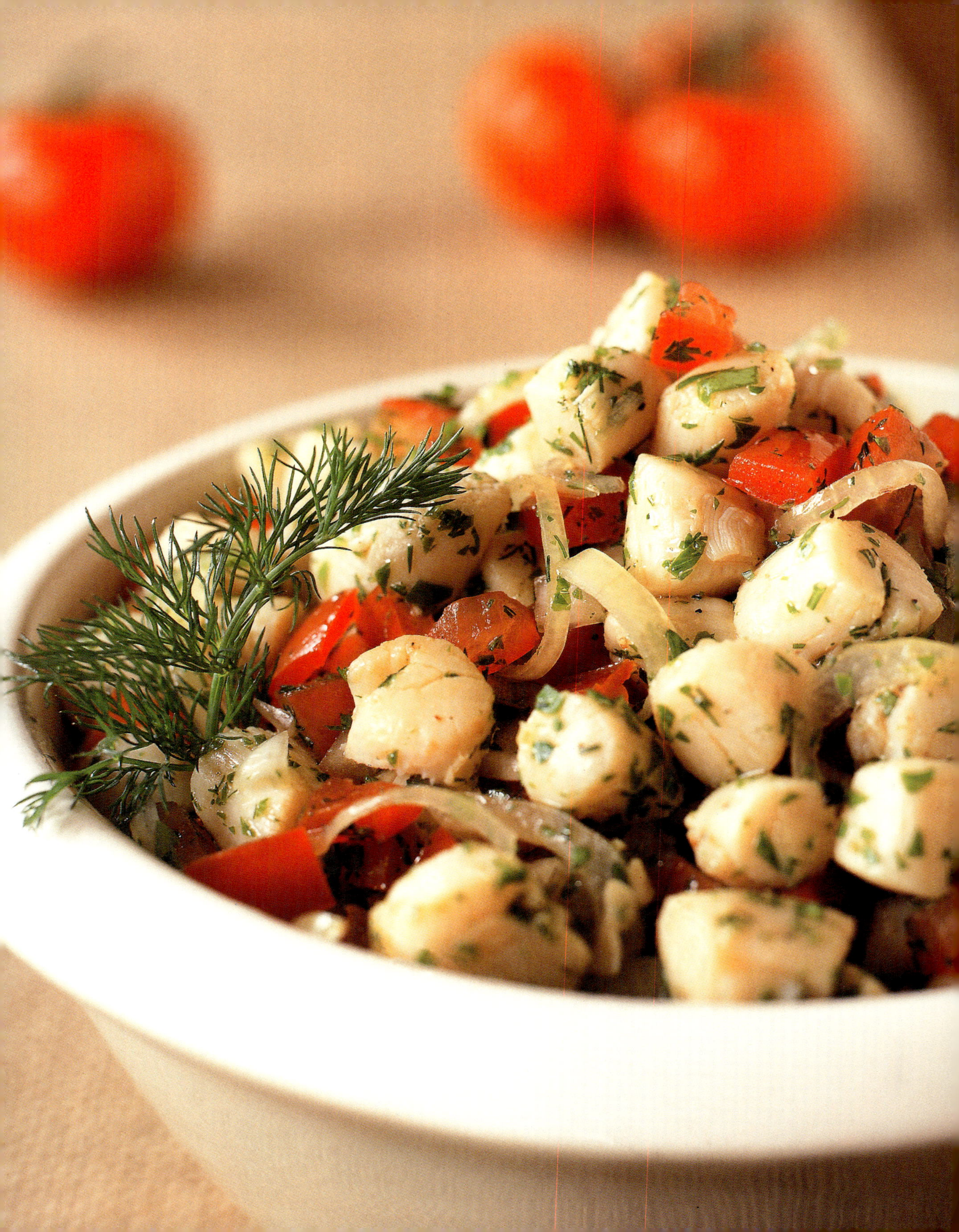

Poached SCALLOP SEVICHE

Bring wine to boil and add bay scallops and fresh bay leaves. Remove from heat. Take out scallops and chill, discarding bay leaves.

To the liquid, add lime and season with salt and pepper. Add tomatoes, red bell pepper, onion, basil, dill, and shallots to liquid. Mix liquid with scallops and chill. Allow 24 hours, or as much time as possible, for flavors to infuse.

SERVES 6 AS A FIRST COURSE OR UP TO 12 AS COCKTAIL APPETIZERS

Bay scallops are sweeter and more delicious than sea scallops. Measuring about 1/2 inch in diameter, they also cook in just a minute or two for a quick and easy meal!

INGREDIENTS

- 2 cups white wine
- 1 1/2 pounds Bay scallops
- 2 fresh bay leaves
- Juice from 1 lime
- Salt and pepper to season
- 3 tomatoes, seeded and chopped
- 2 red bell peppers, seeded and chopped
- 1/2 cup thinly sliced sweet yellow onion
- 1 cup chopped fresh basil
- 1 teaspoon fresh dill, stemmed
- 3 shallots, peeled and chopped

Cajun DIPPED SHRIMP

Mix together mayonnaise, chili sauce, lemon juice, egg yolk, curry powder, and Tabasco sauce.

On a large decorative plate arrange around the rim of the dish the pickled okra and pickled sweet peppers.

Place sauce in a bowl, dip shrimp about halfway into sauce and put onto the center of the serving platter.

Cover and refrigerate until ready to serve.

SERVES 6 AS AN APPETIZER

INGREDIENTS

- 1 cup mayonnaise
- 1/4 cup prepared chili sauce
- Juice from 1 fresh lemon
- 1 hard boiled egg yolk, mashed
- 1/2 teaspoon mild curry powder blend
- Tabasco sauce to taste
- Pickled okra and sweet red peppers, as desired, for garnish
- 1 pound large cleaned, deveined, and cooked cocktail shrimp (tails on), chilled

OYSTERS FLORENTINE with White Truffles

Open oysters with an oyster knife. Run a sharp knife under the oyster meat to detach from cartilage. Discard oyster shell tops. Spread kosher salt in an even layer about 1/2 inch thick over the bottom of a jelly roll pan. Arrange oysters in the salt so that they are level and secure.

Place butter and garlic in heavy, nonstick sauce pan over medium heat and sauté about 4 minutes or until golden. Add baby spinach and fresh basil to pan, and when they begin to wilt, sprinkle flour over the pan. Sauté 2 minutes more to cook flour.

Add whipping cream in a slow stream while stirring to create a smooth, thick sauce and bring to a simmer. Season with salt and pepper. Shave truffles into sauce and spoon over each raw oyster. Sprinkle breadcrumbs over top and run under broiler until brown and bubbly.

SERVE 6 TO 8 AS AN APPETIZER

INGREDIENTS

12-16 large, gorgeous, live oysters

1 box of kosher salt

3 tablespoons butter

1½ - 2 tablespoons minced or sliced fresh garlic

3 cups fresh baby spinach

1 cup fresh basil

2 teaspoons unbleached flour

1 cup heavy whipping cream

Salt and pepper to taste

½ to 1 ounce fresh white truffles (optional)

⅔ cup plain breadcrumbs

Southern Style CRAB CAKES

Rinse and drain the crabmeat and check for pieces of shell. Mix together with breadcrumbs the cumin, onion, bell pepper, relish, eggs, Worcestershire sauce, and mayonnaise. Add cayenne pepper to taste for desired spice.

Form 2- or 3-inch round cakes. Fry in heavy nonstick sauté pan or griddle over medium-high heat, using butter generously. Brown about 4 minutes per side, turning once. Makes about 16 cakes.

SERVES 4 TO 8

INGREDIENTS

12 ounces fresh crabmeat

⅔ cup plain breadcrumbs

½ teaspoon ground cumin

½ cup minced white onion

1 red bell pepper stemmed, seeded, and chopped

¼ cup sweet pickle relish

3 eggs, slightly beaten

1 teaspoon Worcestershire sauce

¼ cup mayonnaise

Cayenne pepper to taste (optional)

Butter for frying

Tennessee Whiskey CHICKEN CUTLETS

The Chicken

Dust chicken cutlets in sweet paprika, black pepper, and salt. Melt butter and olive oil in sauté pan. Sear chicken cutlets in the pan, which should be very hot.

Put chicken aside, keeping warm on a heat-proof platter in the oven.

The Sauce

In the same pan, sauté garlic and scallions.

Add chicken stock and simmer for 10 minutes. Stir in the whiskey to infuse the flavors.

Add tomato paste, honey, parsley, basil, and Italian herb blend. Simmer for 10 minutes, season with salt and pepper. Serve hot over chicken.

SERVES 8

INGREDIENTS

THE CHICKEN

- 8 chicken cutlets
- 1 teaspoon sweet paprika
- Black pepper and salt to taste
- 1 tablespoon butter (or margarine)
- 2 tablespoons extra virgin olive oil

THE SAUCE

- 1 teaspoon of jarred minced garlic or 2 fresh cloves
- 1 bunch fresh green scallions
- 2 cups chicken stock (buy canned or use fresh)
- 1 cup bourbon whiskey
- $1/8$ cup tomato paste
- 1 tablespoon honey
- $1/2$ cup freshly chopped parsley
- $1/2$ cup freshly chopped basil leaves
- 2 teaspoons dried Italian herb blend

Besides great food, when I conjure up an image of the deep South it always includes a blues bar, where the blues truly began.

Red Currant BARBECUED RIBS

The Ribs

Cut each slab into two pieces and boil in lightly salted boiling water for 45 to 55 minutes, or until cooked and tender. Drain and cool.

Combine the cumin, ginger, coriander, paprika, salt, pepper, and cloves and rub over top of ribs. Refrigerate for at least 2 hours.

Bring ribs back to room temperature and grill over medium-hot coals, turning occasionally until charred and slightly crisp on the edges.

The Glaze

Meanwhile, heat oil in a small saucepan to medium-high and sauté scallions and garlic until golden and slightly toasted. Reduce heat to low and stir in jelly and lemon juice. Bring to simmer and slowly simmer for 5 minutes. Remove from heat and stir in mustard.

Glaze ribs just before removing from grill and again after removing from grill to a warm platter. Serve remaining glaze with ribs.

SERVES 4

INGREDIENTS

THE RIBS

- 2 slabs baby back ribs
- 1 teaspoon ground cumin
- 1 teaspoon ground ginger
- 1 teaspoon ground coriander
- 1 teaspoon paprika
- 1 teaspoon each, salt and fresh cracked pepper
- 1 dash ground cloves

THE GLAZE

- 1 tablespoon extra virgin olive oil
- 1 bunch scallions, chopped
- 1 teaspoon minced fresh garlic
- 1 cup red currant jelly
- Juice from 1 fresh lemon
- 1 tablespoon Dijon mustard

Shellfish **GUMBO**

Heat the oil in a heavy stockpot over medium-high heat. Add celery and onion and sauté until golden. Add vermouth and reduce heat to medium. Stir in parsley, basil, sage, tarragon, rosemary, oregano, and paprika.

Sauté 1 to 2 minutes. Stir in crushed tomatoes and bay leaves and bring to a simmer, stirring frequently. Stir in sugar. Season with salt and pepper.

Simmer gently for 1 to 3 hours.

To serve: add okra, shrimp, scallops, and rice to simmering gumbo and serve when shrimp and scallops are hot.

SERVES 8 TO 10

INGREDIENTS

- 2 tablespoons extra virgin olive oil
- 1 cup chopped celery
- 1 cup chopped onion
- 1 cup extra dry vermouth
- 1 cup minced fresh parsley
- ½ cup chopped fresh basil leaves
- ¼ cup chopped fresh sage
- 2 tablespoons minced fresh tarragon
- 1 teaspoon minced fresh rosemary leaves
- 2 tablespoons minced fresh oregano
- 2 tablespoons paprika
- 84 ounces crushed tomatoes (fresh or canned)
- 2 bay leaves
- 2 tablespoons granulated sugar
- Salt and pepper to taste
- 2 cups chopped fresh or frozen okra
- 1 pound freshly cooked and cleaned tiger shrimp (or any firm, cooked seafood will do)
- 1 pound steamed and cooled bay scallops
- 2 to 3 cups cooked brown rice

KITCHEN KLIPS

Fortified wines such as vermouth and sherry add the flavors of many herbs and spices with just one splash.

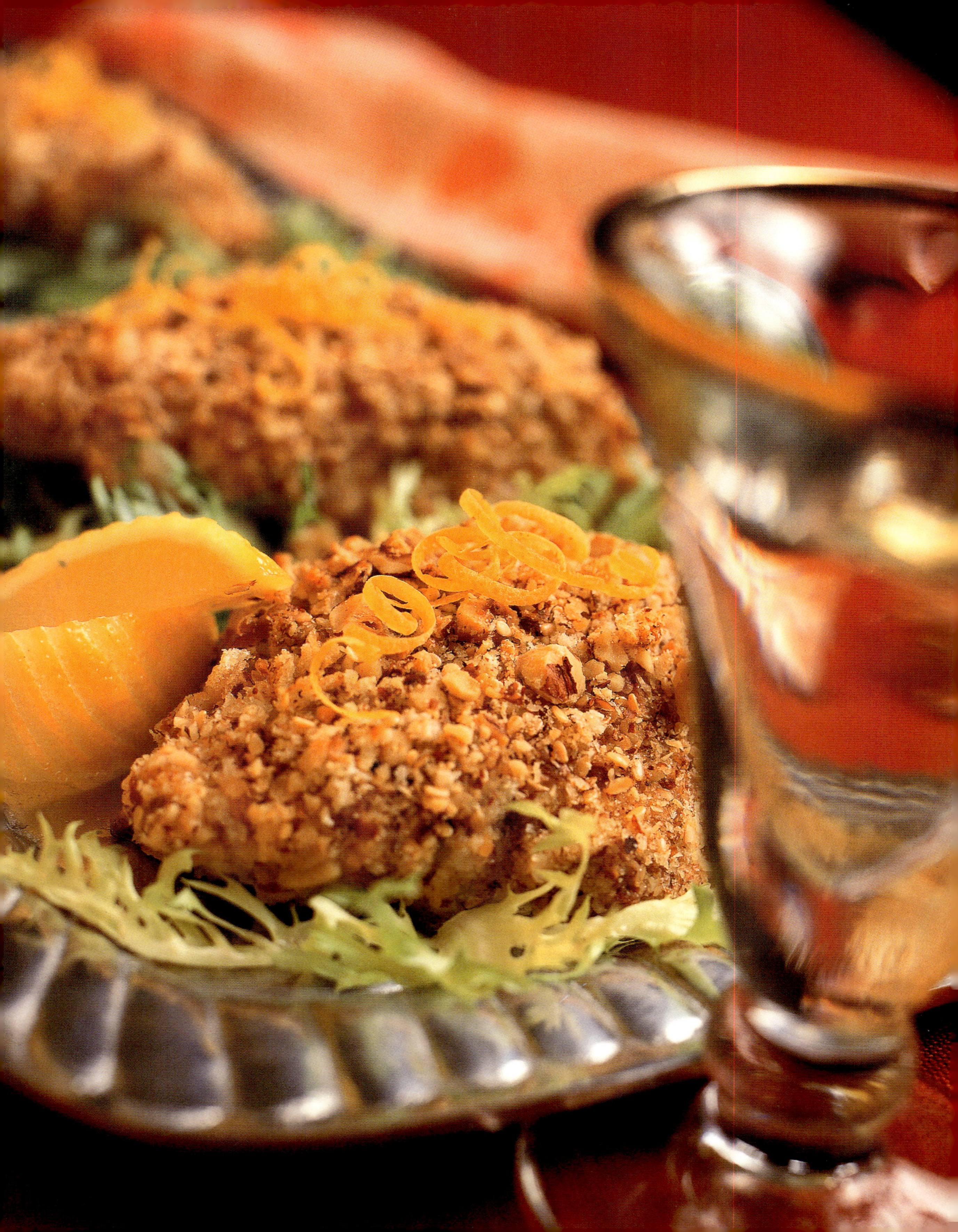

HAZELNUT
Grouper

In a nonstick sauté pan over medium heat, carefully toast the hazelnuts until they are golden brown, shaking the pan often to turn nuts. Remove from pan and cool.

Place cooled hazelnuts in the bowl of a food processor fitted with a steel blade and pulverize. Add breadcrumbs and sesame seeds to the bowl, and pulse just enough to combine with the nuts.

Rinse the grouper filets and place in a glass or ceramic dish. Squeeze lemon juice over the fish and then drizzle with soy sauce. Turn to coat. Sprinkle with garlic powder. Allow to stand for 10 minutes.

Preheat oven to 400°. Dip filets in beaten egg and dredge in hazelnut/breadcrumb/sesame mixture, coating fish heavily with mixture. Place on oiled broiling pan or similar rack for baking. Bake in 400° oven until fish is browned, about 15 to 20 minutes, depending on thickness of filets.

SERVES 6

INGREDIENTS

2 cups hazelnuts

1 cup fine breadcrumbs, unseasoned

½ cup toasted sesame seeds

6 8-ounce grouper filets

3 lemons, cut in halves

1 tablespoon soy sauce

1 teaspoon garlic powder

4 eggs, slightly beaten

KITCHEN KLIPS

Toasting nuts in a sauté pan over medium-high heat will bring out their flavors and natural oils. But, be careful because they quickly and easily burn!

Southern Comfort CHICKEN

Rinse the chicken breasts and split each breast into 2 pieces, for a total of 6 breast halves. Marinate in a mixture of soy sauce, vegetable oil, and garlic.

Grill chicken and chicken sausages over medium heat coals until just cooked. Cool. Chop into large bite-sized pieces.

Place olive oil in a large, nonstick skillet over medium to high heat. Sauté shaved garlic, onions, and scallions for about 5 minutes. Add mushrooms, herbs, cayenne pepper, and meat. Cook until hot. Pour Southern Comfort Whiskey over pan. Simmer 1 or 2 minutes. Serve hot over rice.

SERVES 6 TO 8

INGREDIENTS

- 3 whole boneless, skinless chicken breasts
- 1/4 cup soy sauce
- 2 tablespoons vegetable oil
- 1 tablespoon minced garlic
- 4 hot and spicy chicken sausages
- 3 tablespoons extra virgin olive oil
- 6 cloves garlic, shaved or thinly sliced
- 1 white onion, chopped
- 1 bunch green scallions, chopped
- 1 cup Chanterelle mushrooms or mushrooms of your liking, washed, brushed, and trimmed
- 2 tablespoons fresh minced thyme leaf
- 1 teaspoon dried Italian herb blend
- Cayenne pepper to taste
- 3/4 cup Southern Comfort Whiskey
- Salt and pepper to taste

Kitchen Klips

Libations such as Southern Comfort added to a sauce help tenderize meat and poultry in addition to adding deep, rich flavor. The alcohol burns off, leaving just the wonderful taste and tender texture.

Caramelized GREENS and ONIONS

In a large, heavy, nonstick sauté pan over medium-high heat, melt butter and stir in the onions and garlic. Sauté for 2 minutes and stir in soy sauce. Reduce heat to medium-low and continue to cook the onions, stirring frequently, until they cook down to a fraction of their original volume and they become dark brown in color. This process takes between 60 and 90 minutes. At this point, onions may be placed in a heatproof bowl, covered, and refrigerated up to one day until ready to complete recipe.

Trim and soak collard, turnip, and mustard greens to remove all dirt. Wash thoroughly after soaking.

Arrange the onions in an even layer over the bottom of the sauté pan and increase heat to medium.

Lay the greens over the onions and allow to stand for about 90 seconds. As they begin to wilt, stir the greens into the onions and cook until greens are soft and tender, about 15 minutes.

Pour vermouth over the greens and cook 5 minutes more. Season with salt and pepper.

SERVES 6 TO 8

INGREDIENTS

8 ounces unsalted butter

4 to 5 large white onions, sliced

2 cloves crushed garlic

1 tablespoon soy sauce

6 ounces collard greens

6 ounces turnip greens

6 ounces mustard greens

½ cup extra dry vermouth

2 tablespoons butter

Many recipes cooked in the back kitchens of these blues bars would be passed down from generation to generation as traditional Southern dishes.

Blue Grass **PASTA**

Using thread or dental floss, slice the goat cheese into ¾-inch thick slices. Dip cheese in beaten eggs and then breadcrumbs to coat well. In a large, heavy, nonstick skillet over medium-high heat, melt the butter and brown the goat cheese slices on both sides, about 3 minutes per side.

Put oil in a large, heavy, nonstick skillet over medium-high heat. Add garlic and sauté until golden. Stir in herbs and peppers and cook for 1 minute. Add the cooked pasta and heat just until hot. Season with salt and pepper. Place on warm serving plates and top with the slices of toasted goat cheese.

SERVES 6 TO 8 AS A SIDE DISH

[*"Orecchiette" means little ears—that's just what the pasta looks like!*]

INGREDIENTS

1 18-ounce log goat cheese

2 eggs, lightly beaten

1½ cups plain breadcrumbs

3 tablespoons butter

4 tablespoons extra virgin olive oil

1 tablespoon minced fresh garlic

1 cup chopped fresh basil leaves

½ cup chopped fresh parsley leaves

1 tablespoon chopped fresh oregano leaves

1½ cups chopped roasted red peppers (from a jar is fine)

1 pound Orecchiette pasta, cooked al dente, drained and rinsed in cold water to stop the cooking. Toss with a little oil to prevent sticking.

KITCHEN KLIPS

Pasta may be cooked even a day in advance if cooked to al dente, or just slightly tough, and tossed with a little olive oil, to keep it from sticking together. Added to a sauce right before serving, and cooking—just long enough to heat—takes all the guesswork out of timing the dish as well as simplifying clean-up.

Black-Eyed PEAS and BEANS

Place oil in a heavy nonstick sauté pan over medium heat. Sauté shallots and garlic until slightly browned.

Add black-eyed peas and black beans. If using fresh sprouted peas, allow to cook about 10 minutes, or until tender. (If using canned, no extra cooking time is necessary.) Add bell pepper, parsley, oregano, balsamic vinegar, and sugar. Continue to cook an additional 5 minutes to fuse flavors. Serve warm or cold.

SERVES 8 TO 10

[*Black-eyed peas are cooked up in the South on many holidays, especially at New Year's, to bring good luck.*]

INGREDIENTS

- 2 tablespoons extra virgin olive oil
- 1/2 cup minced fresh shallots
- 1/2 cup minced fresh garlic
- 1 1/2 cups black-eyed peas, fresh sprouted or canned (if canned, rinse and drain)
- 1 1/2 cups black beans
- 1/2 cup minced roasted bell pepper
- 1 cup fresh chopped parsley leaves
- 1 tablespoon chopped fresh oregano leaves
- 1/2 cup balsamic vinegar
- 1 tablespoon sugar
- Salt and pepper to taste

Orange Sesame YAM PUDDING

Preheat oven to 350°. Whip all ingredients except sesame seeds, salt and pepper, and place in lightly oiled medium-sized baking dish. Sprinkle sesame seeds over yams.

Bake in preheated 350° oven for about 20 minutes, or until hot and lightly browned on top.

SERVES 8 TO 12

INGREDIENTS

- 4 medium yams, peeled and cut into chunks, and poached until tender
- 1 cup vegetable stock
- 2/3 cup orange all-fruit preserves
- 2 tablespoons maple syrup
- 2 slightly beaten egg whites
- 1 tablespoon minced fresh ginger
- 1/2 teaspoon ground cinnamon
- 1/4 cup toasted sesame seeds
- Salt and pepper to taste

Quick Ginger **PECAN PIE** Crust

Pulse nuts and cookies in a food processor fitted with a steel blade until pulverized. Add butter and cinnamon and process until the mixture will hold a shape. Press into bottom and sides of pie pans or dishes.

Makes enough for 2 pie crusts.

[*You can freeze one pie crust, or make a second pie using a delicious filling on the next page.*]

INGREDIENTS

4 ounces pecan halves or pieces

8 ounces gingersnap cookies

4 ounces (1 stick) unsalted butter, cut into pieces

1 teaspoon ground cinnamon

Coconut **CUSTARD** Pie

Preheat oven to 350°. Place coconut, coconut milk, and vanilla in bowl of a food processor fitted with a steel blade, and process to blend well. Add the eggs and process just enough to blend.

Pour into a Quick Ginger Pecan Pie Crust and bake in preheated 350° oven until set, about 50 to 55 minutes.

You can make the crusts in the food processor and then scrape out the bowl with a rubber spatula. No need to wash it before making the coconut filling. Then scrape it well again.

INGREDIENTS

- 8 ounces unsweetened coconut (available at health and natural food stores)
- 14 ounces unsweetened coconut milk
- 14 ounces sweetened condensed milk
- 1 teaspoon vanilla extract
- 3 eggs
- 1 prepared Quick Ginger Pecan Pie Crust

Sweet **POTATO PIE**

Preheat oven to 350°. Place the sweet potato, sugar, syrup, vanilla, and cloves in the bowl of a food processor fitted with a steel blade and process, blending well.

Add eggs and process just enough to blend. Spoon into 1 Quick Ginger Pecan Pie Crust and spread, making an even layer in the shell.

Bake in preheated 350° oven until set, about 45 minutes.

SERVES 8 TO 12

INGREDIENTS

- 9 ounces prepared sweet potatoes, drained, or 4 cups peeled and poached sweet potatoes, cooled and mashed with a fork
- 1½ cups brown sugar
- ¼ cup maple syrup
- 1 teaspoon vanilla extract
- 1 pinch powdered cloves
- 3 large eggs
- 1 prepared Quick Ginger Pecan Pie Crust

CHAPTER 4

VERY VEGETARIAN

I'M NOT A VEGETARIAN, but I do love vegetarian dishes and the benefits a vegetarian diet offers to our bodies and our psyches.

Very Vegetarian introduces you to my extremely easy and very satisfying vegetarian recipes. On a recent *Chef Harry & Friends* show I prepared a delightful vegetarian meal with Patrick Bauchau, a vegan vegetarian and star of the hit TV show *The Pretender*. Vegan vegetarians choose not to use dairy or animal products.

> GONE ARE THE DAYS WHEN VEGETARIAN MEANT ONLY BLAND BROWN RICE, TOFU BURGERS, AND PLAIN STEAMED VEGGIES.

Today having the occasional vegetarian friend is no longer the novelty it was just a decade ago. The popularity of vegetarianism is growing, in part as a result of peoples' lifestyle changes, including weight-watching and a greater awareness of the health benefits that fruits, vegetables, beans, tofu, and nuts can provide.

There is no question that vegetarian dishes have a lot to offer. Low in saturated fat and packed with plenty of fiber, they are just what the doctor ordered for the recommended five-to-nine daily servings of vegetables and fruits. Research shows that a diet rich in grains, fruits, and vegetables can even help prevent chronic illnesses such as heart disease, diabetes, and in some cases cancer. But the most surprising thing I have found about vegetarian dishes is how delicious they can be. Gone are the days when vegetarian meant only bland brown rice, tofu burgers, and plain steamed veggies. With my recipes you can cook simple veggie meals in no time, and your family will love every morsel. I guarantee it!

Now On to The **STARS**

THE PRETENDER STAR Patrick Bauchau and his lovely wife Mijanou live a very 'European' lifestyle. They split their time between a wonderful Hollywood Hills home and a pied-à-terre in Louveciennes, a city just west of Paris. Raised in Belgium, Patrick spent a good deal of his youth in Europe. To Patrick and to Mijanou, a native of France, their Louveciennes residence feels more like home. But even in Hollywood, they live in a very French way. Their home, built in the 1920s and formerly owned by Zsa Zsa Gabor, is grand in stature and magnificent in detail. ■ You enter through a charming gate. The gate opens into an entry courtyard, offering a serene and luxurious feel. The heart of the stone-floored mansion is most certainly this beautiful center courtyard, around which the home is arranged. In their courtyard, Patrick and Mijanou have created a place to work together, practice yoga, have coffee, and share his wonderful vegetarian creations with a glass of

In their courtyard Patrick and Mijanou have created a place to work together, practice yoga, have coffee, and share his wonderful vegetarian creations with a glass of wine.

VERY VEGETARIAN

wine. "While I occasionally stray, I feel better eating vegetarian and have leaned in that direction for many years. I love to garden and enjoy creating with the fruits of the earth. It is satisfying and rewarding, even more pleasant when enjoyed "en plein air"—in the open air," Patrick says. ■ While we prepared a vegan dinner with Patrick in their cozy, earth-toned kitchen, we unexpectedly had another helper. It seems that their dog, Clarinet, is the official Bauchau taste tester, and eagerly awaited his duties! ■ The Bauchaus are warm and wonderful people. Patrick is a brilliant actor and Mijanou is a creative, gentle, woman with a warm heart. They are passionate about living and, most of all, each other. This fact caused me to speculate: Maybe there *are* hidden romantic benefits to eating vegetarian!

VERY VEGETARIAN 75

Winter Squash SOUP

Preheat oven to 350°.

Split the squash and remove the seeds and stringy center by scraping with a spoon. Rub flesh with oil and minced garlic. Sprinkle herbs, salt, and pepper over to taste. Roast squash in 350° oven until flesh is tender, about 20 to 25 minutes. Cool scooped out flesh and mash or purée.

Place in a soup pan over medium heat and slowly stir in vegetable stock to desired thickness. Bring to slow simmer. Season again with salt and pepper, and, if desired, stir in vermouth just before serving. Serve with crusty bread.

SERVES 6 TO 8

INGREDIENTS

2 or 3 winter squash (such as acorn, butternut, etc.)

1 tablespoon extra virgin olive oil or canola oil

1 tablespoon minced fresh garlic

1 teaspoon dried Italian herbs

Salt and pepper to taste

4 to 6 cups vegetable stock (canned is fine)

4 tablespoons vermouth (optional)

PUMPKIN SOUP in Pumpkin Bowls

Preheat oven to 350°.

Slice pumpkins in half through the stem. Scrape out seeds and stringy material. Brush pumpkin flesh with olive oil and sprinkle with salt and pepper. Place a sprig of tarragon in the center of each half. Cover pumpkin halves loosely with foil and bake in preheated 350° oven until tender, about 30 to 45 minutes.

Scoop out the flesh of 6 pumpkin halves, reserving the other 6 with flesh intact to use as bowls for serving the soup.

Puree pumpkin flesh with ginger and garlic. Discard tarragon. Place pureed pumpkin flesh into heavy saucepan and slowly stir in the vegetable stock. Add lime juice to taste. Season with salt and pepper. Serve hot.

Warm remaining pumpkin halves and use as soup bowls.

SERVES 6

INGREDIENTS

6 sugar pie pumpkins

6 tablespoons extra virgin olive oil

Salt and pepper

12 fresh tarragon sprigs, stemmed

2 tablespoons finely minced ginger

1 tablespoon finely minced garlic

3 cups vegetable stock (canned is fine)

Juice from 1 small lime

White RADISH SALAD

Split the peppers in half, seed, and trim. Place peppers in a sealable plastic bag with ½ cup soy sauce, 1 tablespoon garlic, and canola oil.

Grill over hot coals until tender, about 4 minutes per side. Cool and cut into small strips (removing the skin is optional).

Scrub and trim radishes and slice into thin slices. Place radishes, red pepper, tomatoes, scallions, and parsley in a bowl. In a separate bowl, mix together the lemon juice, ½ tablespoon garlic, salt, cracked pepper, and sugar. Whisk in the olive oil in a slow stream until dressing is slightly thickened. Pour over radish mixture and toss to coat with dressing. Serve over a mound of greens.

SERVES 6 TO 8

INGREDIENTS

4 red bell peppers

½ cup, plus 1 tablespoon, soy sauce

1½ tablespoons minced fresh garlic

2 tablespoons canola oil

2 bunches white radishes

¾ cup vine ripened tomatoes, seeded and chopped

¾ cup chopped scallions

½ cup chopped fresh parsley leaf

Juice from 2 fresh lemons

½ teaspoon salt

1 teaspoon fresh cracked pepper or to taste

½ teaspoon granulated sugar

¼ cup extra virgin olive oil

6 ounces organic baby greens, rinsed and spun dry

Kitchen Klips

A mushroom brush is a great thing to use when scrubbing radishes because the soft brush will remove dirt but not damage the skin.

Thrice-Cooked ARTICHOKES

Trim all but 1 inch of the stem from artichokes and drop into rapidly boiling water with 2 of the lemon halves. Boil until tender, about 12 minutes. Cool until you can touch them.

Carefully halve the artichokes and remove the hairy choke. Squeeze remaining lemon halves over cut side of artichokes. Mix together the soy sauce, garlic, and canola oil. Drizzle over the cut side of the chokes.

Grill over medium-hot coals, cut side down, for 4 minutes. Place in roasting pan and arrange herbs in center of each artichoke and drizzle with olive oil.

Preheat oven to 375°. Dust artichokes with breadcrumbs and bake in 375° oven until browned. Makes a unique appetizer arranged in a center bowl with crusty bread on the side.

SERVES 4

INGREDIENTS

- 4 medium artichokes
- 4 lemons, cut in half
- ¼ cup soy sauce
- 1 tablespoon minced fresh garlic
- 2 tablespoons canola oil
- 1 bunch fresh thyme
- 1 bunch fresh oregano
- 1 bunch fresh sage
- 8 sprigs fresh rosemary
- 2 tablespoons extra virgin olive oil
- 1 cup Italian seasoned breadcrumbs

The popularity of vegetarianism is growing, in part as a result of peoples' lifestyle changes, including weight-watching and a greater awareness of its health benefits.

Lentil and **CORN CHUTNEY**

Poach corn in water for 15 minutes. Drain and cool. Place in a dish and sprinkle with ½ cup soy sauce, 1 tablespoon garlic, and canola oil. Toss to coat and marinate for 1 hour.

Grill corn over medium-hot coals until toasted, about 5 minutes per side. Cool corn and remove kernels by running a sharp knife down the cob and rotating to remove all kernels. Repeat with all four ears.

Mix corn kernels with lentils, cilantro, and basil in a bowl. In separate bowl, mix together remaining garlic and soy sauce. Whisk in the olive oil and lime juice. Pour over corn and lentil mixture and toss to combine flavors. Allow to stand 15 minutes and toss again before serving, or cover and refrigerate overnight. Remove from refrigerator 20 minutes before serving. Makes about 4 cups.

SERVES 8 TO 10

INGREDIENTS

4 ears fresh white or yellow corn, cleaned

½ cup, plus 1 tablespoon soy sauce

2 tablespoons minced fresh garlic

2 tablespoons canola oil

3 cups fresh organic sprouted salmon-colored lentils (prepared regular lentils may be substituted)

½ cup chopped fresh cilantro leaves

1 cup chopped fresh basil leaves

2 tablespoons extra virgin olive oil

Juice from 2 limes

Quick Tofu **LASAGNA**

Preheat oven to 350°.

Crumble the tofu and mix with the ricotta, peppers, basil and sauce. Place a thin layer of the mixture in the bottom of an 8-inch by 8-inch lasagna pan or baking dish. Alternate layers of noodles and sauce mixture, allowing for a thin layer of sauce over the top noodles. Sprinkle cheese over the top and bake in preheated 350° oven until puffed up and cheese browns, about 40 minutes. Allow to stand 5 minutes before cutting.

SERVES 6 TO 8

INGREDIENTS

1 14-ounce block soft tofu, drained

15 ounces fat-free ricotta cheese

1 12-ounce jar roasted red peppers, drained and chopped

1 cup chopped fresh basil leaves

3 cups tomato sauce

4 8 x 8 no-boil lasagna noodles

1 cup shredded low-fat mozzarella cheese

Rosemary **ROASTED** Winter **VEGETABLES**

Preheat oven to 325°.

Wash roots well and cut into 1-inch cubes. Toss with oil, garlic and parsley to taste. Spread on a jelly roll pan in an even layer. Season with salt and pepper to taste. Sprinkle rosemary leaves over the top and roast in 325° oven until tender and brown, about 60 to 80 minutes.

SERVES 8 TO 12

INGREDIENTS

Potatoes, parsnips, carrots, turnips, yams, beets, or your other favorite root vegetable, about 5 pounds total

$1/4$ cup extra virgin olive oil

1 tablespoon minced fresh garlic

1 cup chopped fresh parsley

Salt and pepper to taste

2 tablespoons fresh rosemary leaves, stemmed

Vegetable EGG FOO YOUNG

The Pancake

Toss eggs with scallions, snow peas, yams, broccoli, sesame seeds, and soy sauce. Gently mix in sprouts. Heat a ¼-inch layer of canola or peanut oil in a large, heavy, nonstick skillet until very hot. Gently spoon in vegetable/egg mixture to create 4-inch patties, and brown on both sides. Drain on paper towel and keep warm while frying balance of pancakes. Serve hot. Makes about 8 pancakes.

The Egg Foo Young Sauce

Heat oil in a small saucepan over medium-high heat, add scallions and garlic, and sauté until golden. Reduce heat to medium.

Separately, mix the cornstarch with soy sauce to create a smooth paste. Stir paste into vegetable stock. Pour stock into pan and cook until thickened, about ten minutes. Stir in sesame seeds. Makes 2 cups.

SERVES 4 AS AN ENTRÉE; 8 AS A SIDE DISH

INGREDIENTS

THE PANCAKE

- 3 eggs, lightly beaten
- ½ cup chopped scallions
- 1 cup fresh snow peas, trimmed and rinsed
- 1 cup shredded yam or sweet potato
- 1 cup finely chopped broccoli
- ¼ cup sesame seeds
- 1 tablespoon soy sauce
- 1½ cups fresh bean sprouts, rinsed and patted dry
- Peanut or canola oil for frying

THE SAUCE

- 2 tablespoons canola oil
- 1 cup chopped scallions
- 1 tablespoon minced fresh garlic
- 1 tablespoon corn starch
- 1 tablespoon soy sauce
- 1½ cups vegetable stock
- ¼ cup toasted sesame seeds

KITCHEN KLIPS

Use a slotted spatula to turn anything you're frying in oil to reduce spatters and make flipping easy.

VERY VEGETARIAN

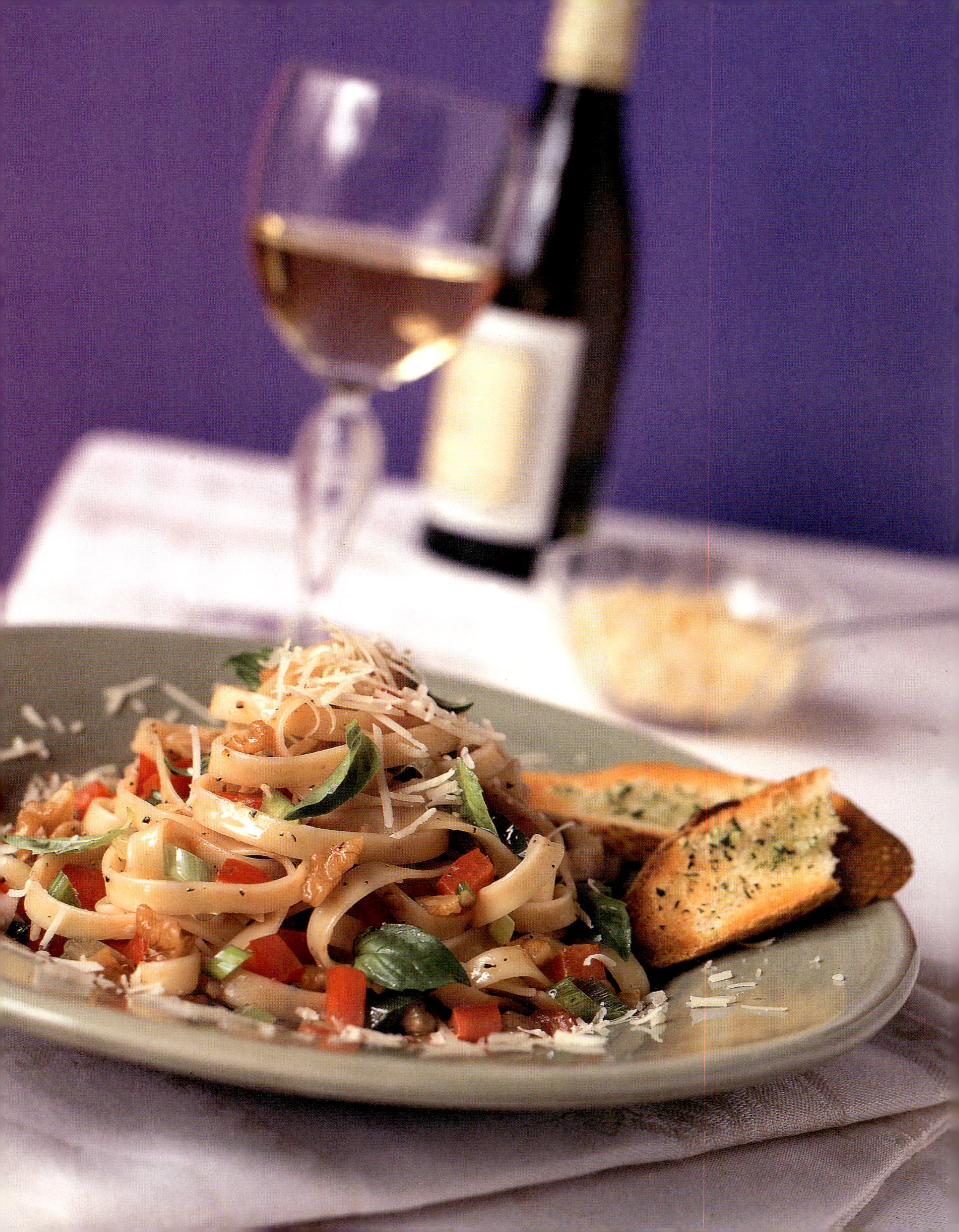

FETTUCCINE with Toasted WALNUT SAUCE

Put 2 tablespoons olive oil into sauté pan and toss in the preboiled pasta. Sauté just until hot and add herbs and remaining ingredients. Continue to sauté another minute while adding remaining olive oil.

Serve hot and add salt and pepper to taste.

SERVES 4 TO 6

INGREDIENTS

- 1 pound fettucine, cooked and drained
- 4 tablespoons extra virgin olive oil
- 2 tablespoons minced garlic
- 1/2 cup chopped red bell pepper
- 1/2 cup fresh scallions
- 1 cup chopped walnuts
- 1/4 cup fresh whole basil leaves
- 2 tablespoons minced tarragon,
- 1 teaspoon minced fresh oregano leaves
- Salt and pepper to taste

Kitchen Klips

Use kitchen shears to chop herbs right into a dish or pan. They are also great for cutting pizza and quesadillas.

Easy Soy BURGER

Grill the burger until cooked to desired doneness. Toast bread. Arrange the burger on one slice of toast and top with tomato, avocado, soy bacon strips, and onion. Spread mustard to taste on bottom of remaining slice of toast and place on top of burger. Serve with low-fat chips or carrot sticks.

1 SERVING

INGREDIENTS

- 1 frozen soy burger with mushrooms
- 1 slice tomato
- 1/2 avocado, sliced
- 3 strips cooked crisp soy bacon
- 1 sliced red onion
- 2 slices hearty rye bread
- Dijon mustard to taste

Balsamic GRILLED VEGGIES

Mix together the vinegar, garlic, honey, herbs, and oil. Arrange the vegetables on a shallow baking tray and drizzle the marinade over the vegetables.

Allow to marinate for up to 1 hour.

Grill over medium-hot coals in batches until tender, about 3 to 5 minutes per side.

SERVES 8 TO 10

INGREDIENTS

- 2 cups balsamic vinegar
- 2 tablespoons minced fresh garlic
- ½ cup honey
- 1 teaspoon dried Italian herb blend
- 3 tablespoons extra virgin olive oil
- 1 medium eggplant, cut into 1 inch slices
- 2 medium zucchini, cut into 1 inch slices
- 1 red onion, sliced
- 2 yellow or green bell peppers, seeded and quartered
- 2 heads radicchio, rinsed and quartered
- 4 Belgian endive, trimmed, rinsed and split

PASTA à la Melanzane

In a large sauté pan over medium heat, add oil, garlic and onions, and sauté until golden.

Stir in the chopped eggplant and sauté 2 minutes more.

Add basil, herb blend, and tomato sauce.

Slowly stir in sour cream. Heat until very hot, but not boiling.

Add freshly cooked pasta and Parmesan to pan and mix well.

SERVES 6 TO 8

INGREDIENTS

- 2 tablespoons extra virgin olive oil
- 1 tablespoon minced fresh garlic
- 1 medium white or yellow onion, chopped
- 2 eggplants, grilled and chopped (see receipe on page 86)
- 1 cup chopped fresh basil
- 1 tablespoon dried Italian herb blend
- 3 cups tomato sauce
- 2 cups light sour cream
- 1 pound pasta of choice, cooked al dente
- 1 cup shredded Parmesan cheese

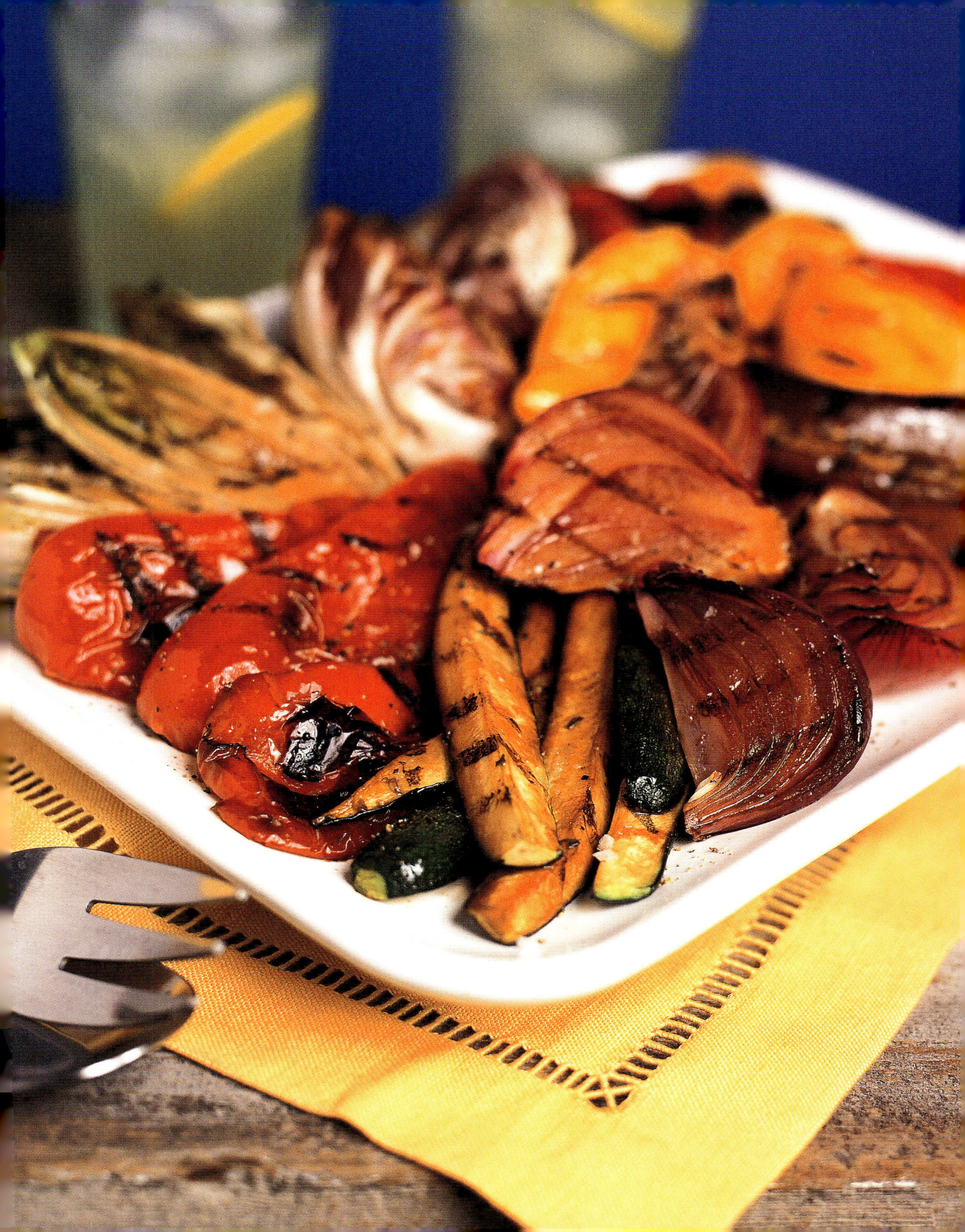

Grilled EGGPLANT

Place eggplant, oil, soy sauce, garlic, and pepper in sealable plastic bag and shake to coat. Drain off any excess oil.

Grill over medium-hot coals, turning once, until tender when poked with the tip of a sharp knife, about 4 minutes per side.

INGREDIENTS

2 eggplants, cut into 1-inch thick slices

⅛ cup extra virgin olive oil

⅛ cup soy sauce

2 tablespoons minced fresh garlic

Pepper to taste

Toasted TOFU and Friends

The Toasted Tofu

Heat a 4- to 5-inch deep pool of oil in a wok or Dutch oven over medium-high heat until hot but not smoking.

While oil is heating, drain tofu well on paper towel and cut into 1-inch cubes. Carefully drop tofu chunks into the oil, which should be bubbling. Be careful not to burn yourself. Maintain heat to keep oil bubbling actively and fry tofu, stirring gently now and then to keep pieces apart.

After about 6 minutes, add garlic cloves to pan and stir again. Fry garlic and tofu for 5 more minutes. Add scallions and parsley to the oil. Fry an additional 5 minutes until mixture is golden brown.

Using a slotted spoon or deep frying screen, remove contents to paper towel-lined tray. Serve hot over a bed of bean sprouts and drizzle with sauce.

SERVES 4 AS AN ENTRÉE OR 8 AS AN APPETIZER

The Drizzle Sauce

Mix wasabi paste with soy sauce until smooth. Stir in ginger, garlic, vinegar, and sesame seeds.

Serve over Toasted Tofu or with sushi or Asian dumplings.

INGREDIENTS

THE TOASTED TOFU

1 8-to-12 ounce cubed extra firm tofu

1½ cups peeled garlic cloves

3 bunches fresh scallions, trimmed and cut into 2 inch lengths

1 cup fresh parsley sprigs

Peanut oil for frying

Fresh bean sprouts for garnish

THE DRIZZLE SAUCE

½ teaspoon wasabi paste

1 tablespoon soy sauce

1 tablespoon minced fresh ginger

1 teaspoon minced fresh garlic

½ cup seasoned rice vinegar

2 tablespoons toasted sesame seeds

Caramelized BRUSSELS SPROUTS

Trim sprouts and split into halves. Rinse well and drain.

Place sprouts, onion, and butter in a sauté pan and sauté over medium low heat for 45 to 50 minutes, or until browned and very tender. Season with salt and pepper. Even the kids will love them!

SERVES 6 TO 8

INGREDIENTS

- 1 pound Brussels sprouts
- 1 medium onion, chopped
- 4 ounces butter
- Salt and pepper to taste

Mom's KASHA

Heat oil in a Dutch oven over medium-high heat. Add onion and celery and sauté until tender and golden.

Stir in soy sauce and kasha and sauté for 3 minutes more, or until kasha begins to toast.

Stir in stock, bring to boil, stir, cover, and reduce heat to maintain a simmer. Simmer for 20 minutes or until liquid is absorbed and kasha is tender.

Stir in parsley and corn and season with salt and pepper.

Serve hot or warm.

SERVES 4 TO 6

INGREDIENTS

- 3 tablespoons extra virgin olive oil
- 1 small white onion, chopped
- 1 cup chopped fresh celery
- 1 teaspoon soy sauce
- 1 cup kasha (buckwheat groats)
- 2 cups vegetable stock
- 1/2 cup chopped fresh parsley leaves
- 1 cup canned corn kernels, drained
- Salt and pepper to taste

Cashew BROWN RICE

Heat the butter in a large, heavy sauté pan with tight-fitting lid over medium-high heat. Sauté the garlic and onion until golden. Add the water, bring to boil, and stir in rice.

Bring to simmer and cover. Simmer slowly, covered until liquid is absorbed and rice is tender, about 35 to 40 minutes. Fluff with fork and stir in cashews and parsley.

SERVES 8 TO 10

INGREDIENTS

2 ounces butter

1 teaspoon minced fresh garlic

1 medium onion, chopped

4 cups water

2 cups brown rice

2 cups roasted and salted cashews

½ cup minced fresh parsley

Salt and pepper to taste

Cream Cheese BROWNIES and RASPBERRY Sauce

The Brownies

Preheat oven to 350°. Melt the chocolate and butter in a small pan over the lowest heat. Place sugar in a mixing bowl and stir in melted chocolate/butter mixture.

Blend in cream cheese. Blend in eggs and vanilla and mix well. Stir in sifted flour and pour into buttered 8-inch square pan.

Bake in preheated 350° oven for 40 minutes. Remove from oven to rack.

Serve warm with raspberry sauce.

The Raspberry Sauce

Place berries in a heavy, nonstick saucepan over medium heat. Pour sugar over the berries and Cognac over the sugar. Shake the pan a few times and allow to come to a simmer very slowly. Stir and simmer gently for 10 minutes.

Makes about 2 cups.

SERVES 8 TO 12

INGREDIENTS

THE BROWNIES

4 squares semisweet baking chocolate

1 cup butter

2 cups sugar

4 ounces cream cheese, softened to room temperature

3 eggs, slightly beaten

1 teaspoon vanilla

1 cup flour

THE SAUCE

4 cups fresh raspberries

1 cup sugar

½ cup Cognac

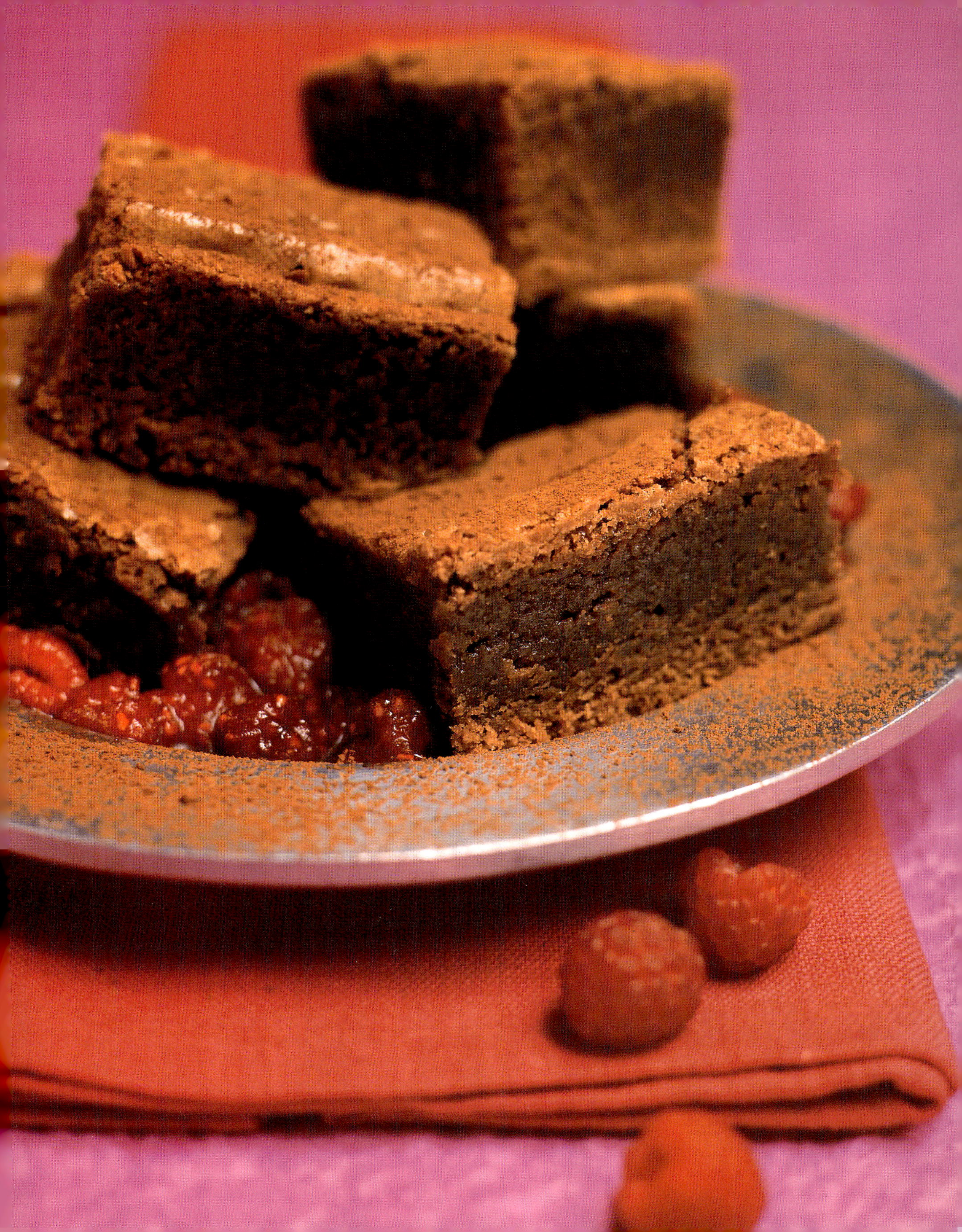

TEQUILA Drenched FRUIT

Place all ingredients except sorbet/ice cream/pound cake into food process bowl fitted with steel blade. Pulse until smooth.

Pour over sorbet or ice cream or serve over pound cake slices.

MAKES ABOUT 3 CUPS OF SAUCE
OR ENOUGH FOR 6 TO 8 SERVINGS

INGREDIENTS

16 ounces frozen sliced strawberries in syrup, almost thawed

1 cup frozen raspberries

1 cup peeled and chunked kiwi

2 tablespoons powdered sugar

1 cup shredded sweetened coconut

Juice from 2 fresh limes

6 ounces high quality tequila

2 ounces Cognac

Lime sorbet, vanilla ice cream, and/or slices of pound cake

Ginger BAKED APPLES

Preheat oven to 325°.

Place a cinnamon stick in the core of each apple. Decoratively insert 2 or 3 cloves in each apple.

Place apples in a deep baking dish with lid. Pour ginger ale over the apples and place lemon half in the center of the apples.

Sprinkle a dash of vanilla over the apples and cover.

Bake in preheated 325° oven for 90 to 120 minutes or until apples are soft but not mushy. Serve with warm caramel sauce (see receipe on page 91).

SERVES 4

INGREDIENTS

4 firm apples, cored

4 cinnamon sticks

8 to 12 whole cloves

10 ounces ginger ale

½ lemon

Dash vanilla extract

Quick Warm CARAMEL SAUCE

Mix ingredients together in a saucepan over medium-low heat and stir until mixture reaches a simmer. Simmer 10 minutes.

Cool to warm before serving over ice cream, bananas, or ginger baked apples. Makes about 1 2/3 cups of sauce.

INGREDIENTS

1 cup light brown sugar

1 stick unsalted butter

1 cup heavy whipping cream

½ teaspoon vanilla extract

Date GRANOLA SHAKE

Blend ingredients together until smooth. Pour into mugs and garnish with sprigs of mint.

Makes 2 or 3 shakes. It's a great way to start the day!

INGREDIENTS

12 to 14 pitted dates

2 cups low- or no-fat lemon yogurt

1 cup granola of choice

1 teaspoon vanilla extract

1 banana

1 cup orange juice

Fresh mint sprigs for garnish

Low in saturated fat and packed with plenty of fiber, vegetarian dishes are just what the doctor ordered.

CHAPTER 5

LATIN
LOVERS

"IT'S HOT, IT'S REALLY HOT." That is, the popularity of the Latin culture. Not only has Latin music and fashion become hip, but Latin food is happening in a big way. Since Latina singers Gloria Estafan and Selena "crossed-over" to mainstream pop, Latin has come to mean cool attitude, sexy clothes, and very sensuous food. In this chapter, with star presence from musician Nestor Torres, I'll introduce you to a range of spicy—and not-so-spicy—Latin recipes. The term "Latin" today has evolved into a broader meaning, embracing cultural aspects not only from Mexico, but also from Spain, and Central and South America. Latin food blends the best of these cultures, with drinks that make you want to dance and dishes that add an element of surprise to your palate. I've combined the vibrant flavors of Mexico with cooking techniques imported from other Latin countries to give you recipes that will taste authentic, but cook-up in a contemporary, easy style. Ah, the aromas, the textures, the appetite appeal! These recipes will bring out the "Latin Lover" in all of us and add adventure to any meal—even an everyday dinner! So travel into the kitchen with me to discover some vibrant south-of-the-border meal ideas.

> LATIN FOOD EMBRACES THE BEST OF THESE CULTURES, WITH DRINKS THAT MAKE YOU WANT TO DANCE AND DISHES THAT ADD AN ELEMENT OF SURPRISE TO YOUR PALATE.

LATIN LOVERS 93

Now On to The **STARS**

LATIN JAZZ ARTIST NESTOR TORRES lives in charming Corals Gables, Florida in a Colonial-style bungalow. The home opens onto a foyer that serves as a spectacular setting for Nestor and his love, Patricia's, art collection. Eclectic, colorful, romantic art—the collection boasts pieces from all over the world. "We like our home to reflect our taste, our travels and our lives together," Nestor explains to me as we toured his home. ■ Dark wood floors provide contrast to the white plaster walls, creating a perfect background for the magnificent art collection. Architectural details, including archways and wood beams, make the home a work of art in itself.

■ "Even around our table there are things from all over the world. I think the world comes together around the table. Food, music, and wine build a universal bridge," Nestor comments. It's evident his creativity goes beyond his song writing, music making, and poetic words. In the kitchen, Nestor is quite capable and eager. "I love combining flavors and experimenting. There is no end to learning and creating recipes!" Nestor says. ■ Their kitchen is cozy with tiles and a brand new gas range. It opens onto a tiled patio landscaped like a Latin tropical paradise. There is a breakfast area with a window seat, and cupboards loaded with spices hinting at Nestor's passion for intense flavors and high heat. "You can spice it up for me! I love it hot, hot, and more hot," he declares. ■ Patricia is quite decisive when it came to choosing a dessert recipe. "Chocolate! It has to be chocolate! And please don't ruin it with nuts, berries, or other flavors. Just chocolate. Pure and simple," she implores. When she took her first bite of our creation—chocolate crusted chocolate cheesecake swimming in chocolate fudge sauce—(see page 112) she closed her eyes, entering what appeared to be a trance. Her lips parted and she said, "Oh, yes. Oh Harry. Oh yes." Nester looked at me and remarked, "Well, I know what we need to name this dessert. I am just not sure you will be able to print it!"

In the kitchen, Nestor is quite capable and eager. "You can spice it up for me! I love it hot, hot, and more hot," he declares.

LATIN LOVERS **95**

Tortilla SOUP

Heat the oil in a nonstick sauté pan over medium-high heat and sauté the onion and garlic until golden, about 10 minutes. Stir in the tomato and tomatillo and sauté 3 minutes more. Remove from heat and cool.

Place mixture in blender or food processor. Blend or process until smooth. Heat stock in a soup pot and stir in tomato mixture. Heat until almost simmering but do not boil.

Fry the tortilla strips in peanut oil until brown and crisp. When ready to serve the soup, squeeze lime juice into soup. Ladle soup into warm bowls and place a comfortable amount of tortilla strips in each bowl. Divide the cheese on top and pass the minced jalapeños for garnish and heat to taste!

SERVES 6 TO 8

INGREDIENTS

2 tablespoons safflower oil

1 large onion, chopped

2 garlic cloves, sliced

2 small, firm tomatoes, peeled and seeded

2 tomatillos, peeled and chopped

2 quarts chicken or vegetable stock

6 corn tortillas cut into thin strips

Peanut oil for frying tortillas

1 1/2 cups shredded pepper jack cheese

2 limes, cut in half

Minced fresh jalapeños as garnish

Kitchen Klips

To easily peel and seed a tomato, drop firm ripe tomatoes into boiling water for 1 minute. Drain and cool under cold water and peel off skin. Cut off the top and stick index finger in seed cavities and the seeds just pop right out.

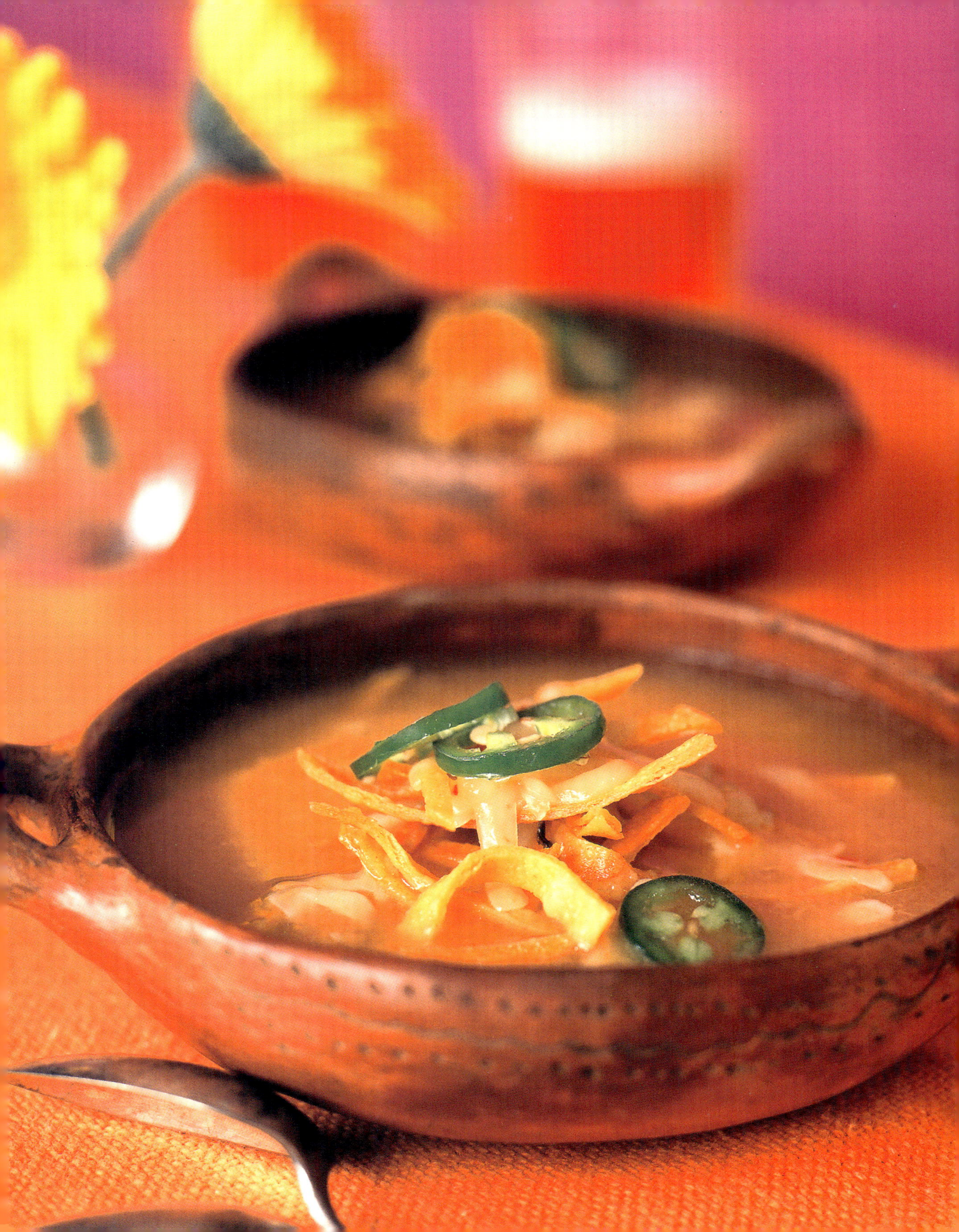

Muy Picante SALSA

Heat oil in heavy saucepan over medium-high heat and sauté onion and garlic until golden.

Stir in chiles and sauté 2 minutes more. Reduce heat to medium and stir in chipotle peppers in sauce and cumin. Simmer 10 minutes.

Cool. Process lightly in food processor with minced jalapeños to taste. Serve warm or cold. Makes 3 cups.

SERVES 12 TO 16

INGREDIENTS

- 1 tablespoon extra virgin olive oil
- 1 large onion, chopped
- 1 tablespoon minced fresh garlic
- 1 ounce dried chiles
- 3 7-ounce cans chipotle peppers in Adobo sauce
- 2 tablespoons ground cumin
- Minced jalapeños to taste

Yellow Tomato SALSA

Mix ingredients together and season with salt and pepper. Add jalapeño pepper, if desired. Makes about 2 cups.

SERVES 8 TO 12

INGREDIENTS

- 4 firm yellow tomatoes, seeded and chopped
- 2 mild green chiles, seeded and chopped
- 1/4 cup chopped fresh cilantro leaves
- 1 teaspoon ground cumin
- 1 teaspoon ground mild chili powder
- 1 teaspoon crushed dried Mexican oregano
- Juice from 2 fresh limes
- Salt and pepper to taste
- Chopped, seeded jalapeño to taste (optional)

Harry's SALSAS

USE THESE FRESH tangy salsas for dipping with a variety of chips. Or use them for garnishing tacos, tostadas, and burritos. Better yet I like to spoon the salsas over eggs, roasted meats, or over a hot or cold seafood dish.

Tomatillo Salsa

Toss ingredients together and season with salt. Makes about 3 cups.

Tomatillos are also called Mexican green tomatoes and resemble small green tomatoes. They have a thin, parchment-like covering, which is removed and discarded. The flavor has hints of lemon and apple. Choose firm tomatillos with tight-fitting husks. Store in a paper bag in the refrigerator for up to one month.

Papaya Salsa

Add all ingredients to bowl and stir. Let sit for a couple of hours if time allows for flavors to fuse.

Serve with large tortilla chips.

SERVES 12 AS AN APPETIZER

Use papaya seeds for pepper and also in vinaigrettes.

INGREDIENTS

TOMATILLO SALSA

- 1 pound fresh tomatillos, peeled and chopped
- 1 onion, minced
- 2 mild green chili peppers, minced
- 1/2 cup chopped fresh cilantro leaves
- 1 teaspoon ground cumin
- Juice from 2 fresh limes
- Salt to taste

PAPAYA SALSA

- 1 cup papaya—keep seeds if desired and add to recipe
- Juice from 3 medium limes
- 1/2 cup red tomato, seeded and chopped
- 1/2 cup chopped fresh cilantro
- 1/4 cup minced fresh white onion
- 1 teaspoon sugar
- 1 teaspoon cumin

"Por favor"—try it; es delicioso!"

Quick and Cheesy JALAPEÑO ROLL-UPS

In food processor, blend cream cheese, olives, cilantro, and cumin.

Spread onto tortillas and roll up. Cut at an angle and serve as appetizer.

Serve with guacamole, fresh salsa, and chips. Throw in some Mexican margaritas for a real fiesta!

SERVES 8 TO 12 AS AN APPETIZER

INGREDIENTS

- 8 ounces cream cheese, softened to room temperature
- 5 ounces jalapeño stuffed olives
- ¼ cup fresh cilantro
- 1 tablespoon ground cumin
- 4 medium-sized fresh wheat tortillas

Kitchen Klips

Always wear rubber, plastic or vinyl gloves when handling any hot peppers. If the juices get on your fingers and you rub your eyes it can be dangerous and will definitely hurt!

Latin has come to mean cool attitude, sexy clothes, and very sensuous food.

Crab FIRECRACKERS

Carefully slit chiles the entire length of one side and remove seeds and insides.

Mix together the goat cheese with crabmeat and hot pepper sauce. Stuff each chile with the mixture, just enough so that they will close tightly.

Mix together olive oil and garlic and soy sauce.

Place chiles on the grill over medium-hot coals, and paint each chile with the liquid.

Grill chiles, turning once, until skin begins to form black blisters and cheese starts to melt out from the chile opening. Serve hot or warm. Can be kept up to 30 minutes on a serving platter in warm oven.

SERVES 8 AS A FIRST COURSE OR 4 FOR LUNCH

INGREDIENTS

8 mild to medium green chiles

8 ounces herbed goat cheese, softened to room temperature

4 ounces boiled crabmeat, rinsed, picked over and chopped

1 teaspoon (or to taste) hot pepper sauce

3 tablespoons extra virgin olive oil

1 teaspoon minced fresh garlic

1 tablespoon soy sauce

Shooter SHRIMP

Mix together lime juice, tequila, sesame oil, cumin, and paprika.

Dip tomato slices in mixture, allowing marinade to drain back into bowl. Put tomatoes aside. Put shrimp in tequila mixture and allow to marinate 1 hour.

Place 3 shrimp and 2 tomato slices on bamboo skewers until all are used and grill over medium-hot coals until shrimp are just done, about 2 or 3 minutes per side.

SERVES 8 AS AN APPETIZER

INGREDIENTS

Juice from 3 fresh limes

½ cup high quality tequila

1 tablespoon sesame oil

1 teaspoon ground cumin

1 teaspoon sweet paprika

6 small, firm Roma tomatoes, cut into 3 thick slices each

About 30 large shrimp (1 pound), peeled and deveined

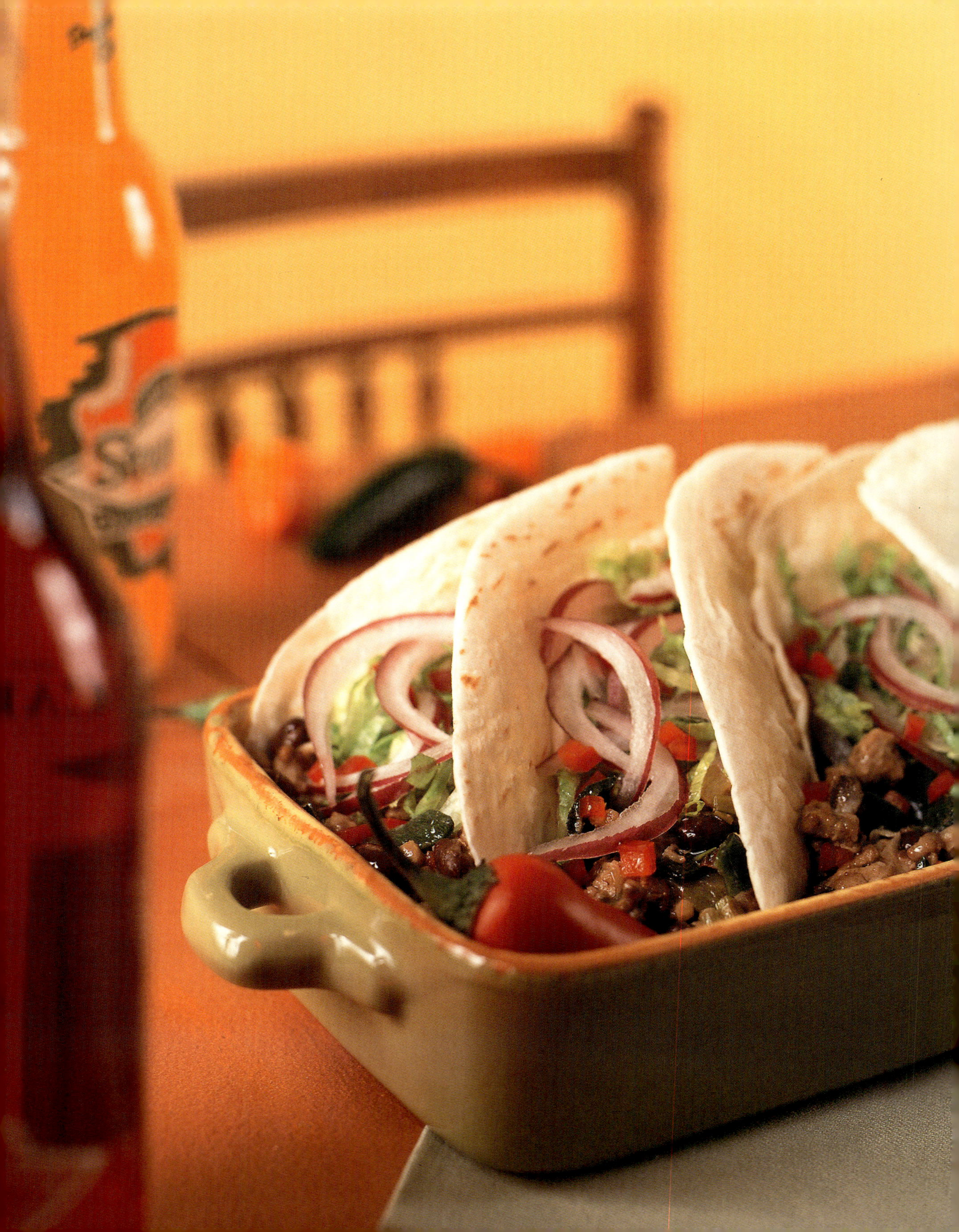

QUESO FUNDIDO

Brown ground pork in a heavy, nonstick skillet until very well done, scrambling constantly to break apart. Stir in garlic and scallions and sauté for a few minutes more. Add vinegar, cumin, and black beans. Sauté. Add poblano peppers and green chiles. Sauté until peppers are tender.

Turn heat to low and top with cheese. Sauté until melted.

Put tortillas in separate pan or microwave oven to warm while cheese melts.

Place a spoonful of meat filling in a tortilla and eat like a taco.

Serve with sour cream, guacamole, shredded lettuce, and chopped onions.

A NOTE *to those who like it hot: Add a few sliced jalapeños!*

SERVES 6 TO 8 AS AN APPETIZER

INGREDIENTS

- 1 pound lean ground pork
- 2 tablespoons minced fresh garlic
- 1/2 cup chopped fresh scallions
- 1/8 cup balsamic vinegar
- 1 tablespoon ground cumin
- 1 cup prepared black beans, rinsed and drained
- 2 poblano peppers, seeded and diced
- 2 mild green chiles, seeded and diced
- 2 cups shredded Mexican blend melting cheese, or substitute jack or mild cheddar
- 8 soft, fresh, small flour tortillas

KITCHEN KLIPS

Brown large amounts of meat all at once. Cool and separate into 1-pint freezer containers. Once frozen, the meat can be thawed overnight for a quick fix the next day.

Shredded Beef and **BRIE TOSTADAS**

Preheat oven to 275°. Arrange onions in the bottom of a high-sided roasting pan that will hold brisket. Rinse brisket and lay on top of onions fat side up.

Pour water into pan and place bay leaves in water. Arrange garlic over the top of meat and sprinkle with salt and pepper.

Seal pan tightly with foil and roast in preheated 275° oven overnight (for 8 to 10 hours).

Cool meat and trim away the remaining fat. Refrigerate until fully chilled.

Preheat grill to medium-high. Grill brisket until crisp and beginning to char on both sides. Meat should be on the dry side, and falling apart. Grill 7 to 8 minutes per side.

Cool about 10 minutes and cut beef into 1-inch thick slices across the grain, which will allow the beef to fall apart into shreds.

Preheat oven to 325°. Slice Brie into thin slices and arrange with shredded beef on top of the tostada shells.

Bake in preheated 325° oven until cheese melts and shells are crisp.

Serve immediately with garnishes. Any leftover beef can be used in tacos, soup, or quesadillas.

SERVES 8 TO 12

INGREDIENTS

2 large onions cut into thick slices

1 5-7 pound beef brisket

4 cups water

2 bay leaves

2 cloves fresh garlic, sliced

1 tablespoon kosher salt

1 tablespoon fresh cracked pepper

8 ounces chilled ripe Brie cheese

12 tostado shells

Garnishes of yellow tomato salsa, shredded lettuce, sour cream, and guacamole

KITCHEN KLIPS

Make your own tostada shells by frying corn tortillas in hot peanut oil until golden and crispy. Drain on paper towel and store in an airtight container for up to 5 days. They can be recrisped in a warm oven if necessary.

Cha-cha Carrot MANGO SALAD

Combine all ingredients except greens in a bowl. Let sit for 20 minutes or so for flavors to fuse. Serve on a bed of greens.

SERVES 6 TO 8

INGREDIENTS

1 ripe, fresh mango, chopped into small chunks

¼ cup chopped fresh cilantro leaves

Juice from 3 medium limes

¼ cup minced white onion

1½ cups shredded carrots

1 tablespoon sugar

Salt and pepper to taste

Organic mixed baby greens

> I've combined the vibrant flavors of Mexico with cooking techniques imported from other Latin countries.

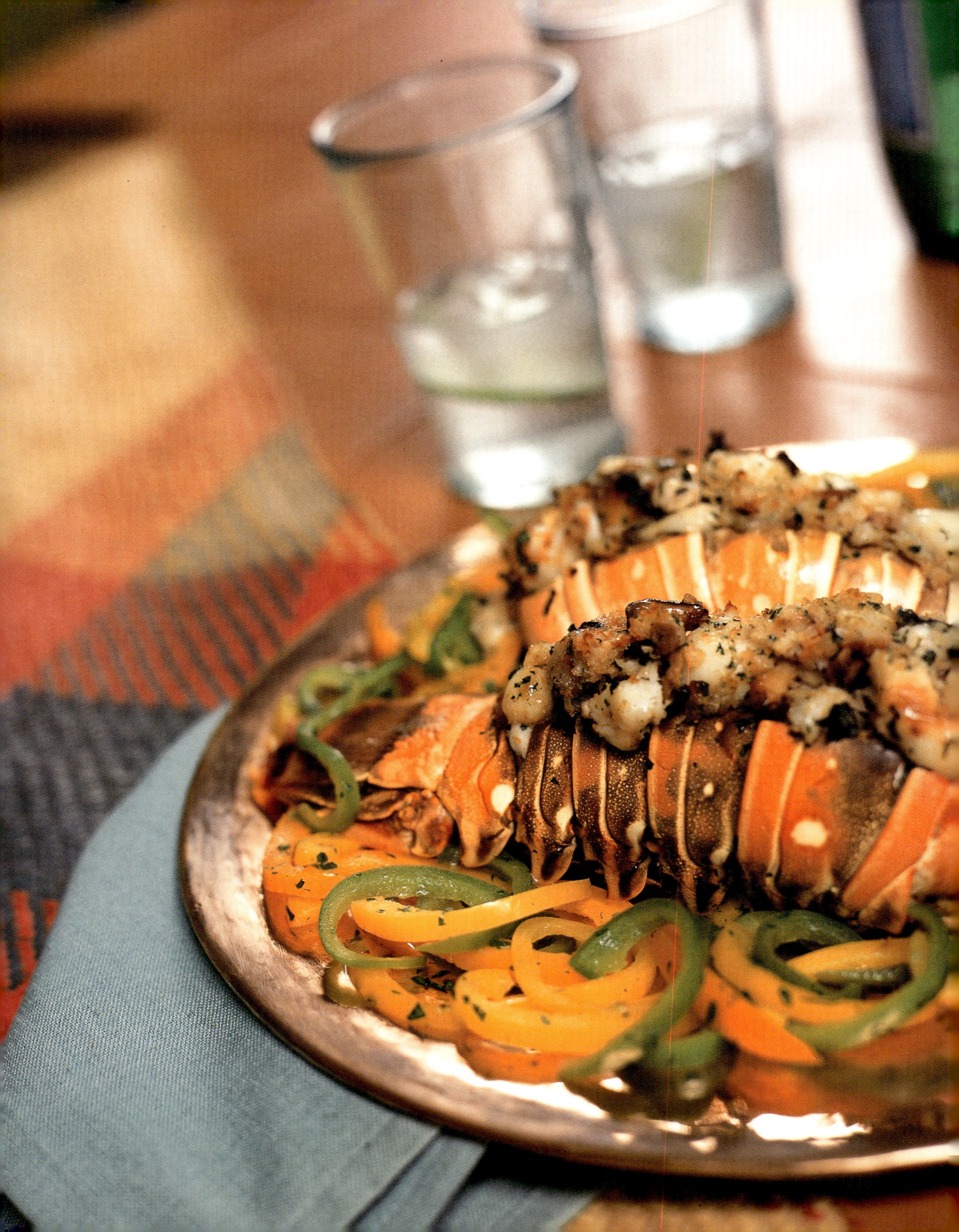

Baked Stuffed **LANGOSTA**

Using kitchen shears, cut lobster tail down the center of the back of the shell and remove meat.

Cut meat into chunks and reserve shells.

In a large, nonstick sauté pan over medium-high heat, melt butter and stir in garlic. Sauté 1 to 2 minutes and add parsley and basil. Add mushrooms and soy sauce to the pan. Stir in hearts of palm. Add lobster chunks, stir over heat 1 minute and remove from heat.

Preheat oven to 350°. Sprinkle breadcrumbs lightly onto lobster. Fill lobster shells with lobster filling.

Place on a baking sheet and bake in a preheated 350° oven for about 10 to 15 minutes or until done and slightly browned on top.

SERVES 6.

INGREDIENTS

- 6 8-ounce langosta or lobster tails
- 8 ounces unsalted butter
- 2 tablespoons minced fresh garlic
- ¼ cup chopped parsley
- ½ cup chopped fresh basil leaf
- 1 cup shiitake mushrooms, stemmed and wiped clean
- 2 to 3 tablespoons soy sauce, or to taste
- ¾ cup hearts of palm, chopped
- ½ cup plain breadcrumbs

KITCHEN KLIPS

Some hearts of palm are tough and woody and should be thrown away. Always check hearts of palm for texture by cutting off a small piece of one end to make sure they are tender.

South-of-the-Border POSOLE

Heat oil in a large soup pot over medium-high heat and sauté onion and garlic until golden. Reduce heat to medium and add hominy and corn to pot.

Stir in cumin, chili powder, and tomato puree. Bring to a simmer and stir in remaining ingredients, except garnishes.

Simmer gently about 90 minutes, stirring often.

Dish out into soup bowls and top with shredded lettuce and sour cream.

Add sliced, grilled chicken (or even leftover beef from tostadas, see recipe on page 104) for a one-dish meal that will please the whole family!

Squeeze limes as desired.

SERVES 8 TO 10

INGREDIENTS

- 1 tablespoon extra virgin olive oil
- 1 large onion, chopped
- 1 tablespoon minced fresh garlic
- 60 ounces prepared Mexican-style Hominy, drained
- 15 ounces corn kernels, drained
- 2 tablespoons ground cumin
- 1 tablespoon mild chile powder
- 14 ounces tomato puree
- 6 ounces tomato paste
- 3 cups chicken or vegetable stock
- 1 teaspoon dried oregano
- 1 teaspoon Worcestershire sauce
- Shredded lettuce and sour cream for garnish
- 2 limes for garnish

Kitchen Klips

Posole, traditionally served at Christmas, originated in Jalisco, in the middle of Mexico's Pacific coast. The key ingredient in Posole is hominy and was one of the first gifts that Native Americans gave to the colonists. Ground up and cooked, hominy is called grits.

CHILAQUILES

Heat oil in large, heavy, nonstick sauté pan over medium-high heat until hot. Stir in garlic, onion, and peppers. Sauté for 4 or 5 minutes.

Remove pan from heat and stir in tomato puree and cumin. Lower heat to medium and return pan to heat, stirring constantly. Stir in sour cream. Keep stirring. Just before the mixture simmers, stir in the tortilla chips to coat.

Sprinkle with cheddar and jack cheeses and cover loosely with foil and cook until cheese melts and chips soften slightly. Serve with garnishes as desired.

SERVES 4 TO 6

INGREDIENTS

- 1 tablespoon extra virgin olive oil
- 1 teaspoon minced fresh garlic
- 1 onion, chopped
- 1 mild green chile pepper, minced
- 1 red bell pepper
- 2 cups tomato puree
- 1 teaspoon ground cumin
- 1 cup sour cream
- 8 to 10 ounces tortilla chips
- 1/2 cup shredded cheddar cheese
- 1/2 cup shredded jack cheese
- Fried eggs to serve on top of Chilaquiles, as desired
- Extra sour cream for garnish, if desired
- Chopped lettuce, tomato, and jalapeño pepper for garnish, if desired
- Guacamole, fresh salsa, black pitted olives, and chopped cilantro for garnish, if desired

KITCHEN KLIPS

To slice and chop an onion without many tears, cut off the top and peel and pull the outer layer down to the root end. Use as a handle and slice the onion as desired toward the root end. Cut the stacked sliced onions cross-wise to chop.

Jumping Refried BEANS

Heat oil in large nonstick skillet and sauté garlic until golden. Stir in beans and mix in tomato paste and syrup. Mash together.

Preheat oven to 300°. Remove to baking dish, sprinkle cheese over the top and bake in preheated 300° oven until hot and cheese bubbles.

SERVES 6 TO 8 AS A SIDE DISH

INGREDIENTS

- 1 tablespoon extra virgin olive oil
- 2 tablespoons minced fresh garlic
- 60 ounces prepared black beans, drained
- 6 ounces tomato paste
- ½ cup maple syrup
- 1 cup shredded jack cheese

BROWN RICE Latin Style

In a large, heavy nonstick saucepan, sauté the scallions in olive oil. Add green chiles, parsley, and spices, and sauté.

Add rice, stir, and slowly add corn and nuts. Sauté until all ingredients are mixed and done to taste.

SERVES 8 TO 10

INGREDIENTS

- 2 tablespoons extra virgin olive oil
- ½ cup chopped fresh scallions
- ½ cup sweet mild green chiles, deseeded and sliced thinly
- ¼ cup fresh parsley, stems removed
- 1 tablespoon Mediterranean or Greek oregano
- 1 teaspoon freshly ground black pepper
- 6 cups cooked brown rice
- 2 cans corn kernels
- 1 cup shelled pistachio nuts

CHOCOLATE
Cheese Flan

Have all ingredients and equipment ready. Preheat oven to 350°. In a small saucepan over medium high heat, add sugar and tequila, stirring continuously until sugar is slowly boiling. Cook until mixture is pale golden in color. Keep warm and quickly move on.

Preheat oven to 350°. In a food processor fitted with a steel blade or blender, add condensed milk, cream cheese, and cocoa and pulse until smooth. Add eggs, milk, and vanilla extract and again pulse until mixture is smooth. Pour melted sugar into custard cups or round flan mold. Pour flan mixture into custard cups on top of the melted sugar.

Place cups into another large ovenproof container and fill container with water surrounding the cups up to 1 or 2 inches from the top of molds. Bake in a preheated 350° oven for 40 minutes or until firm to the touch. Remove from oven and cool. Chill cups in the refrigerator until thoroughly cooled.

Run a sharp knife around sides of the cups to loosen flan. Being careful not to get any water in the flan, dip cups into hot water for 15 seconds and invert onto serving plates or platters.

SERVES 8

INGREDIENTS

- 2/3 cup tequila
- 2/3 cup granulated sugar
- 1 14 ounce can sweetened, condensed milk
- 8 ounces cream cheese, softened to room temperature
- 2/3 cup cocoa
- 1 tablespoon vanilla extract
- 4 eggs
- 14 ounces of whole milk (use the can from the condensed milk to measure)
- 2/3 cup granulated sugar

Patricia's CHOCOLATE ECSTASY

The Crust

Place chocolate wafers in food processor bowl, and, using the steel blade, process into fine crumbs. Add butter in pieces and pulse until butter binds to the crumbs.

Wrap aluminum foil around the outside edges and bottom of a nine-inch spring pan. Scrape crumbs into the pan and press the crumbs firmly against sides and bottom.

The Filling

Preheat oven to 325°. Place cream cheese and sugar into food processor bowl and puree until smooth.

Add sour cream, vanilla, and cocoa and process to blend. Place eggs in the bowl and pulse just to combine. Scrape bowl. Give a few more pulses, then pour the batter into crust.

Bake in preheated 325° oven until cake completely domes up on top, about 2 hours.

Cool and refrigerate fully before unmolding and serving.

The Fudge Sauce

Stir together all ingredients in a small, heavy, nonstick saucepan over medium-low heat until simmering. Simmer very gently for 10 minutes, being careful not to scorch.

Remove from heat and cool about 10 minutes before serving over the chocolate cake. Makes about 1½ cups fudge sauce.

SERVES 8

INGREDIENTS

THE CRUST

1 9-ounce package of chocolate wafer cookies (like Famous Chocolate Wafers)

4 ounces unsweetened butter

THE FILLING

16 ounces cream cheese, softened to room temperature

1⅔ cups granulated sugar

8 ounces of sour cream

1 teaspoon vanilla extract

½ cup Dutch processed cocoa

4 eggs

THE SAUCE

1 cup granulated sugar

½ cup Dutch processed cocoa

½ cup light Karo syrup

2 ounces unsweetened butter

½ cup heavy whipping cream

Chef Harry's FROZEN MARGARITAS

A MEXICAN MEAL just has to start with a real Tex-Mex, South-of-the-Border margarita. I've devised some of my best original margaritas at celebrity parties. A margarita can be served shaken, straight-up, on the rocks, or very frosty and blended. Try 'em all, you can't lose. Have your very own taste-test when it's a stay-by-the-pool day! Just remember, if you drink don't drive!

Plain Margaritas

In a food processor fitted with a steel blade, pulse together the tequila, sugar, Triple Sec, lime juice, grape juice, and ice until smooth.

Using the lime wedge, moisten the rim of a glass and dip the moistened rim in kosher salt, if desired. Fill glass with frozen margarita.

Watermelon Margaritas

In a food processor fitted with a steel blade, pulse together the tequila, sugar, watermelon liquor, watermelon, lime juice, and ice until smooth.

Using the lime wedge, moisten the rim of a glass and dip the moistened rim in kosher salt, if desired.

Fill glass with frozen margarita.

Raspberry Margaritas

In a food processor fitted with a steel blade, pulse together the tequila, sugar, raspberry liquor, raspberries, lime juice, and ice until smooth.

Using the lime wedge, moisten the rim of a glass and dip the moistened rim in kosher salt, if desired.

Fill glass with frozen margarita. Top with three fresh raspberries.

ALL RECIPES ARE FOR 1 MARGARITA

INGREDIENTS

PLAIN MARGARITAS

- 2 ounces high quality tequila
- 1 teaspoon sugar
- ½ ounce Triple Sec
- Juice from one fresh lime
- 1 ounce white grape juice
- Crushed ice
- 1 wedge of lime
- Kosher salt (optional)

WATERMELON MARGARITAS

- 2 ounces high quality tequila
- 1 teaspoon sugar
- ½ ounce watermelon liquor
- 1 3-inch seedless piece of watermelon
- Juice from one fresh lime
- Crushed ice
- 1 wedge of lime
- Kosher salt (optional)

RASPBERRY MARGARITAS

- 2 ounces high quality tequila
- 1 teaspoon sugar
- ½ ounce Framboise (or raspberry liquor)
- ½ cup fresh raspberries
- Juice from one fresh lime
- Crushed ice
- 1 wedge of lime
- Kosher salt (optional)
- 3 fresh raspberries, for garnish

CHAPTER 6

LAZY
LUNCHES

LUNCH, NOT BRUNCH! I developed some of the recipes in this chapter especially for my guest, writer Judith Krantz. Judith was raised in Paris and carries on the European tradition of enjoying a large midday meal. And now midday entertaining is becoming more and more popular here. I receive many requests from celebrities to plan a lunch menu, usually emphasizing "light" lunch recipes that can be served with a casual attitude. This latest cuisine trend also emphasizes "let's do lunch-like foods," not the typical weekend brunch dishes. One star said to me, "Just because a meal takes place in early afternoon on a Sunday, it does not mean just eggs!" Although you will find several recipes in this chapter that use eggs, I have intentionally omitted traditional breakfast dishes. Instead, I recommend that you think of my recipes in the *Lazy Lunches* chapter as possibilities for dining light and perfect picnic recipe ideas.

> "JUST BECAUSE THIS MEAL TAKES PLACE IN EARLY AFTERNOON ON A SUNDAY, IT DOES NOT MEAN JUST EGGS!"

Now On to The **STARS**

JUDITH KRANTZ refuses to allow garlic into her home. This directive was clear from the start. Her own personal chef reminded me again as we began preparations for lunch. As the activity in the kitchen reached full speed—and with no garlic in sight—Judith Krantz entered the kitchen looking beautiful in Chanel. Not every one can wear a Chanel suit in the kitchen and look just right! Currently touring for her new novel, *The Jewels of Tessa Kent*, and working on her next, Judith doesn't have much time to spend in the kitchen. Add up all those made-for-TV movies, book promotions, and relentless charity commitments and you have one hard-working woman. ■ The Krantz's Bel Air home is exquisitely decorated. Glazed walls and pastel silk furnishings are accented by antique furniture, fine paintings, and stunning carpets. Complementing the décor are her collections of rare ceramics, silver, and glass. ■ The inspiration for the romance in her novels comes from much of her own life. As the mother of two sons, Judith notes, "I've unconsciously

Judith Krantz entered the kitchen looking beautiful in Chanel. Not every one can wear a Chanel suit in the kitchen and look just right!

been creating the daughters I never had in the form of my heroines." ■ When it comes to food, there is just one thing that really tickles Judith's fancy. "I love caviar. I really do. I could sit in a warm bubble bath with a beautiful large mother-of-pearl shell full of the finest caviar and mother-of-pearl spoon and just eat and eat and eat. I think one of the things that has kept my marriage strong is that Steve doesn't like caviar. He always gives me his when it is served. Who couldn't love that in a man?" she said with a smile. Then she added, "I just love it, I really do. It used to be you could give fine caviar as a gift. Now it has gotten so expensive. And the finest caviar is so hard to get." ■ Lunchtime had arrived and a gorgeous table beckoned. Bud vases holding single blooms of multicolored Gerber daisies surrounded a clay pot brimming with pink cabbage roses. The antique French service plates were adorned with baroque sterling and fine crystal. ■ The first course, an olive pâté served on sesame black pepper flatbreads, was mellow yet flavorful, with roasted red peppers adding a touch of smoky flavor. Next, I offered Judith a main dish of delicious make-ahead potato salad in vinaigrette and salmon cakes topped with a thin slice of goat cheese and a huge dollop of cucumber caviar chutney. Naturally, it was the caviar chutney that Judith liked the best! So the next time your book club meets, make it a *Lazy Lunch* featuring a Judith Krantz favorite dish and book!

Jesse James SOUP

In a large, heavy, soup pot heat the oil over medium-high heat and stir in the onions and chiles. Sauté until slightly golden. Place chicken breasts in pot on top of vegetables and cook for 2 minutes. Sprinkle with salt and cover with water. When water begins to boil, reduce heat to maintain low boil, and cook until chicken is tender, about an hour.

Remove chicken (you can use the chicken for my "Elegant Chicken Salad" recipe on page 127). Strain stock through a cheesecloth and place back into pot. Clean rutabaga and potatoes and cut them into small chunks. Place in stock pot and simmer until tender but still firm. Stir in tomato purée, cilantro, oregano, cumin, paprika, and lemon juice. Simmer slowly for 20 minutes to allow flavors to blend.

Serve in warm bowls and garnish with avocado and sour cream.

SERVES 6

INGREDIENTS

1 tablespoon canola oil

1 large onion, chopped

2 Anaheim chiles, seeded and chopped

4 skinless, boneless chicken breasts, split into halves

1 tablespoon salt

1 and $\frac{1}{2}$ liters of bottled spring water

1 rutabaga

1 pound new potatoes

24 ounces tomato purée

$\frac{1}{2}$ cup chopped fresh cilantro leaf

1 teaspoon dried oregano

$\frac{1}{8}$ cup ground cumin

1 teaspoon paprika

Juice from 3 fresh lemons

2 sliced avocados, for garnish

1 cup sour cream, for garnish

Bordeaux OLIVE PÂTÉ and Herb Toasts

The Pâté

In a food processor bowl fitted with a steel blade, pulse the olives until minced. Add lemon juice and oregano and process until a paste in formed. Pulse in red pepper. Add oil in a slow stream while processing.

Serve with a crisp plain sliced baguette or my tasty herb toasts. Makes about 1½ cups.

The Herb Toasts

Preheat oven to 350°. Arrange the breads on a buttered tray. Melt the butter with the garlic and herbs and sauté just to mix flavors, about 3 minutes.

Remove from heat and, using a pastry brush, 'paint" the tops of the breads with all the garlic herb butter. Sprinkle with salt and pepper and bake in oven for 20 minutes. Reduce heat to 210° and bake until crisp, about 60 minutes.

Toast keeps in airtight container for up to 5 days. They can be served alone or with an accompaniment, such as my olive pâté recipe.

SERVES 8 TO 12 AS AN APPETIZER

INGREDIENTS

THE PATE

12 to 14 ounces pitted Mediterranean style black olives, drained

Juice from one fresh lemon

1 teaspoon dried oregano

1 roasted red pepper

1 tablespoon extra virgin olive oil

THE HERB TOASTS

18 pieces cocktail bread

3 ounces butter

1 clove garlic, minced

2 teaspoons dried Italian herb blend

KITCHEN KLIPS

Olive pâté is also referred to as tapenade or poor man's caviar. Crispy little toasts are also called crostini.

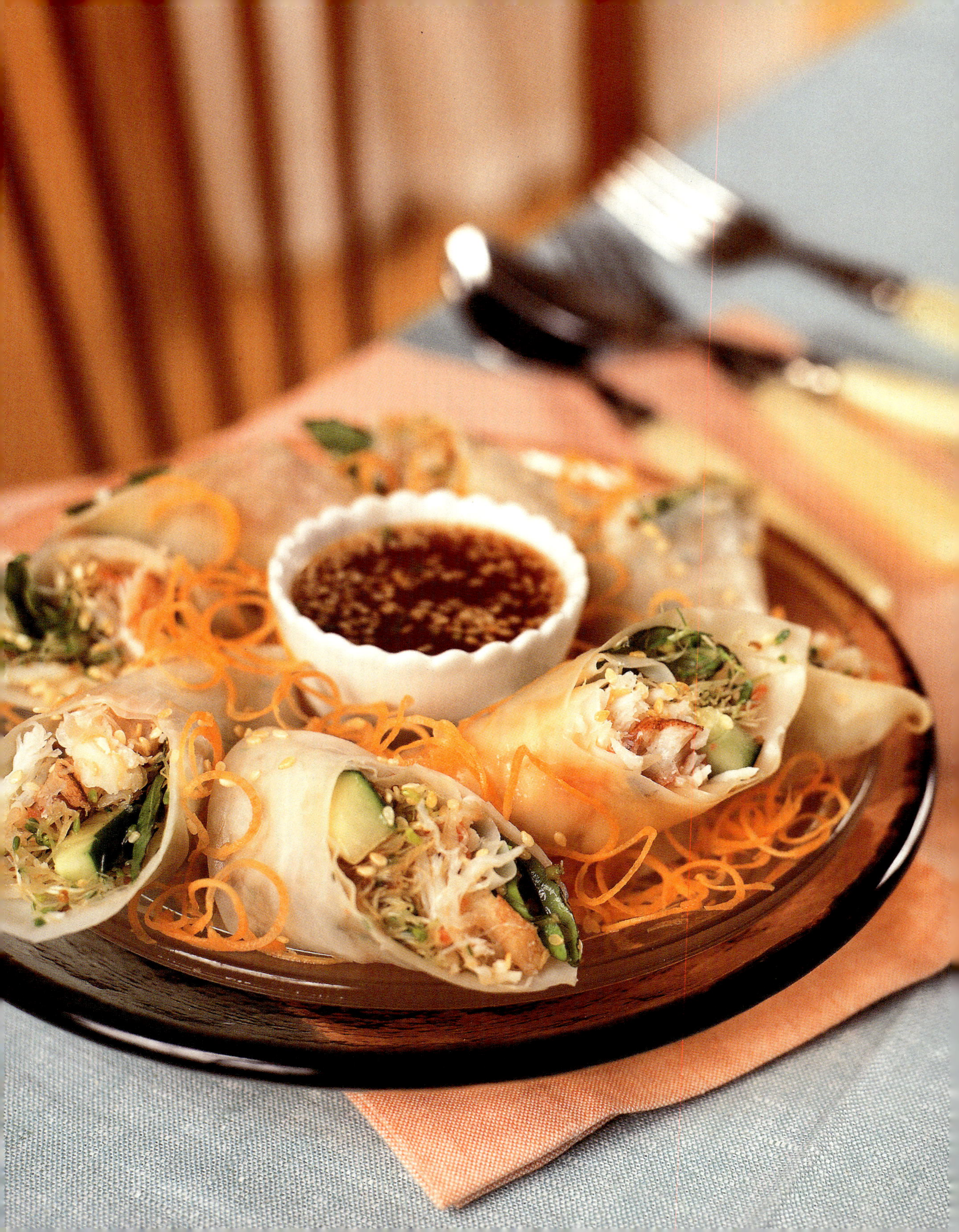

Dungeness CRAB Summer ROLLS

The Crab Rolls

In a shallow baking dish filled with a 1-inch deep layer of cool water, soak the wrappers until pliable but still firm. Drain.

Working quickly, place a finger shaped mound of crab on the rounded side of a wrapper. Arrange a cucumber strip over the crab. Place a smaller row of sprouts next to the crab and cucumber and a couple of basil leaves on top. Sprinkle with sesame seeds. Brush the area next to the crab mound with hoisin. Roll up tightly, folding over edges to enclose filling, like an egg roll. Repeat with remaining ingredients for 18, small, tight summer rolls. Serve with Ginger Dipping Sauce.

The Ginger Dipping Sauce

Mix the ingredients together with a wire whisk. Makes about 1 cup.

SERVES 8

Summer roll wrappers can be found at Asian specialty food markets. They are shaped as quarter circles, and come dehydrated and packaged in clear plastic. They are either called "spring roll wraps" or "summer roll wraps." They are very different from egg roll or wonton wrappers, which are found in the refrigerator cases of a supermarket and will not work as a substitute.

INGREDIENTS

THE CRAB ROLLS

18 summer roll wrappers

1 pound fresh, cooked Dungeness crabmeat, rinsed and picked over for shell bits

18 thin cucumber strips

1 cup assorted sprouts (alfalfa, onion, radish, etc.)

1 cup fresh basil leaves, rinsed and patted dry

¼ cup toasted sesame seeds

¼ cup hoisin sauce

THE DIPPING SAUCE

⅔ cup seasoned rice vinegar (as for sushi)

1 tablespoon soy sauce

2 tablespoons catsup

1 tablespoon powdered or 2 tablespoons minced fresh ginger

2 tablespoons toasted sesame seeds

1 teaspoon minced chives

KITCHEN KLIPS

Ranging from 1 to 4 pounds, Dungeness crab is caught off the Pacific coast from Mexico to Alaska. Its flesh is pink and very sweet.

Curried New POTATOES with CAVIAR

Cut potatoes into halves and poach in lightly salted water until tender but not soft. They are ready when the tip of a knife can go through a potato without resistance.

Drain and run under cold water to stop cooking. Drain again. Mix together the yogurt with the curry blend, lemon juice, and paprika. Toss yogurt mixture with potatoes. Arrange in a layer on a serving plate and top with salmon.

Sprinkle with dill and garnish with dollops of caviar.

SERVES 8 AS A SIDE DISH OR APPETIZER

INGREDIENTS

- 1 pound baby red potatoes
- 1 pound baby gold potatoes
- 2 cups plain non-fat yogurt
- 1 tablespoon curry blend powder or to taste
- Juice from 1 lemon
- 1/2 teaspoon paprika
- 6 ounces smoked salmon, torn into bits
- 1 tablespoon fresh dill, stemmed
- Caviar for garnish—as much as desired! (Judith Krantz loves caviar!)

Chopped COBB SALAD

Be creative when arranging all of the items on top of the Romaine. Present before tossing to your guests, then toss with the desired amount of dressing.

The Buttermilk Dressing

Mix together the sugar, flour, and dry mustard. Bring the vinegar to a boil in a saucepan over medium-high heat and boil for 5 minutes. Add the sugar mixture to the vinegar and stir until smooth. Add the egg and the buttermilk and cook, stirring constantly for 2 minutes more. Season with salt and pepper to taste. Makes 2 cups.

SERVES 8

The Sourdough Croutons

Preheat oven to 300°. Slice baguette into 1/2-inch thick slices. For larger slices, cut baguette at an angle. Melt butter and stir in salt and herb blend. Using a pastry brush, "paint" a cookie sheet or jelly roll pan with the seasoned butter and arrange bread slices on top. "Paint" tops of slices with butter.

Bake for 10 minutes and reduce heat to 250° and bake until crisp, about 45 minutes. Toasts may also be placed in 225° oven and left overnight to crisp. Makes 24 to 36 croutons.

SERVES 8 TO 12 AS A SIDE SALAD

> *The Cobb Salad originated at Hollywood's historic Brown Derby restaurant.*

INGREDIENTS

- 3 cups poached and chilled chicken breast meat, cut into small chunks
- 12 strips bacon, fried until crisp and crumbled
- 1 cup crumbled blue cheese
- 1 cup chopped or grated hard boiled egg
- 2 avocados, cut into small pieces
- 2/3 cup fresh scallions, trimmed and chopped
- 1 cup tomato, seeded and chopped
- 1/2 cup pitted black olives, drained and sliced
- 3 Romaine lettuce hearts, trimmed and finely chopped
- Buttermilk Dressing to taste

THE DRESSING

- 1/4 cup sugar
- 3 tablespoons flour
- 1 teaspoon dry mustard powder
- 2 cups red wine vinegar
- 1 egg, well beaten
- 2/3 cup low-fat buttermilk
- Salt and pepper to taste

THE CROUTONS

- 1 small day-old sourdough baguette
- 4 ounces butter
- 1 teaspoon salt
- 1 tablespoon dried Italian herb blend

SALMON CAKES with Caviar Cucumber Chutney

The Salmon Cakes

In a food processor bowl fitted with a steel blade, pulse salmon, relish, breadcrumbs, and bell pepper until finely chopped. Scrape into a bowl and mix in soy sauce, mayonnaise, eggs, dried herbs, dill, curry powder, and pepper. Form 12 3-inch patties. (Add more breadcrumbs if necessary to form firm patties.)

In a large, heavy, nonstick sauté pan over medium-high heat, add enough butter to generously coat the bottom of the pan. When foam subsides, arrange cakes, not touching, in the pan. Cook until brown on both sides, turning once, about 4 minutes per side. Cakes should be moist but not mushy inside. Top with a slice of goat cheese and a dollop of caviar cucumber chutney.

The Caviar Cucumber Chutney

Mix together sour cream, lemon juice, and cucumber. Just before serving, gently stir in caviar. Makes about 1 2/3 cups.

SERVES 6

INGREDIENTS

THE SALMON CAKES

12 ounces Alderwood smoked salmon

¼ cup sweet pickle relish

½ cup unseasoned breadcrumbs

1 red bell pepper, minced

1 teaspoon light soy sauce

⅓ cup mayonnaise

2 eggs, slightly beaten

1 teaspoon dried Italian herb blend

2 tablespoons minced fresh dill weed

1 teaspoon mild curry powder blend

1 teaspoon ground black pepper

Butter for frying

12 ½-inch thick round slices fresh goat cheese

THE CHUTNEY

1 cup sour cream

Juice from 1 lemon

1 cup finely chopped cucumber, seeded and peeled

4 ounces black caviar of choice

Kitchen Klips

Alderwood smoked salmon is typically from the Pacific Northwest. It is packed and boxed requiring no refrigeration until opened. It has a firm, dry texture that chunks rather than slices.

Citrus SCALLOP Salad

Be creative when arranging all of the items on top of the Romaine. Present before tossing, then toss with the desired amount of dressing.

SERVES 4

The Citrus Vinaigrette

Whisk together all of the ingredients except for the oil. Continue whisking, while slowly adding the oil in a thin stream until dressing is slightly thickened. Season with salt and pepper. Makes about ¾ cup.

The Poached Scallops

Bring white wine, herbs, sugar, and scallops to a simmer for about 5 minutes. Turn off heat.

Season with salt and pepper and chill 24 hours, if time allows, for flavors to infuse.

INGREDIENTS

- 2 to 3 cups poached scallops (see below for recipe), chilled and drained
- 12 strips bacon, fried until crisp and crumbled
- 1 cup crumbled blue cheese
- 1 cup chopped or grated hard boiled egg
- ⅔ cup fresh scallions, trimmed and chopped
- 1 cup Mandarin orange sections
- 1 head Romaine lettuce, trimmed and chopped finely
- Citrus Vinaigrette dressing, to taste

THE VINAIGRETTE

- Juice from 1 fresh lime
- Juice from 1 fresh lemon
- ¼ cup orange juice
- 1 teaspoon minced fresh garlic
- 1 teaspoon dried Italian herb blend
- 1 tablespoon honey
- ⅓ cup extra virgin olive oil
- Salt and fresh cracked pepper to taste

THE POACHED SCALLOPS

- 2 cups white wine
- 1 teaspoon dried Italian herbs
- 1 teaspoon sugar or to taste
- 1 pound bay scallops
- Salt and pepper to taste

CORNED BEEF and CABBAGE Reuben

Heat oil in a nonstick skillet over medium-high heat. Sauté the onion and pepper until tender, about 5 minutes. Stir in the cabbage and sauté until cabbage is tender and soft. Season with salt and pepper. Remove from heat.

Slice the bread through the diameter and create two large round slices of bread. (Use bread trimmings for croutons or breadcrumbs.) Spread one side of each slice with dressing. On one slice of bread, on top of dressing, arrange cheese in a single layer. Top with corned beef, also in an even layer. Place cabbage on top of corned beef, and place other slice of bread, dressing side down, on top of the cabbage.

In a nonstick skillet brushed with butter, toast sandwich until bread is golden and crisp and cheese has melted, turning once to toast both sides. Cut into four pie-shaped wedges and serve hot. Serve with fried or boiled potatoes for a perfect Saint Patrick's Day celebration!

SERVES 4

INGREDIENTS

2 tablespoons extra virgin olive oil

1 chopped onion

1 red bell pepper, seeded and chopped

8 ounces finely shredded cabbage (about $\frac{1}{2}$ medium head)

Salt and pepper to taste

1 large round loaf of bread

$\frac{1}{3}$ cup Thousand Island Dressing

8 slices Swiss cheese

$\frac{3}{4}$ pound thinly sliced corned beef

Butter for frying

Thousand Island DRESSING

Mix all ingredients together well. Makes about $1\frac{1}{3}$ cups.

SERVES 4 TO 6 ON A SALAD OR 4 IN A
CORNED BEEF AND CABBAGE REUBEN

INGREDIENTS

$\frac{3}{4}$ cup mayonnaise

$\frac{1}{4}$ cup sweet pickle relish

3 chopped scallions

1 chopped hard-boiled egg

2 tablespoons catsup

1 tablespoon wine vinegar

Elegant Chicken **SALAD**

Chop chicken into small bites. Grate or chop eggs finely. Mix together mayonnaise, mustard, relish, and nuts and combine with chicken and egg. Allow to stand 1 hour in refrigerator for flavors to blend. Serve over greens or in a sandwich.

SERVES 8

INGREDIENTS

- 4 poached or boiled skinless, boneless chicken breasts
- 6 hard boiled eggs, cooled
- 2½ cups mayonnaise
- ⅛ cup Dijon mustard
- ⅓ cup sweet pickle relish
- ½ cup pine nuts
- 2 cups chopped walnuts

FETTUCCINE with ROASTED VEGETABLES

Preheat an oven to 325°. Toss the vegetables with the garlic and oil. Spread on a baking sheet and sprinkle with cracked pepper and salt. Place in preheated 325° oven and roast until fennel and peppers are tender, about 35 minutes.

Just before vegetables are finished (they may be held in warm oven up to 1 hour) cook pasta in boiling salted water until al dente. Drain pasta. Toss pasta with butter and then with vegetables. Mix together fresh minced herbs and sprinkle liberally over pasta and vegetables. Serve with shaved Parmesan.

SERVES 4 TO 6

INGREDIENTS

1 head fennel, trimmed, rinsed and cut into strips

1 purple onion cut into chunks

1 yellow zucchini, trimmed and sliced

1 red bell pepper, seeded and sliced

1 green bell pepper, seeded and sliced

2 tomatoes, trimmed, seeded and quartered

1 cup large pitted black olives, drained

1 tablespoon minced fresh garlic

⅓ cup extra virgin olive oil

Cracked pepper and Kosher salt, to taste

1 pound dried spinach fettuccine

Salted water for boiling pasta

4 tablespoons butter, melted

½ cup minced fresh basil leaves

1 tablespoon minced fresh oregano leaves

¼ cup chopped Italian parsley leaves

Shaved Parmesan cheese as a garnish

LAZY LUNCHES

EGG SALAD "90265"

Grate the eggs finely and mix with the mayonnaise and mustard until blended. Gently fold in caviar. Divide egg salad mixture among slices of toast and top egg salad with tomatoes. Sprinkle the capers over the tomatoes.

Divide slices of onions into rings and arrange on top of caper dotted tomatoes. Arrange butter lettuce leaf on top and a dollop of crème fraîche or sour cream as a final touch. This sandwich is more easily enjoyed with a knife and fork. Makes 4 sandwiches.

SERVES 4

INGREDIENTS

- 12 hard boiled eggs
- 1½ cups mayonnaise
- ¼ cup yellow mustard
- 1 or 2 ounces caviar of choice
- 4 large ¾-inch thick slices egg bread toast
- 8 thin slices tomato
- 2 tablespoons capers, rinsed and drained
- 2 very thin slices red onion
- 8 butter lettuce leaves
- ½ cup crème fraîche or sour cream

Kitchen Klips

For perfect hard-boiled eggs with bright yellow yolks, place eggs in a pot and cover with cold water. Bring to a boil over medium-high heat. Cover and turn off heat. Allow eggs to sit undisturbed in the hot covered pot for 20 minutes. Drain and run under cold water. They should peel easily and be perfect for your recipe or snack.

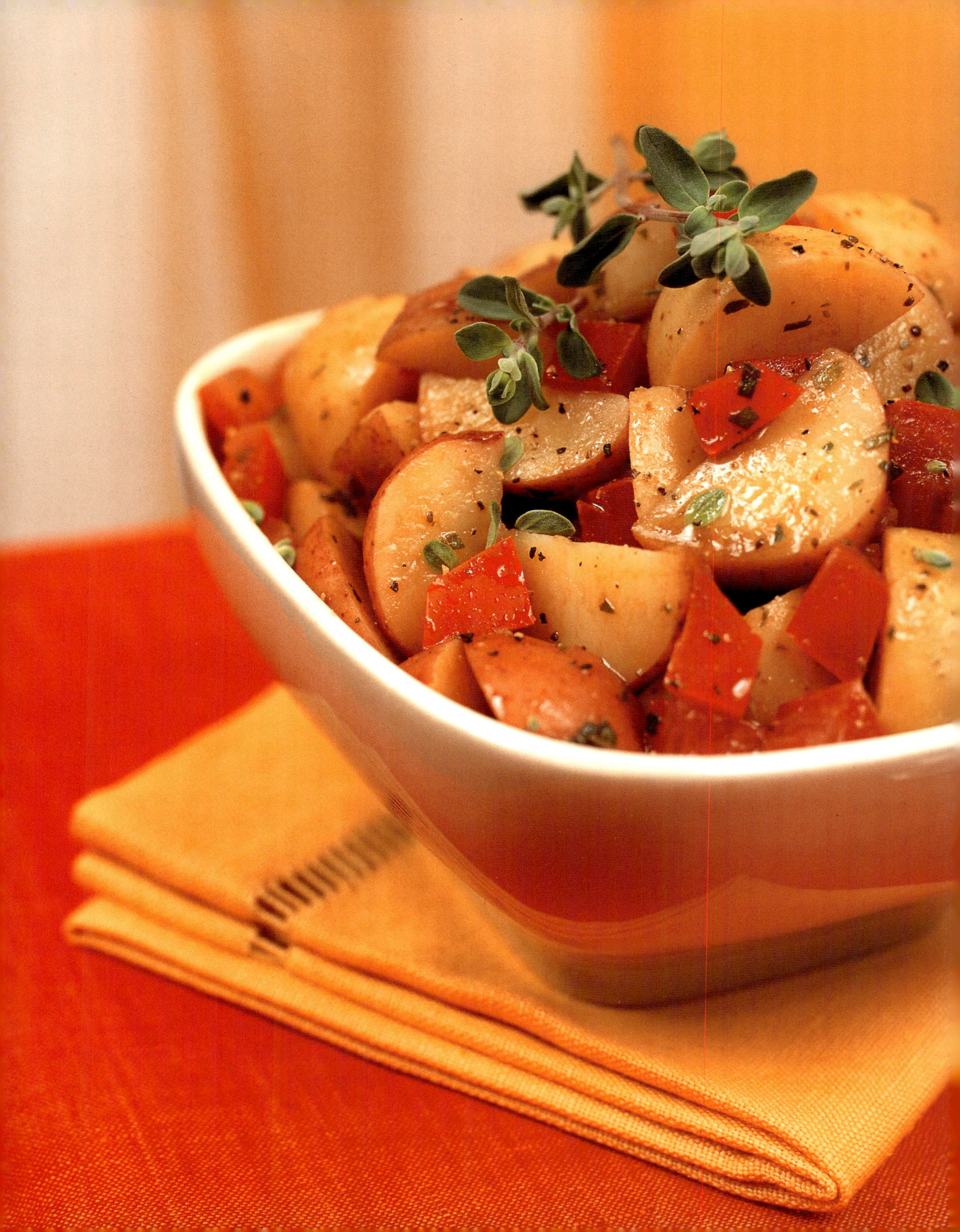

Red and White New POTATO SALAD

Quarter potatoes and poach until tender but not soft. Drain and rinse with cold water to stop cooking process.

Place in glass or ceramic bowl with tomato.

In a separate bowl, mix together vinegar, oregano, basil, celery seed, sugar, and mustard. Whisk in oil slowly and continue to whisk until slightly thickened. Season with salt and pepper. Pour over potatoes and tomato, and toss.

Cover and refrigerate until ready to serve.

SERVES 6 TO 8

INGREDIENTS

12-16 ounces gold new potatoes

12-16 ounces red new potatoes

2 firm tomatoes, seeded and chopped

½ cup balsamic vinegar

1 tablespoon minced fresh oregano leaf

½ cup chopped fresh basil leaf

1 teaspoon celery seed

1 tablespoon granulated sugar

1 tablespoon Dijon mustard

½ cup extra virgin olive oil

Salt and pepper to taste

KITCHEN KLIPS

Poaching potatoes in simmering but not boiling water will allow the skins to remain intact as potatoes cook. Drain the potatoes as soon as firm but not yet soft and cool under gently running cold water.

Poached SALMON WITH Ginger Garlic CHUTNEY

The Poached Salmon

Place the salmon flat, skin side down in a pan (the pan should easily accommodate the fish comfortably and have a tight-fitting lid). Pour the water over the salmon and add the dill. Slice the lemon and float the slices in the water. Sprinkle the salt over the contents. Cover and poach on the stovetop using medium heat.

When water begins to simmer, reduce heat, and simmer until fish is poached, about 25 minutes.

Remove from pan and cool. Chill. Spread chutney over salmon to serve.

SERVES 6

The Ginger Garlic Chutney

Mix together the ingredients and allow flavors to combine for a few hours or overnight. Makes $1^2/_3$ cup, allowing for 8 servings.

INGREDIENTS

THE POACHED SALMON

- 3 pound piece of salmon side fillet
- 4 cups water
- 3 sprigs fresh dill
- 1 lemon
- 1 teaspoon salt

THE CHUTNEY

- $1/_3$ cup minced fresh garlic
- $1/_3$ cup minced fresh ginger
- 2 tablespoons soy sauce
- $1/_4$ cup finely minced fresh cilantro
- $1/_4$ cup seasoned rice vinegar as for sushi
- $1/_2$ teaspoon sesame oil
- 1 finely chopped fresh scallion

KITCHEN KLIPS

Salmon may be poached in white wine or fish stock for a deeper, richer, and fruitier flavor.

Grapefruit CAKE with PINEAPPLE Frosting

The Cake

Cream the butter while slowly adding ⅓ cup sugar, and beat until fluffy. Blend in the vanilla and grapefruit syrup. Sift together all of the dry ingredients except the remaining sugar. Add ¼ cup of the milk and ¼ cup of the sifted ingredients at a time to the butter mixture, blending thoroughly after each addition until all dry ingredients and milk are used.

Beat the egg whites until foamy. Sprinkle in the cream of tartar and beat to peak stage. Fold the egg whites gently into the batter.

Preheat oven to 350°.

Pour batter into two 8- or 9-inch round cake pans that have been greased or well sprayed with nonstick spray. Bake in preheated 350° oven for 50 to 55 minutes or until top springs back in center when gently touched. Cool layers and frost with Pineapple Grapefruit Frosting.

The Pineapple Grapefruit Frosting

Drain the pineapple in a strainer and press out as much juice as possible. Place the pineapple in the center of a square of cheesecloth or clean kitchen towel. Gather corners and side to form a pouch, twisting the top to enclose. Twist over the sink to remove as much juice as possible. Set aside pineapple on paper towel. Whip the cream cheese and butter with the powdered sugar and whip in the vanilla and zest. Beat in the sour cream until frosting is blended and fluffy. Blend in coconut, if desired.

To assemble

Place contents of one pan on cake round or serving platter and spread top with a layer of frosting. Set contents of other pan on top. Spread remaining frosting in an even layer to attractively cover sides and top. Decorate with fresh flowers, if desired.

SERVES 10 TO 12

[*Roll oranges and grapefruit firmly with the palm of your hand while pressing against a countertop or tabletop. This action will loosen the skin and make peeling a breeze!*]

INGREDIENTS

THE CAKE

- ½ pound unsalted butter, softened to room temperature
- 2 cups granulated sugar
- 1 teaspoon vanilla extract
- ⅛ cup grapefruit syrup
- 3 cups cake flour
- ½ teaspoon salt
- 3 teaspoons baking powder
- 1 cup milk
- 7 egg whites
- 1 teaspoon cream of tartar

THE FROSTING

- 1 10-to-12 ounce can crushed pineapple
- 24 ounces cream cheese, softened to room temperature
- 4 ounces unsalted butter, softened to room temperature
- 1⅓ cups powdered sugar
- 1 teaspoon vanilla extract
- 1 tablespoon finely minced fresh grapefruit zest
- ½ cup sour cream
- 2 cups shredded sweetened coconut (optional)

Ginger LEMON TARTS

The Crust

Process ingredients in food processor fitted with steel blade until meal-like in texture. Press mixture into 6 individual tart pans (with removable bottoms) covering sides and bottoms well.

The Filling

In a heavy saucepan, mix together the yolks, flour, sugar, and enough milk to make a smooth paste. Place over low heat and stir constantly, while slowly adding milk in a stream. Continue to stir and raise heat just enough to slowly bring mixture to a simmer.

Simmer for 2 minutes and stir in lemon zest and juice and lastly vanilla. Simmer 30 seconds more. Remove from heat and pour into tart shells. Refrigerate until cold.

The Meringue Topping

Beat egg whites and cream of tartar until frothy. Continue to beat, while slowly adding sugar, one teaspoon at a time. Keep beating until soft peaks are formed. Beat in vanilla.

Divide meringue over tarts evenly, being careful to spread the filling all the way to the edges.

Place on middle rack of oven and turn on broiler. Broil top until golden with toasted highlights.

SERVES 6

INGREDIENTS

THE CRUST

12 ounces low-fat, low cholesterol gingersnaps

3 ounces butter or margarine

THE FILLING

6 egg yolks

2 tablespoons unbleached all-purpose flour

¾ cup powdered sugar

3 cups non-fat or low-fat milk

1 tablespoon finely minced fresh lemon zest

1½ tablespoons fresh lemon juice

1 teaspoon vanilla extract

THE TOPPING

2 egg whites

1 teaspoon cream of tartar

1½ cups granulated sugar

1 teaspoon vanilla extract

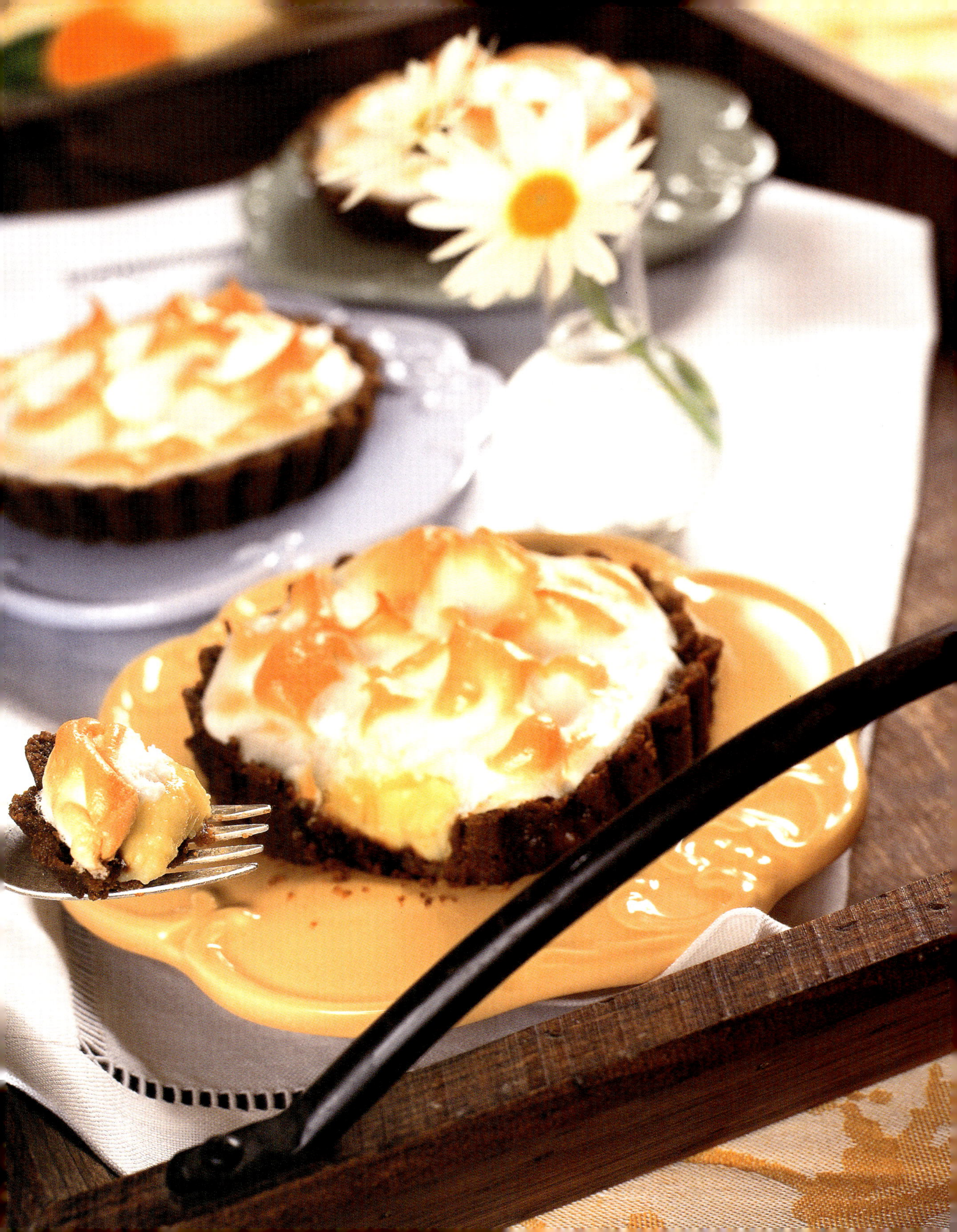

CHAPTER 7

COMFORT
CUISINE

WHEN I THINK OF RAINY DAYS or Mondays, I think of cooking something really good to eat to cheer me up. I think of good old-fashioned meals, nowadays coined "comfort food." And that's what this chapter is about. Preparing to cook with Orson Bean and Alley Mills, we planned recipes that we craved when our body, soul, or emotional spirit needed a "time out" from today's "healthy" gourmet cuisine. So, we dedicated this show to real food for real people—even if the real people just happened to be celebrities! On today's top-ten list of food types, comfort food has got to be up there. What's new about today's comfort food is that those fatty, genuinely non-healthy ingredients have been cut or modified in my recipes. With this in mind, I've taken really traditional dishes and created special Chef Harry recipes. They're perfect for when you're in the mood for something richer than a salad or longing for a traditional dish your mom prepared when you were a kid. This chapter has a range of recipes to hit the spot—no matter what craving or mood you're looking to satisfy.

> WHAT'S NEW ABOUT TODAY'S COMFORT FOOD IS THAT THOSE FATTY, GENUINELY NON-HEALTHY INGREDIENTS HAVE BEEN CUT OR MODIFIED IN MY RECIPES.

Now On to The
STARS

ORSON BEAN AND ALLEY MILLS make a great couple. Both brilliant television and stage actors in their own right, they are even more dynamic when working together. Orson had just finished over six years on *Dr. Quinn Medicine Woman*, only to receive an offer for a leading role opposite Cameron Díaz in a film that begins shooting in the fall. Alley is much loved on reruns of *The Wonder Years*, a critically acclaimed show that ran for many seasons. Together, they recently received standing ovations in a play for the Venice Theatre Ensemble. ■ Their home is situated on one of the charming canals of Venice, California. At first, before their marriage, Orson owned a small, vintage cottage. He soon bought the house next door for more room. Together, Orson and Alley turned his cottage into bedrooms and then connected the adjacent house, which became a wonderful, spacious, and light great-room area. When the next cottage became available it was purchased as a guest suite. They recently acquired a fourth cottage nearby for Orson's daughter and her family, who are moving from Paris back to the U.S. ■ The cottages have all been redone in the period in which they were built, the 1940s.

Orson is a connoisseur of fine wine and Shakespeare. Alley obviously adores him and together they behave like love-struck teenagers.

Orson and Alley's marvelous folk art furnishings and eclectic art complement the wood plank floors and whitewashed ceilings with beams and moldings. Orson loves to cook, and their kitchen was hand-built—not by a craftsman, but by an artist. Outside sits an antique neon sign and a wading pool for their ducks. Their cats (Orson loves cats and has published a humorous cat-lover's book, *25 Ways to Cook a Mouse—For the Gourmet Cat*), live a happy life exploring the grounds and the cottages. The Beans illuminate their canal front decks with antique lanterns and relax outside on teak furniture. ■ They live casually but surround themselves with style. Orson is a connoisseur of fine wine and Shakespeare. Alley obviously adores him and together they behave like love-struck teenagers. I found it a pleasure to be in their company. As we planned their meal, Orson was emphatic that they not be served "That fancy stuff on beds of cilantro and saturated in reduction sauces. I am a meat-and-potatoes kind of guy, and I would prefer meat loaf and mashed potatoes to caviar and foie gras," he added. That made my work very easy. When I arrived, Orson answered the door partially dressed and greeted me like I was family. Alley came out and warmly hugged me and planted a kiss on my cheek. ■ Shortly after my arrival Orson's daughter and her two adorable French-speaking toddlers appeared. Her husband was already hard at work and couldn't join us, so they invited actress friend Katy Selverstone and her friend Jeff Miller. We all had a fine time eating these "Mom's cooking" recipes, which I have shared with you in this chapter. So, light a fire, grab a drink, make some recipes from this chapter, and sit down for some soul-warming comfort food!

Farmer's COTTAGE CHEESE

Mix the vegetables together in a bowl. Sprinkle with herbs, salt, and pepper and mix again. Gently stir in the cottage cheese. Makes about 6 cups. Serve on crackers as an appetizer, or as a side dish with a lean protein dinner to add extra calcium to the meal.

SERVES 4 TO 6

INGREDIENTS

- 1/2 cucumber, seeded and chopped
- 1 bell pepper, seeded and chopped
- 1 bunch fresh scallions, trimmed and chopped
- 2 medium firm tomatoes, seeded and chopped
- 1 teaspoon Italian herb blend
- Salt and pepper to taste
- 16 ounces small curd cottage cheese

Yatze SCHMEAR

Heat the oil in a nonstick sauté pan over medium heat. Stir in the onion and sauté until toasted, about 12 to 15 minutes. Cool. Stir the toasted onion into the sour cream and add the Gorgonzola cheese. Mix in the Worcestershire, paprika, and pepper. Makes about 2 cups.

SERVES 8 AS A SCHMEAR OR DIP

INGREDIENTS

- 1 tablespoon safflower oil
- 1 chopped onion
- 16 ounces sour cream
- 8 ounces crumbled Gorgonzola cheese, room temperature
- 1 teaspoon Worcestershire sauce
- 1/2 teaspoon paprika
- 1 teaspoon fresh cracked pepper

Brooklyn POTATO Latkes

Shred the potatoes using a food processor or grate them by hand.

Stir the onion and eggs into the potatoes. Sprinkle the flour over the mixture along with the salt and pepper and mix in well. Heat to medium-high a 1/2-inch deep layer of oil in a nonstick, heavy, large sauté pan or chicken fryer.

Using a 1/3 cup scoop, place mounds of potato mixture into the hot oil and flatten slightly into pancakes. Fry until crisp and brown on both sides, about 6 to 8 minutes per side.

Drain on paper towel lined tray and hold in warm oven. Repeat with balance of potato mixture and serve as soon as possible. Makes 16 latkes. Try the latkes topped with sour cream or apple sauce.

SERVES 4 TO 6

INGREDIENTS

- 2 large russet potatoes
- 1 small yellow onion, minced
- 2 eggs, slightly beaten
- 1 tablespoon unbleached all purpose flour
- 1 teaspoon salt
- 1/2 teaspoon ground black pepper
- Vegetable oil for frying

Kitchen Klips

Shred potatoes for latkes or hashbrowns just before making and do not rinse away the potato's starch. The starch helps them bind together well and makes them easier to turn!

COMFORT CUISINE

Loaded POTATO SKINS

The key to making potato skins is having baked potato skins available for use. Make this recipe when making mashed potatoes or any other recipe that calls for the flesh from baked potatoes.

Melt butter in a heavy nonstick sauté pan over medium-high heat. Place potato skins in pan, skins side down. Fry until crisp and golden on the bottom. While frying skins, in a large mixing bowl, combine tomatoes, garlic, sugar, bleu cheese, and basil and mix well. Next, drizzle olive oil and vinegar over mixture and toss to combine. Season with salt and pepper to taste.

Fill warm potato skins with mixture and serve.

SERVES 6 TO 8 AS AN APPETIZER

INGREDIENTS

2 tablespoons butter

6 baked potatoes, cut in half lengthwise (scoop out flesh and reserve for another use)

4 tomatoes, seeded and chopped

1 tablespoon minced fresh garlic

2 teaspoons granulated sugar

1½ cups crumbled bleu cheese

1 cup fresh basil leaves, chopped (opal basil, if available, is wonderful in this recipe)

2 tablespoons extra virgin olive oil

2 tablespoons balsamic vinegar

Salt and pepper to taste

KITCHEN KLIPS

For perfect baked potatoes, pierce each potato 3 or 4 times with a sharp knife inserted about 3/4 inch. Bake on middle rack of pre-heated 325° oven for 90 minutes or until tender.

Grilled Pepper STEAK

Melt butter in heavy nonstick sauté pan over medium-high heat and sauté the peppers until tender. Season with salt and ground pepper. Reheat when ready to serve.

Rinse steaks and place in a zip-lock bag or glass dish. Whisk together soy sauce, olive oil, red wine, and garlic and pour over steaks. Refrigerate and allow to marinate from 1 to 12 hours.

Grill over medium hot grill to desired doneness, sprinkling cracked pepper on both sides when turning. For 1½-inch thick steaks, grill about 6 minutes per side for medium. Place steaks on heated serving platter and smother in sautéed red peppers.

SERVES 4

INGREDIENTS

4 ounces butter

4 red bell peppers, seeded and sliced into strips

Salt and ground pepper to taste

4 New York strip steaks, about 8 to 12 ounces each

½ cup light soy sauce

2 tablespoons extra virgin olive oil

1 cup red wine

1 tablespoon minced fresh garlic

Cracked pepper to taste

> We planned recipes that we craved when our body, soul, or emotional spirit needed a "time out" from today's "healthy" gourmet cuisine.

50s MEAT LOAF and Toasted Scallion Mashed Potatoes

The Meat Loaf

Preheat oven to 325°.

Have all ingredients at room temperature and mix together well.

Form a loaf on a greased and sided baking pan.

Bake in preheated 325° oven until cooked through, about 2 hours. Test with meat thermometer if there is any question as to doneness. This makes a generous loaf. It is excellent cold, sliced, and made into sandwiches the next day.

The Toasted Scallion Mashed Potatoes

Peel the potatoes and cut into large chunks. Boil potatoes in lightly salted water until tender and easily pierced with the tip of a knife. Drain.

Heat the butter in a sauté pan over medium-high heat and stir in the scallions. Sauté the scallions until toasted.

With an electric beater, beat the butter and scallions into the potatoes and continue to beat, while adding cream in a stream. Season with salt and pepper and whip until smooth and fluffy. Potato recipe can be placed in a casserole and kept covered in a warm oven until ready to serve.

SERVES 8

INGREDIENTS

THE MEAT LOAF

1½ pounds lean ground pork

1½ pounds ground veal

3 large eggs

1 cup breadcrumbs

2 cups corn kernels, drained

2 tablespoons Worcestershire sauce

⅛ cup steak sauce of choice

Salt and pepper to taste

THE MASHED POTATOES

5 large baking potatoes

1½ sticks unsalted butter

1 cup fresh scallions, chopped

1 cup heavy cream

Salt and white pepper to taste

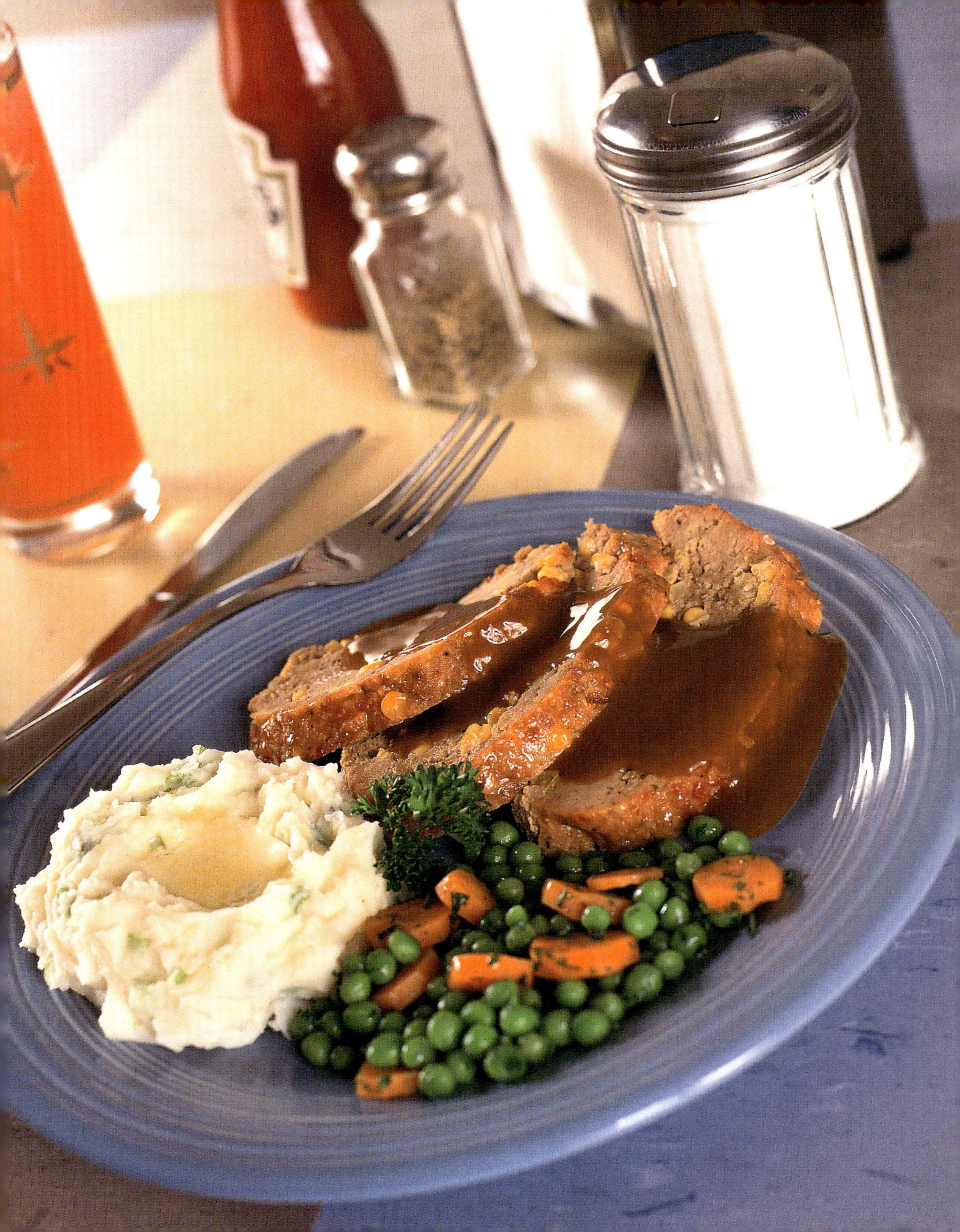

Traditional **TURKEY**

Preheat oven to 350°. Rinse the turkey inside and out and pat dry. Carefully loosen the skin that covers the breast by gently wiggling your fingers between the skin and the meat. Smooth the butter in an even layer over the breast meat and press the skin back down. Rub the bird all over with the olive oil and place in a roasting pan.

Sprinkle with salt and pepper. Place the onion in the cavity along with the fresh herbs. Roast in preheated 350° oven for about 3 hours, or about 8 minutes per pound.

SERVES 12

INGREDIENTS

- 1 16 pound fresh turkey
- 2 sticks unsalted butter, softened to room temperature
- 1 tablespoon extra virgin olive oil
- 1 tablespoon coarse salt
- 1 tablespoon fresh cracked pepper
- 1 small onion, peeled
- 1 sprig rosemary
- 1 small bunch fresh basil

Many people believe that it is unsafe to eat dressing that has been cooked in the cavity of a turkey. An unstuffed bird cooks more quickly and evenly, and there is less chance of getting sick. I recommend cooking the dressing separately from the bird.

Garlic and Chive **MASHED POTATOES**

Melt butter in a small pan over medium heat and add garlic. Sauté garlic until toasted. Add chives to pan and remove from heat. Whip potato flesh with melted garlic chive butter. Slowly whip in milk or cream. Season with salt and pepper to taste.

SERVES 12 AS A SIDE DISH

INGREDIENTS

- 1 stick unsalted butter
- 2 tablespoons minced fresh garlic
- $\frac{1}{2}$ cup finely chopped fresh chives
- Flesh from 6 baked potatoes
- 1 cup whole milk or cream
- Salt and pepper

Grandma's CORN BREAD Dressing

Preheat oven to 300°. Cut cornbread into small pieces and place on large pan in oven for 30 or 40 minutes or until slightly toasted and dried. Turn off oven and leave cornbread until ready to make dressing.

Increase heat to 325°.

In a large, heavy, nonstick skillet or Dutch oven over medium-high heat, melt butter and stir in onions and celery. Sauté until golden brown. Stir in herbs, paprika, and parsley. Season with salt and pepper. Reduce heat to medium and stir in cornbread. Pour stock over mixture and stir until absorbed. Place in buttered casserole that will accommodate mixture, and bake uncovered in preheated 325° oven until hot and crisp on top, about 30 minutes.

SERVES 8 TO 10

For quick cornbread that is perfect for cornbread stuffing, use an all-natural mix and stir in an onion that has been chopped and toasted with a little butter. Then follow the package directions to create an extra-tasty flavor!

INGREDIENTS

- 2 8-inch x 8-inch cornbread, store-bought or homemade
- 2 sticks unsalted butter
- 2 medium onions, chopped
- 1 cup chopped celery
- 1 tablespoon dried Italian herb blend
- 1 teaspoon sweet paprika
- ½ cup chopped fresh parsley
- Salt and pepper, to taste
- 3 cups chicken or vegetable stock, canned is fine

Cranberry Citrus RELISH

Rinse cranberries and place in heavy saucepan. Pour in sugar, lemon juice, and orange juice. Cook over medium-high heat until simmering, stirring occasionally. Stir in lemon zest, cinnamon, and cloves. Reduce heat to slow simmer and simmer 15 additional minutes. Pour into heatproof bowl. Cool and refrigerate until ready to serve. Makes about 3 cups.

SERVES 8

INGREDIENTS

- 1 pound fresh cranberries
- 1 cup granulated sugar
- Juice from 1 lemon
- ¼ cup orange juice
- Zest from 1 lemon
- ½ teaspoon cinnamon
- 1 dash ground cloves

Veggie Egg White OMELET

Heat a medium-sized nonstick omelet or sauté pan over medium-high heat and brush with butter. Add vegetables and sauté for 2 minutes. Stir in basil. Beat egg whites until slightly foamy and pour over vegetables.

Flip in sides to create burrito-shaped omelet or fold in half for half moon shape. Flip and brown on both sides.

SERVES 1

INGREDIENTS

- ¼ teaspoon butter
- 2 chopped scallions
- ¼ cup chopped red pepper
- ¼ cup chopped broccoli or cauliflower
- A few chopped basil leaves
- 4 to 6 egg whites
- Salt and pepper to taste

Roasted Chicken
POTATO PIE

Preheat oven to 350°. In medium-sized saucepan over medium heat, sauté onions, garlic, carrots, celery, and peas in butter for 3 minutes.

Add chicken and flour and stir well. Pour in cream and simmer while stirring for 2 or 3 minutes.

Spoon mixture into a deep 9x13 roasting pan that will accommodate it and cover evenly with a thick layer of the mashed potatoes. Bake, uncovered, in preheated 350° oven until golden brown, about 30 minutes.

SERVES 8

INGREDIENTS

1 Rosemary Roasted Chicken, cooled, meat removed from bones, and cut into chunks

1 chopped onion, white or yellow

2 cloves minced garlic

1 cup baby carrots, cut into small pieces

1 cup chopped celery

1½ cup fresh shelled peas

1 stick unsalted butter

2 tablespoons flour

1 cup heavy whipping cream

Salt and pepper to taste

Garlic and Chive Mashed Potatoes (see recipe on page 146)

Rosemary Roasted
CHICKEN

Preheat oven to 325°. Place chicken in roasting pan. Drizzle olive oil over the bird and rub salt and pepper into skin. Place rosemary in cavity with garlic, allowing about 1 inch of rosemary to stick out for garnish. Bake for 90 minutes or until done and juices from chicken run clear.

INGREDIENTS

1 medium roasting chicken, giblets and neck removed

3 tablespoons extra virgin olive oil

Salt and pepper to taste

2 generous sprigs fresh rosemary

3 whole garlic cloves, peeled

Cheese SOUFFLÉ in a Pan

Heat sauté pan over medium-high heat and brush with butter. Beat egg whites until soft peaks are formed. Pour into hot sauté pan. Sprinkle cheese over top.

Run under broiler until top is golden brown.

SERVES 2

INGREDIENTS

¼ teaspoon butter

4 egg whites

1 tablespoon shredded Parmesan cheese

Quick Pickled French GREEN BEANS

Place beans lengthwise in a jar with tight fitting lid. Beans should fit somewhat tightly in jar. Pour in vinegar, and add sugar, onion, dill, and salt and pepper to jar.

Add water to fill jar and seal. Shake jar to blend ingredients and refrigerate up to 3 days before serving. (Overnight works fine, too!)

SERVES 4 TO 6

INGREDIENTS

8 ounces French green beans, trimmed and rinsed

2 tablespoons red wine vinegar

1 teaspoon or one cube sugar

¼ cup chopped purple onion

2 tablespoons minced fresh dill

Salt and pepper to taste

1 cup water

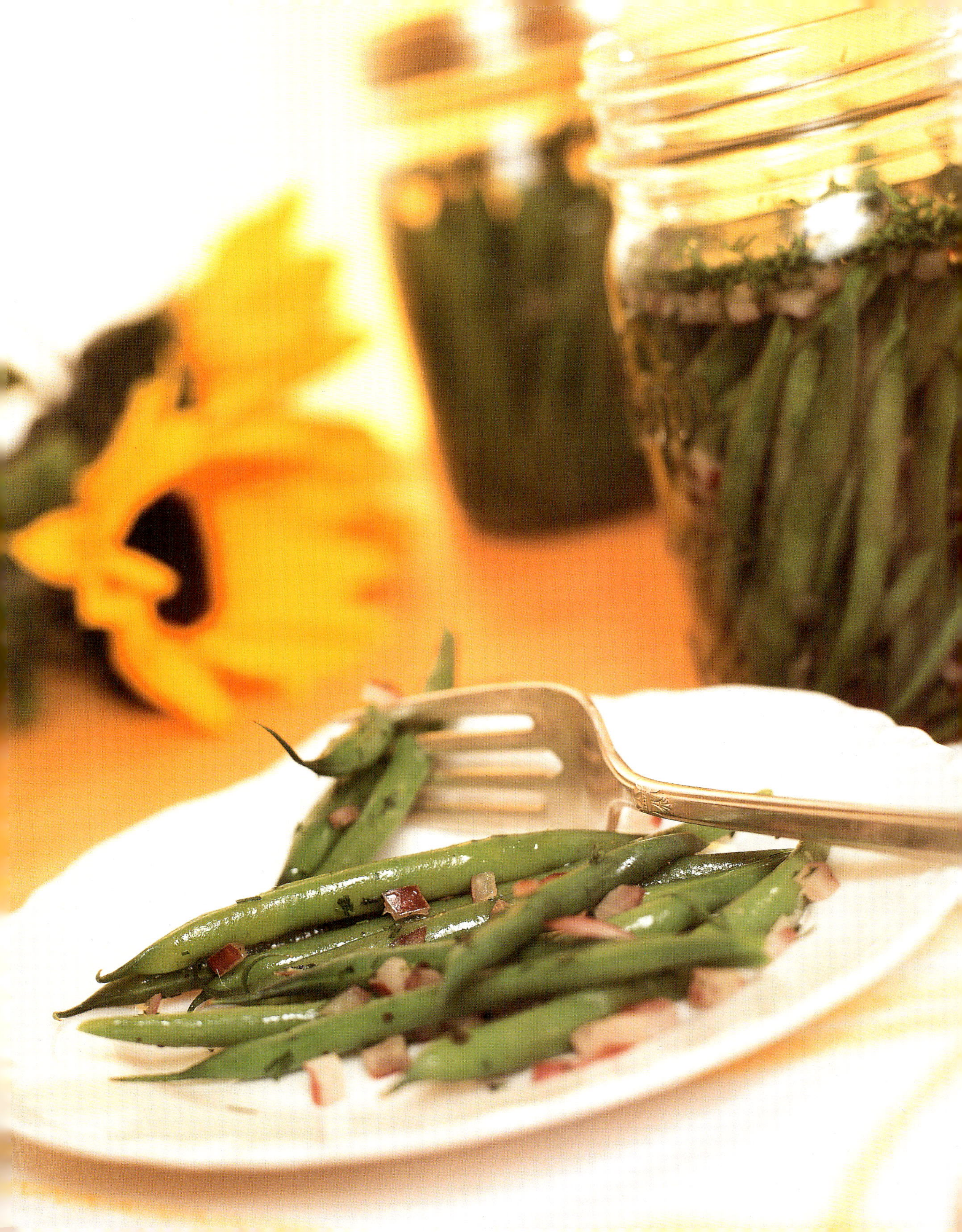

Pecan GARLIC SPINACH Sauté

In heavy nonstick sauté pan over medium heat, melt butter and stir in garlic and pecans and sauté for 3 minutes.

Add baby spinach, and drizzle vermouth over greens. Sauté for 2 more minutes or until spinach starts to wilt.

Season with salt and pepper to taste. Serve warm.

SERVES 4

Use prewashed baby spinach for salads and sautés. It reduces prep time and the baby spinach doesn't have tough stems like adult spinach.

Sautéing pecans with extra virgin olive oil brings out the oil from the pecans for a rich and aromatic flavor that goes perfectly in dressings and over goat cheese!

INGREDIENTS

- 3 tablespoons unsalted butter
- 2 sliced fresh garlic cloves
- 1 cup pecan halves
- 1 8 ounce bag prewashed baby spinach
- ½ cup dry vermouth
- Salt and pepper to taste

KITCHEN KLIPS

Garlic becomes very bitter and unpleasant if even slightly burned. Always watch carefully when sautéing garlic and never cook very long over high heat.

Black Bottomed Lemon MERINGUE PIE

In a food processor fitted with a steel blade, process cookies, butter, cinnamon, and almond extract until the mixture resembles a coarse meal. Press into a deep pie dish.

In a heavy saucepan over medium-low heat, mix together egg yolks, flour, powdered sugar, and enough of the milk to create a smooth texture. Continue to stir while slowly adding the rest of the milk and then the lemon juice. Do not stop stirring! Bring the mixture to a simmer, adjusting heat as necessary, and gently boil for 2 minutes.

Pour into a glass or ceramic bowl and cover with plastic wrap that touches the surface of the custard. When still warm but not hot, pour custard into chocolate crust. Refrigerate until chilled thoroughly.

Preheat oven to hottest setting.

With an electric mixture, beat the egg whites with the cream of tartar and slowly add the sugar. Continue to beat until stiff peaks are formed. Spoon the meringue over the lemon filling and make sure to seal all edges, with the meringue touching the edge of the pie dish. No filling or crust should be exposed. Make decorative peaks with a spatula. Place pie in oven preheated to hottest setting just until meringue turns golden and peaks brown.

Serve as soon as possible.

SERVES 8 TO 10

INGREDIENTS

1 9-ounce package of chocolate wafer cookies (like Famous Chocolate Wafers)

1 stick unsalted butter, cut into chunks

1 teaspoon cinnamon

1 teaspoon almond extract

5 egg yolks

2 tablespoons unbleached all-purpose flour

$2/3$ cup powdered sugar

2 cups milk or cream

Juice from 3 lemons

10 large egg whites

1 teaspoon cream of tartar

1 cup granulated sugar

Berry PEACH CRUMBLE

The Filling

Preheat oven to 350°. Toss berries, peaches, and orange zest with juice. Sprinkle with powdered sugar and 1/4 cup flour. Toss to coat. Place in buttered deep baking dish that will accommodate it comfortably, about 10 x 14 inches.

The Topping

Pulse topping ingredients in a food processor until they become the texture of coarse meal. Place in an even layer, covering berries.

Place dish in preheated 350° oven until bubbly and brown on top, about 40 minutes. Serve à la mode.

SERVES 8 TO 12

INGREDIENTS

THE FILLING

3 pints fresh strawberries, rinsed and hulled

4 cups sliced fresh peaches (you may substitute frozen)

1 tablespoon orange zest

2 tablespoons orange juice

1 cup powdered sugar

1/4 cup unbleached all purpose flour

THE TOPPING

1 stick butter, cut into pieces

1 cup flour

1 cup oatmeal

1 cup brown sugar

1 cup granulated sugar

1 teaspoon cinnamon

Kitchen Klips

Use a foil liner under casseroles and pies when baking to catch any spill over. Any spill over that hits the bottom of the oven will cause smoke and change the flavor and color of the dish.

COMFORT CUISINE

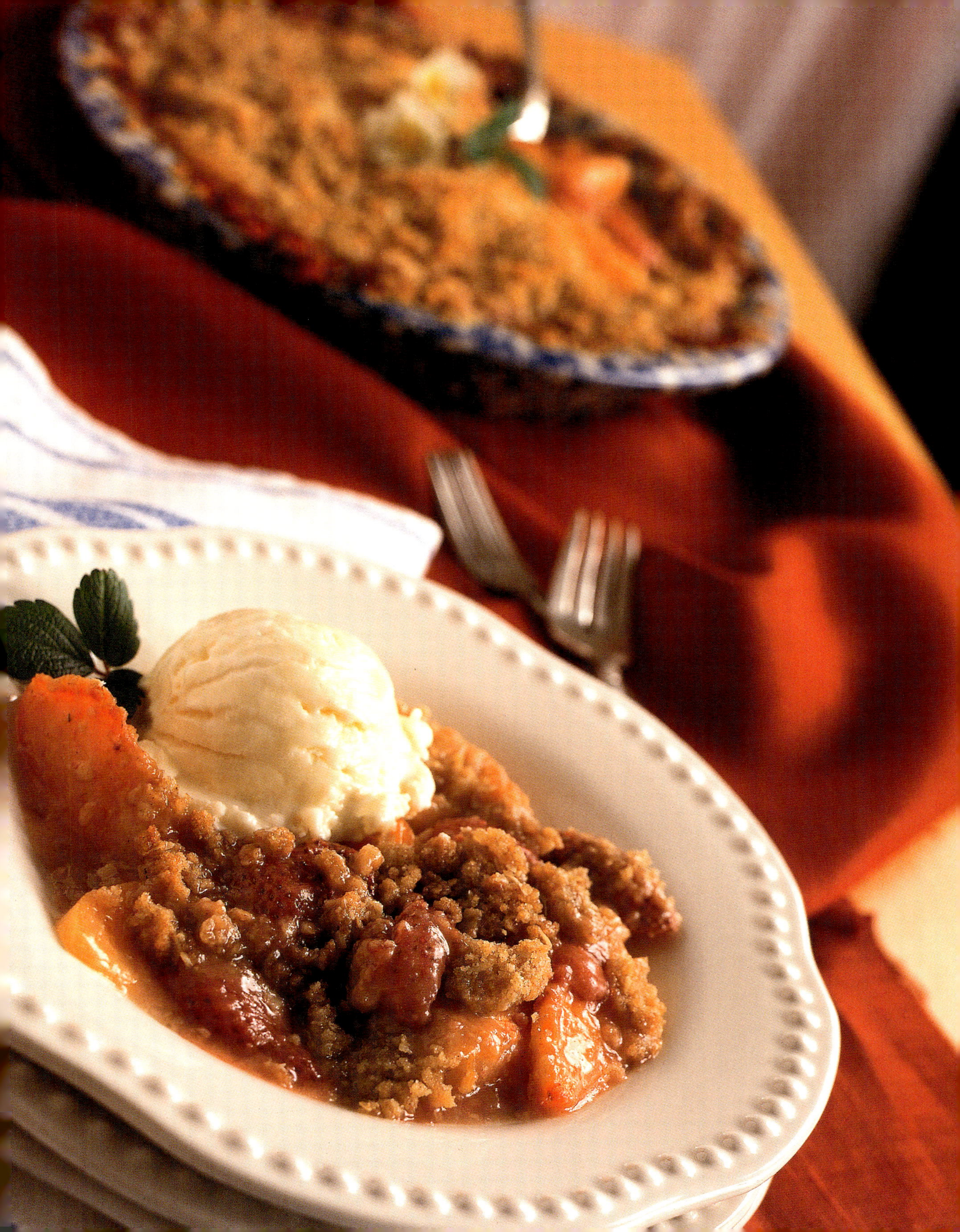

Brown RICE CUSTARD

Cook ingredients except brown sugar over medium heat, stirring constantly until slow boil is reached (approximately 20 minutes).

Pour into heatproof bowl or individual cups and sprinkle brown sugar over the top. Serve warm.

SERVES 6 TO 8

INGREDIENTS

4 cups leftover cooked brown rice

1 can sweetened condensed milk (14 ounces)

2 cups regular milk

3 egg yolks slightly beaten

½ teaspoon cinnamon

½ teaspoon vanilla extract

¼ cup brown sugar

Barry's IRISH COFFEE

Whisk the cream, powdered sugar, and vanilla until frothy and thick but not whipped stiff.

Divide the granulated sugar and whiskey between four mugs or Irish coffee glasses. Place one cup of coffee in each mug and stir gently.

Divide cream mixture on top of mugs. Serve immediately. Makes 4 cups.

SERVES 4

INGREDIENTS

1 cup heavy whipping cream

3 tablespoons powdered sugar

½ teaspoon vanilla extract

4 tablespoons granulated sugar

4 ounces Irish whiskey

4 cups hot coffee

Spiced Citrus **CIDER**

Place cloves, cinnamon sticks, and zests in a cheesecloth bundle tied with cotton thread. Put in saucepan with apple cider, and heat until just barely simmering. Keep at slow simmer for 20 minutes. Discard bundle.

Divide red hots between 4 mugs. Ladle hot spiced cider into mugs and serve. Makes 4 to 6 cups.

SERVES 4

[*To turn this cider into a delicious libation, add one ounce of peppermint schnapps to each serving.*]

INGREDIENTS

8 cloves

2 cinnamon sticks, broken into pieces

Zest from 2 oranges

Zest from 1 lemon

Zest from 1 lime

4 to 6 cups apple juice or cider

¼ cup cinnamon red hots (candy)

KITCHEN KLIPS

The zest is the outermost skin layer of citrus fruit. When making zest, avoid the white inner "pith," which is very bitter. Use a vegetable peeler to remove the thin layer of zest and chop finely in a food processor or cut into thin strips with a sharp knife.

CHAPTER 8

SIMPLY
SCANDINAVIAN

SCANDINAVIANS HAVE LONG BEEN KNOWN AS **brilliant designers of porcelain, silverware, crystal, linen, and wood furnishings—creative efforts that add style and flare to a table setting. It's logical to assume that a people who design things to beautify a table would care about the food they serve. Bearing this in mind, I thought that I would explore the mystery of Scandinavian cuisine. When Caroline Lagerfelt agreed to be a guest on my show, it was a perfect opportunity to introduce my viewers to Scandinavian food. And what a savory experience it became for me—and will be for you! What ingredients do Scandinavians use to cook? They use salmon, herring, pork, poultry, beets, potatoes, cucumbers, dill, lingonberries, almonds, sour cream, and butter. Their cooking is pure and simple, resonating from the sea and complemented by riches from their forests. Their native liquor, Aquavit, enhances the vivid flavors of Denmark, Norway, Sweden, and Finland (the primary countries thought of as Scandinavian, though Iceland is also included in this group). Called "the water of life," Aquavit is tipped quickly from glass to mouth and swallowed in a gulp. This beverage jolts and stimulates the appetite—and brings out the flavor of each ingredient. Aquavit is imbibed in a custom called "skoaling." I must add that if you need some justification to indulge, the Scandinavians believe that Aquavit aids digestion!**

THEIR COOKING IS PURE AND SIMPLE, RESONATING FROM THE SEA AND COMPLEMENTED BY RICHES FROM THEIR FORESTS.

Now On to The
STARS

CAROLINE LAGERFELT IS SMART, sexy, classy, talented, and witty—all in a very beautiful, Scandinavian package. Playing Cheech Moran's wife on the popular TV show *Nash Bridges*, she has also a great sense of humor. ■ Talking about her first exposure to fine food, Caroline notes, "I was the child of a diplomat. My parents decided it would be best if I attended boarding school in England at a very young age. I went home for holidays and we would have this marvelous French food prepared by the great chefs of Europe. Then, I would go back to school in England where I was served mystery meat and suet pudding!" ■ She currently owns a loft in Manhattan, a home in west Los Angeles, and an old farmhouse she and her family are restoring on a small Swedish island. "I love it there, " Caroline says. "Lots of stone and wood and beautiful land and wonderful fresh foods to cook great meals. The fish is awesome on the island. But, you know what we say about Scandinavian food? Enough dill, chives, and sour cream can make anything wonderful!" ■ Her home in Los Angeles is cozy with elegant touches. Caroline spends very little time in LA since *Nash Bridges* shoots in San Francisco. " They fly me up and treat me like royalty. How lucky I am—it's great!" ■ But she does love to cook. Her small kitchen, enhanced by white tiles and European cupboards, still has the look of a serious chef's workplace, with a gas cooktop, double ovens, and a butcher-block work space. Scattered around are lots of candles and small collections of unusual artifacts from all over the world. She says she uses many of these decorative items when she sets her table. "I love to gather around the table with friends and family. What better way to share than together with good food and a splash of Aquavit?" I agree—so once again let's "skoal"!

"My parents decided it would be best if I attended boarding school in England at a very young age. I went home for holidays and we would have this marvelous French food prepared by the great chefs of Europe."

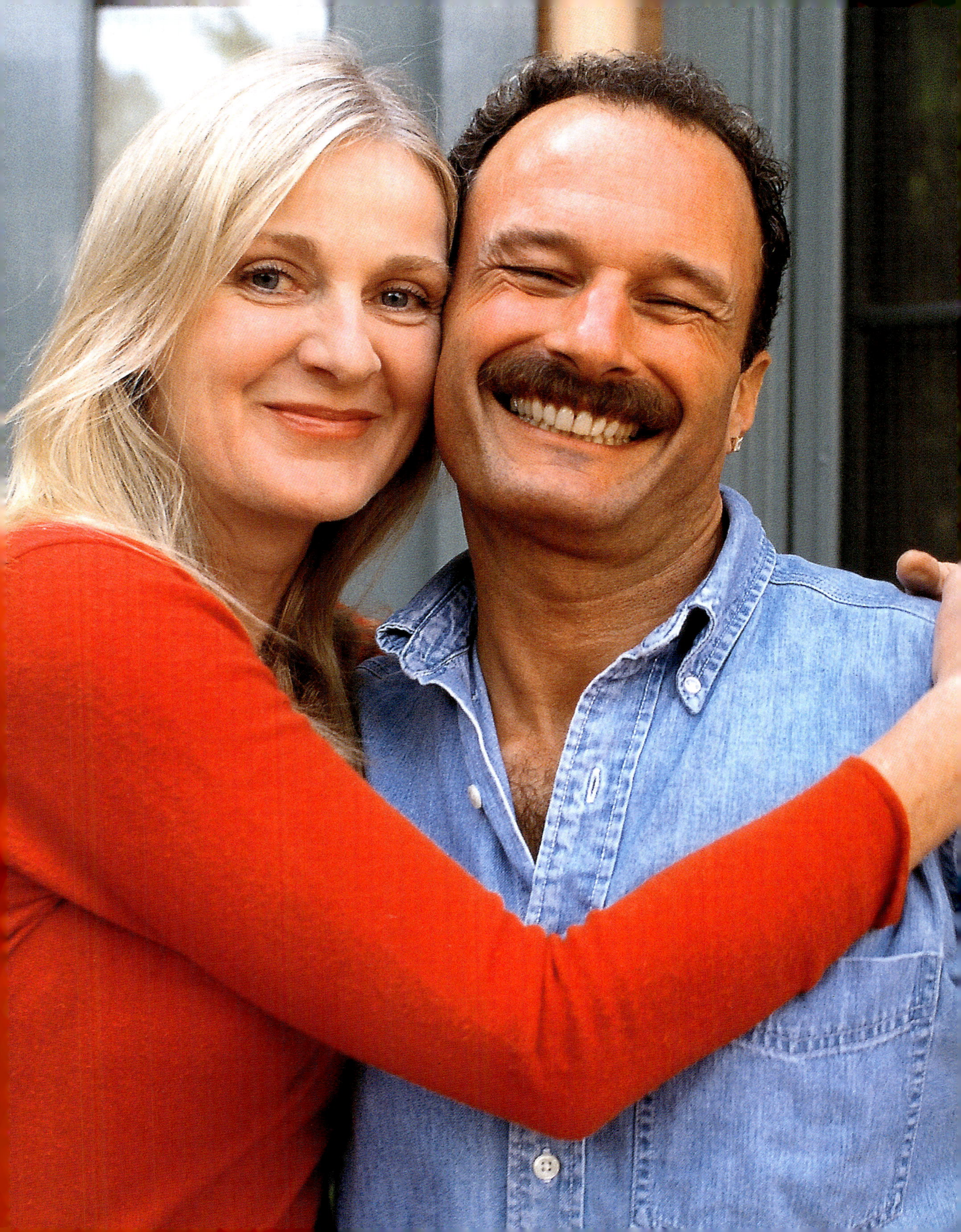

Bergen Shellfish SOUP

Heat the oil in a heavy stockpot over medium-high heat and stir in the celery and onion. Sauté until golden.

Add wine and reduce heat to medium. Stir in bay leaves, herb blend, parsley, basil, and paprika.

Sauté and stir in crushed tomatoes and bring to a simmer. Stir in sugar and season with salt and pepper. Simmer gently for 1 to 3 hours. Remove bay leaves.

To serve: Add shrimp, scallops, and lobster to simmering gumbo and serve as soon as shellfish is hot.

SERVES 6 TO 8

It's a good idea to precook the shellfish, and then add it to soups just prior to serving (make sure to keep the pot on the stove long enough to heat up the shellfish). Precooking the shellfish will shorten the cooking steps and eliminate any guesswork about the timing!

INGREDIENTS

- 2 tablespoons extra virgin olive oil
- 1 cup chopped celery
- 1 cup chopped onion
- 1 cup white wine
- 2 bay leaves
- 1 tablespoon dried Italian herb blend
- 1 cup minced fresh parsley
- ½ cup chopped fresh basil leaves
- 2 tablespoons paprika
- 64 ounces crushed tomatoes
- 2 tablespoons granulated sugar
- Salt and pepper to taste
- 1 pound freshly cooked cleaned tiger shrimp (any firm, cooked seafood will do)
- 1 pound steamed and cooled bay scallops
- 2 to 3 cups cooked lobster meat, cut into chunks

Alderwood Smoked SALMON SALAD

In bowl of food processor fitted with a steel blade, pulse salmon fillet, dill, chives, lemon juice, and capers until chopped finely. Season with black pepper. Serve with flatbread or pumpernickel toast.

SERVES 8 AS AN APPETIZER

INGREDIENTS

- 1 8-ounce Alderwood or other dry smoked salmon fillet, broken into chunks
- ¼ cup chopped fresh dill leaf
- ⅓ cup chopped fresh shallots
- Juice from 2 lemons
- ¼ cup capers, drained
- Freshly cracked black pepper to taste

Chopped **HERRING**

Drizzle apple cider vinegar over pieces of rye bread. Allow vinegar to soak into bread and then gently squeeze out excess. Add moist bread, herring, onion, apple, and egg to processor and pulse. Add enough herring juice to moisten well and pulse again. Season with pepper to taste. Makes about 2 1/2 cups.

Serve with pumpernickel bread or bagel toasts.

SERVES 8 AS AN APPETIZER

INGREDIENTS

- 1/2 cup apple cider vinegar
- 2 pieces of rye bread
- 1 16-ounce jar pickled herring, drained and juice reserved
- 1 cup chopped white onion
- 1 green apple, cored and chopped
- Hard boiled eggs, chopped
- Fresh cracked black pepper, to taste

Crawfish and Wild **RICE SALAD**

Toss the rice with the olive oil and stir in fennel, tomato, pine nuts, dill, and scallions. Mix together the lime and lemon juice, sugar, and salt and pepper. Toss with rice mixture and crayfish and serve, or cover and refrigerate up to 24 hours. Serve at room temperature.

SERVES 6

INGREDIENTS

- 3 cups cooked wild rice, cooled
- 1 tablespoon extra virgin olive oil
- 1 cup diced fresh fennel bulb
- 1 cup yellow or red tomato, seeded and chopped
- 1/4 cup pine nuts
- 1/4 cup fresh dill
- 1/2 cup chopped fresh scallion
- 1/4 cup lime juice
- Juice from 1 lemon
- 1 tablespoon sugar or honey
- Salt and pepper to taste
- 1 pound cooked crayfish, cleaned and chilled

Potato PEA SOUP

Preheat oven to 400°. Clean potatoes well and poke with a fork. Bake for 70 to 90 minutes or until soft. When cooled, slice off just the tops of the potatoes and scoop out the potato flesh into a bowl. Leave a good ¼ inch of flesh and skin, since you will be using the shells to present the soup.

In a large stockpot over medium heat, melt butter and stir in the onions. Sauté until golden. Add potato flesh and peas and chives. Add the cream and milk slowly while stirring and mashing soup with the back of a wooden spoon. Bring soup to a simmer. Add Aquavit and season with salt and pepper to taste.

Simmer slowly for 25 minutes and serve in potato shells. Garnish with sour cream and caviar.

SERVES 6 TO 8

INGREDIENTS

6 to 8 large baking potatoes

2 sticks butter

1 medium white onion, minced

8 ounces sweet peas, shelled, fresh or frozen

½ cup chopped fresh chives

2 cups heavy whipping cream

2 cups milk

¼ cup Aquavit

Salt and pepper, to taste

Sour cream and caviar for garnish

Scandinavian beers range from the lightest of pilsners to the heaviest of lagers.

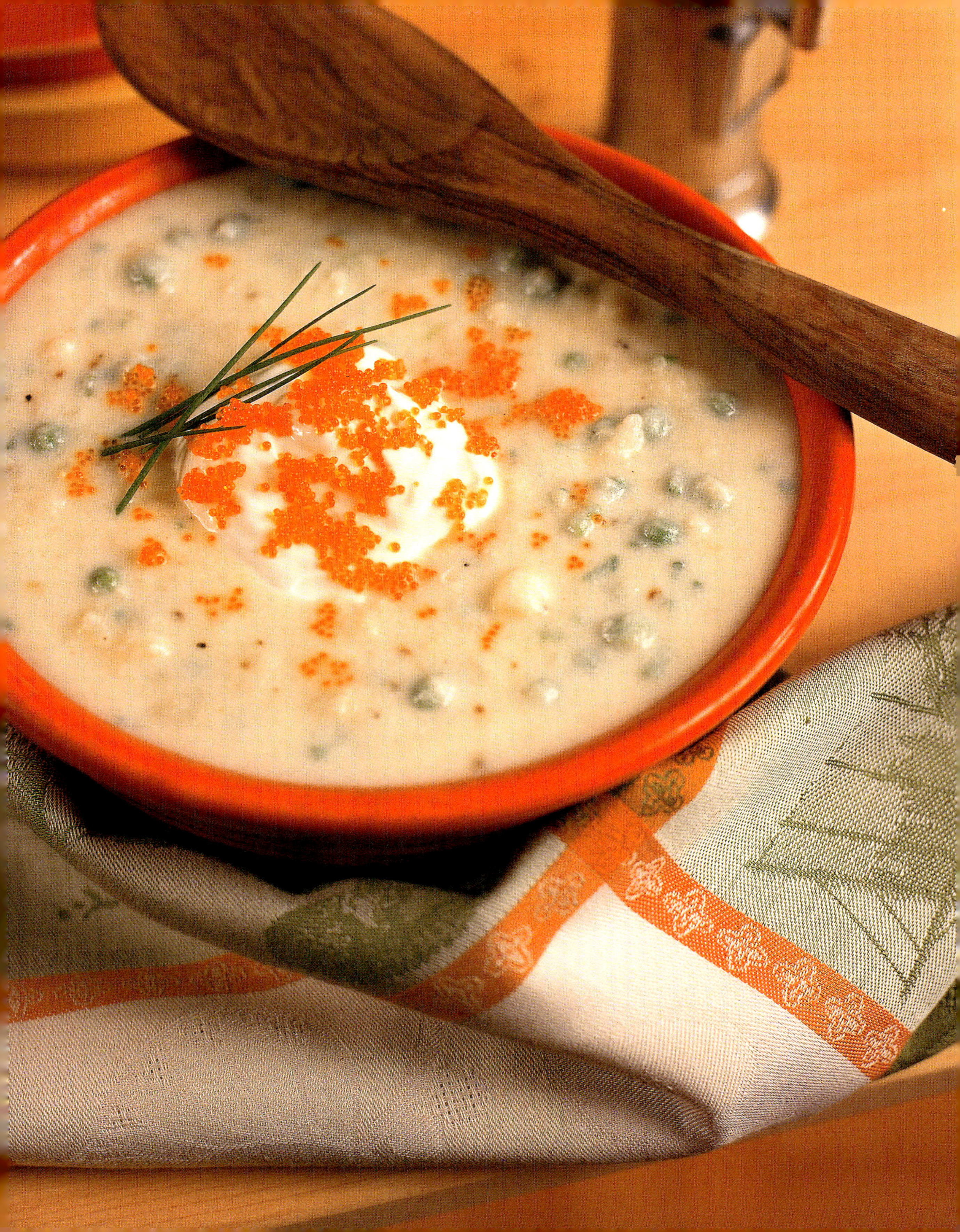

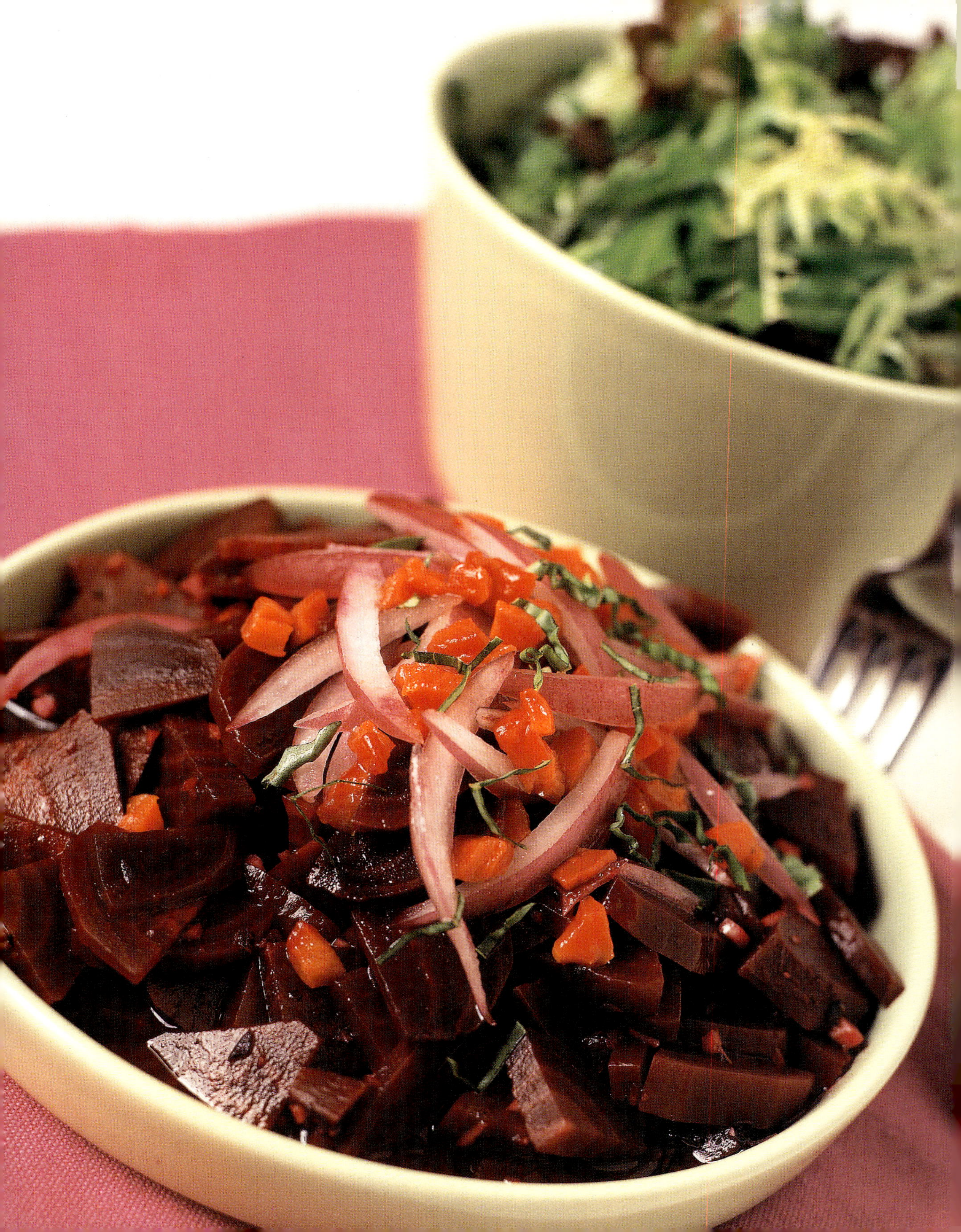

SALAD of Pickled Beets

Mix together vinegar, sugar, oregano, garlic, and salt and pepper. Slice beets into half-moon shapes and place in glass or ceramic container with vinegar mixture. You may add a bit of water if necessary to cover the beets.

To serve: Arrange beets over baby greens and top with pimento and red onion slices. Drizzle any marinade left from beets over salad. Garnish with fresh basil leaves and grated hard-boiled egg, if desired.

SERVES 8

INGREDIENTS

- $2/3$ cup red wine vinegar
- $1/8$ cup granulated sugar
- 1 teaspoon dried oregano
- 1 tablespoon minced fresh garlic
- 1 teaspoon salt, or to taste
- Fresh cracked pepper, to taste
- 4 medium beets, peeled, quartered and boiled in salted water until tender but not soft, drained and cooled
- 6 ounces fresh baby mixed greens
- $1/2$ cup chopped pimento
- 1 thinly sliced red onion
- Fresh basil leaves for garnish, as desired
- Grated hard boiled egg, as desired

Cabbage, Apple, and Onion SALAD

INGREDIENTS

- 2 tablespoons extra virgin olive oil
- 1 tablespoon minced fresh garlic
- 1 white cabbage, shredded
- 3 cups thinly sliced red onion
- 3 Granny Smith apples, cored and sliced
- $1/2$ cup Aquavit
- 2 tablespoons caraway seeds
- $1/2$ cup fresh dill
- 1 tablespoon brown sugar
- Salt and pepper, to taste

Heat oil in a large heavy sauté pan over medium-high heat and sauté garlic until golden. Add cabbage and onion and sauté until tender. Add apples and Aquavit and simmer until apples soften, about 5 minutes. Stir in caraway seeds, dill, and brown sugar. Season with salt and pepper. Serve warm.

SERVES 8

Aquavit is a colorless Scandinavian liquor, distilled from grain or potatoes and traditionally flavored with caraway seed. It is stored in the freezer and should be enjoyed very cold.

Fjord's **FISH AND CHIPS** with Dilled Tartar Sauce

Slice the fillets into 1-inch wide strips. Mix together yogurt and Tabasco sauce and marinate fish strips for 1 hour. In a food processor fitted with a steel blade, process the macadamia nuts until ground.

Add crumbs, cornmeal, and seasoning to bowl and process to combine. Roll strips in crumbs to coat.

Heat a ½ inch deep layer of oil in a deep pan over medium-high heat and fry fish strips in batches until golden brown and crispy, turning once, about 4 minutes per side.

Drain on a paper towel-lined tray and keep warm in oven while frying fish. Serve with dilled tartar sauce.

SERVES 8 AS AN APPETIZER OR 4 AS AN ENTRÉE

The Chips

Slice potatoes into ½-inch thick slices. Melt butter in large, heavy, nonstick skillet over medium-high heat and layer the potatoes, overlapping the edges, and in a single layer. Sprinkle with salt and pepper. Sauté until golden browned and crisp on the bottom.

Drizzle melted butter over the top and run potatoes, still in the pan, under the broiler until lightly browned on top.

SERVES 8 AS AN APPETIZER OR 4 AS AN ENTRÉE

The Dilled Tartar Sauce

Mix ingredients together. Cover and refrigerate a few hours or overnight.

Stir gently before serving. Makes 1½ cups.

SERVES 8 WITH AN APPETIZER OR 4 WITH AN ENTRÉE

INGREDIENTS

2 skinless catfish fillets

2 cups low- or non-fat lemon flavored yogurt

Tabasco sauce, to taste

4 to 6 ounces macadamia nuts

1 cup plain breadcrumbs

1 cup cornmeal

1 tablespoon garlic seasoning

Canola oil for frying

THE CHIPS

2 baked potatoes, cooled

4 tablespoons butter

Salt and pepper to taste

4 tablespoons melted butter

THE SAUCE

1 cup mayonnaise

1 tablespoon coarse mustard

¼ cup pickle relish

2 tablespoons catsup

2 minced shallots

2 tablespoons fresh dill, stemmed

2 tablespoons capers, drained

Sweet and Sour SWEDISH MEATBALL STEW

The Stew

Heat oil in a large, heavy, nonstick Dutch oven or soup pot over medium-high heat. Sauté onions in oil until toasted. Add cabbage to pot, pour stock over cabbage. Cover and reduce heat to simmer until cabbage is tender, about 30 minutes.

Add lemon juice, brown sugar, and tomato sauce. Season with salt and pepper to taste. Bring to simmer and drop in meatballs one at a time. Simmer until meatballs are well cooked, about 1 hour. Serve hot.

SERVES 6 TO 8

The Meatballs

Mix ingredients together and form 2-inch round meatballs. Drop into simmering stew. Makes about 16 small meatballs.

INGREDIENTS
THE STEW

- 2 tablespoons extra virgin olive oil
- 1 cup minced onion, red or white
- 6 cups shredded white cabbage
- 2 cups beef, chicken, or vegetable stock
- Juice from 4 lemons
- 1 cup brown sugar
- 64 ounces of tomato sauce
- Salt and pepper, to taste
- Meatballs (see recipe below)

INGREDIENTS
THE MEATBALLS

- 1 pound extra lean ground beef
- 1 cup fresh or prepared breadcrumbs
- 1 tablespoon dried Italian herb blend
- 3 eggs, lightly beaten
- 2 tablespoons Worcestershire sauce

KITCHEN KLIPS

Meatballs for stews or sauce can be made in advance, browned in a little hot oil in a skillet and cooked until firm. They can then be cooled and refrigerated or frozen for a quick and easy addition to a recipe.

Country MEATLOAF in Sour Cream Pastry

The Pastry

Place sifter over food processor and sift flour into tub. Add 12 tablespoons butter and process until mixture is combined and texture of meal. Remove.

In a separate bowl, mix together the egg and sour cream and stir this into the flour-butter mixture. Pulse until you can gather the dough into a soft, pliable ball. Wrap in plastic wrap and refrigerate 1 hour.

Cut the chilled dough in half and roll out each half to rectangles of 6 by 14 inches each, setting aside any scraps. Butter the bottom of a jellyroll pan with 1 tablespoon of soft butter. Lift 1 sheet of the pastry over the rolling pin, and unfold it into the pan.

The Filling

Melt the 4 tablespoons of butter in a 10- to 12-inch skillet. When the foam subsides, add chopped mushrooms and cook them over moderate heat, stirring frequently, for 6 to 8 minutes or until they are lightly colored.

Add ground pork and sirloin to the skillet and cook, stirring occasionally, for another 8 to 10 minutes or until the meat loses its red color and any accumulated liquid in the pan cooks completely away. Stir in flour.

Scrape the meat mixture from the skillet (or the mushrooms and already cooked meat) into a large mixing bowl and stir in the chopped onions, parsley, cheese, and milk. Gather this meat mixture and place it in the center of the dough in the pan. With your hands, pat the meat into a narrow loaf extending lengthwise down the center of the dough from one end to the other. Lift the second sheet of pastry over the pin and gently drape it on top of the meatloaf, pressing the edges of the 2 sheets together.

Dip a pastry brush into the egg-and-milk mixture and moisten the edges of the dough. Press down on the edges all around the loaf with the back of a fork. (The tines will seal the edges securely). With a fork prick the tip of the loaf in several places to allow steam to escape.

Continues

INGREDIENTS

THE PASTRY

2¼ cups unbleached flour

12 tablespoons chilled, unsalted butter, cut into ¼-inch bits

1 egg

1 cup sour cream

1 tablespoon soft butter (to grease pan)

Preheat oven to 375°. Gather together into a ball all of the excess scraps of dough and roll it out to a thin rectangle. With a pastry wheel or small, sharp knife cut this dough into long, narrow strips. Brush the loaf with more of the egg and milk mixture and crisscross the pastry strips over the top of the loaf in an attractive pattern.

Brush the strips with milk and egg mixture and set the jellyroll pan in the center of the oven. Bake for 45 minutes, or until the loaf has turned a golden brown.

Serve thick slices of the hot meat loaf, accompanied by a bowl of cold sour cream and a side dish of lingonberries.

SERVES 8 TO 10

THE FILLING

1 cup sour cream

Salt and pepper for seasoning

4 tablespoons butter

¾ cup finely chopped mushrooms (about ¼ pound fresh mushrooms)

1 pound each of ground pork and ground sirloin

2 tablespoons all-purpose flour

⅓ cup finely chopped onions

¼ cup finely chopped parsley

1 cup freshly grated Cheddar, Swiss, or Gruyere cheese

½ cup milk

1 egg combined with 2 tablespoons milk

Kitchen Klips

Sour cream pastry and pâte brisée dough can be made in advance, wrapped tightly in plastic wrap and then foil and frozen for up to 45 days. Thaw over-night in the refrigerator and then roll away!

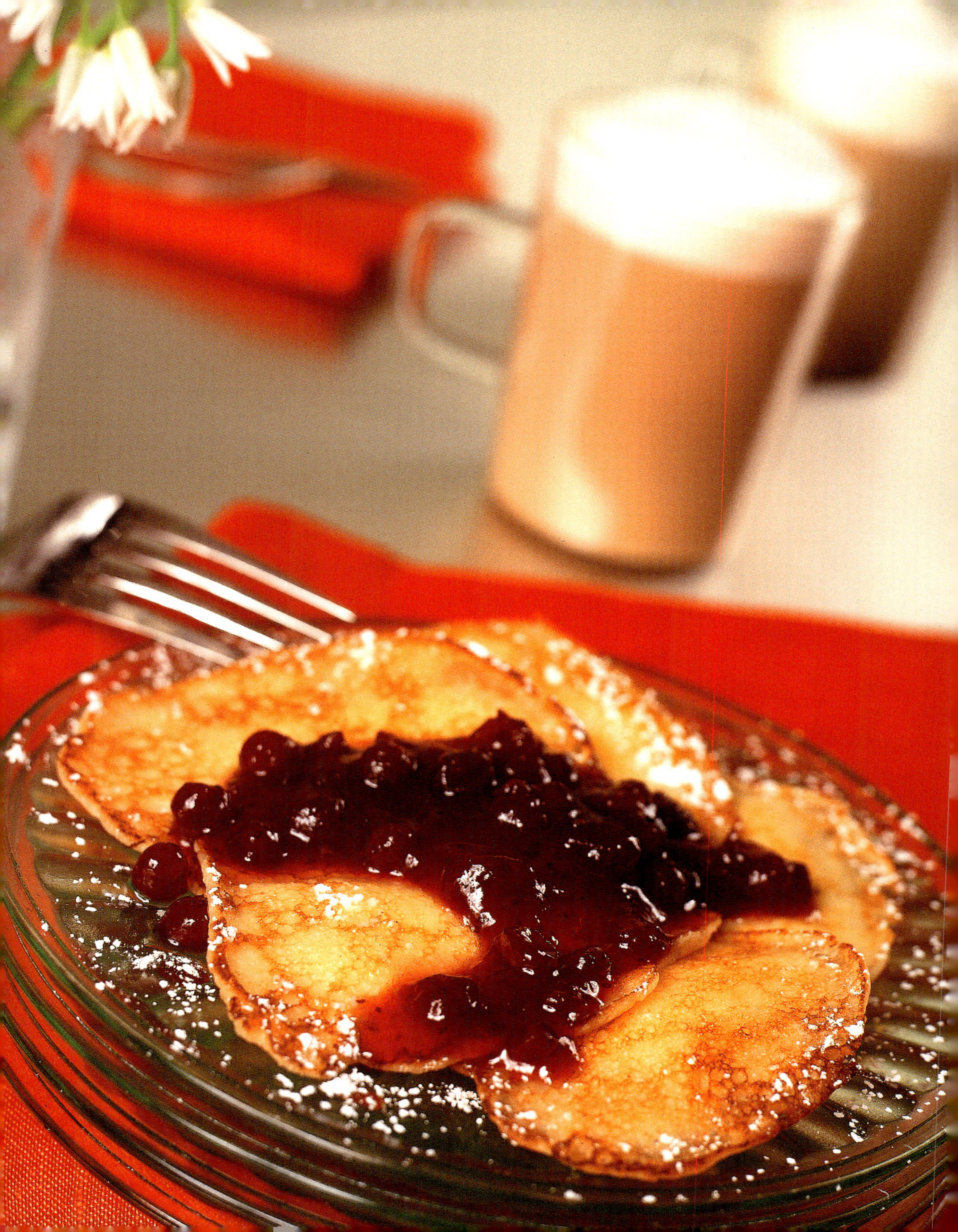

Danish **PANCAKES**

Lightly beat eggs and whisk in the cream. Stir in flour and whisk in milk, melted butter, and sugar until smooth. Drop tablespoonfuls of batter onto lightly buttered hot griddle and cook about 2 minutes per side. Keep cooked pancakes on warm platter until all are done.

Serve with lingonberry preserves.

SERVES 8

INGREDIENTS

3 eggs

1 cup heavy whipping cream

1 cup flour

1 cup regular or low-fat milk

6 tablespoons melted butter

1 tablespoon sugar

Lingonberry preserves

INGREDIENTS

5 large apples, peeled, cored, and thinly sliced

1/8 cup unbleached all purpose flour

1 cup granulated sugar

1 teaspoon cinnamon

Zest from 1 orange

Juice from 1 orange

1 teaspoon almond extract

1 cup sour cream

1 tablespoon powdered sugar

1 cup ground almonds

Apple Almond **ORANGE LOAF**

Preheat oven to 350°. Toss together all ingredients except sour cream, powdered sugar, and almonds and press into buttered loaf pan to accommodate. Cover with foil and bake in preheated 350° oven for 60 minutes.

Mix together sour cream and powdered sugar. Remove loaf from oven, uncover, and spread sour cream mixture over top. Sprinkle almond crumbs over sour cream.

Return loaf to oven uncovered and bake 15 to 20 minutes more, until top begins to brown. Remove from oven and run sharp knife around edges of pan. Let sit for 10 minutes and serve like a pudding. Serve warm with ice cream, if desired.

SERVES 8

Fruit CONFIT

In a saucepan over medium heat, mix together the sugar, orange juice, and brandy until sugar dissolves. Add remaining ingredients and bring contents to a simmer.

Continue to simmer until fruit is tender and mixture resembles the texture of preserves.

Remove cinnamon sticks and serve warm over ice cream or sponge cake. Keeps covered in the refrigerator for one week.

SERVES 8

INGREDIENTS

1 cup sugar

2 cups orange juice

½ cup brandy

2 cups dried pitted apricots

1 cup dried sliced apples

1 cup dried pitted prunes

1 cup dried peach slices

1 tablespoon finely chopped lemon zest

2 cinnamon sticks

Peach Ginger MUFFINS

Preheat oven to 375°. Soak peach slices in boiling water until tender, about 10 minutes. Drain well and chop into bits.

Mix together the raisins, flour, baking powder, ginger, and cinnamon in a large mixing bowl.

In a smaller bowl, whisk together eggs, sugar milk, vanilla, and butter. Add to the dry ingredients and stir just enough to mix well. Fold in peach pieces.

Spoon mixture into 12 greased muffin tins, filling each tin about ⅔ full. Bake in 375° oven until firm to the touch in the center, about 20 minutes. Remove from oven, sprinkle each muffin with a little brown sugar. Cool about 10 minutes and remove from pan. Makes 12 muffins.

SERVES 6 TO 12

INGREDIENTS

4 ounces dried peach slices

1 cup raisins

2 cups unbleached all purpose flour

2 teaspoons baking powder

1 teaspoon dried ginger

1 teaspoon dried cinnamon

2 eggs

1 cup sugar

½ cup milk

1 teaspoon vanilla extract

4 tablespoons butter, melted and cooled

½ cup brown sugar

Orange Almond **DANISH**

The Short-Cut Dough

In the bowl of a processor fitted with a steel blade, place the flour, 1/3 cup sugar, and butter and pulse until the mixture is the texture of coarse meal.

Stir together the yeast, remaining 1 teaspoon sugar, and warm water together until dissolved.

Add yeast mixture, sour cream, egg yolks, vanilla and poppy seeds to bowl with flour mixture. Pulse a few times just until mixture forms a loose ball. Remove from processor, divide dough into 2 balls, wrap separately in plastic wrap and refrigerate 1 hour or overnight.

The Orange Filling

In a small saucepan over medium heat, warm the preserves until very liquid.

Stir in almond extract. Keep warm.

To Assemble and Bake

Preheat oven to 375°. Lightly flour a work surface and roll each ball of dough into a 12-inch circle. Gently divide the preserves over the top as if saucing a pizza. Sprinkle with almonds, brown sugar, and cinnamon. Cut each circle into 12 pieces as if cutting a pizza. Starting at wide end of triangle, roll up toward point like little crescent rolls. Place on baking sheets lined with parchment paper.

Using a pastry brush, brush each pastry with egg white and sprinkle the unrefined sugar over the pastries. Place in oven and reduce heat to 350°. Bake until golden brown, about 25 minutes. Makes 2 dozen pastries.

SERVES 12

INGREDIENTS

THE DOUGH

3 cups unbleached all purpose flour

1/3 cup granulated sugar plus 1 teaspoon

8 ounces butter, cut into bits

4 to 5 teaspoons quick rise yeast

1/4 cup 105° to 115° (lukewarm) water

1/2 cup sour cream or crème fraîche, room temperature

2 egg yolks

1 teaspoon vanilla extract

1/2 cup poppy seeds

THE FILLING

1 cup orange preserves

1 teaspoon almond extract

TO BAKE

Flour for dusting work surface

1 cup ground almonds

3/4 cup brown sugar

1 tablespoon cinnamon

2 egg whites, slightly beaten until watery

2 tablespoons unrefined (turbinado) granulated sugar

CHAPTER 9

PARTY
CENTRAL

WHEN IT CAME TIME TO PLAN the last chapter of *Star Grazing* I thought, what better way to end a cookbook created in the homes of celebrities than with a chapter devoted to party food. And what a successful party you can have with the recipes in this chapter. A cocktail party serving a variety of appetizers can offer guests the fun of informally grazing while socializing together. There are many benefits to this type of entertaining. You don't need a huge dining room table or matching dinnerware to pull off your party. Easy to prepare, and simple to serve and eat, appetizers are the main criteria for party food. Plan your food as you would a dinner party—in courses. Serve a first course of cold appetizers that you can have available as your guests arrive and have their first drink. My Jazzy Cheddar Spread or my Three Cheese Pâté with Toasted Leeks are excellent starters. (It's also good to have them out to make sure your guests get some food as well as alcohol in their digestive systems right away.) The dishes that make up the second course should be served warm—think about Shrimp Toasts, Brie Topped with Peaches in Phyllo Pastry, and my Blue Cheese Wheat Tart with Caramelized Onions. Round out the party food with dishes that are crowd-pleasing and hearty. The Roasted Pepper Lasagna, my Scalloped Potatoes with Pork Sausages, or Maple Barbecued Pork are excellent suggestions. And finally, complete your party as you would any dinner party with something sweet—a dessert tray. And don't forget to tell your guests that you plan to serve a meal of appetizers. That way they know not to eat beforehand!

PLAN YOUR PARTY FOODS AS YOU WOULD A DINNER PARTY— IN COURSES.

Now On to The
STARS

CINDY WILLIAMS AND HER FAMILY live in a fabulous, Malibu cliff-side Cape Cod compound that is totally charming. The gated entrance protects the privacy of the home's front lawn, which boasts stables, an enormous trampoline, and a basketball set-up. ■ To the rear of the home is a grassy yard ending at a cliff, dropping far down to the Pacific Ocean. The setting is breathtaking. Standing with Cindy at a perfect vantage point, she said, "This house keeps calling us back. My husband (Bill Hudson of the Hudson Brothers) built this house. We have rented it out and moved several times. But we keep coming back. He really didn't build it for such a large family, but we just love it here. This view, the property, the location, well, they are very hard to beat. Plus, it is just so darn comfortable, too!" ■ Inside are grand spaces with huge stone fireplaces and furniture that is comfortable and overstuffed. French doors display the spectacular ocean views. Wood floors and beams emphasize the home's Cape Cod motif. A winding staircase leads to an art gallery with unique and very precious pieces of work, including a collection of John

> "My husband built this house. We have rented it out and moved several times. But we keep coming back."

PARTY CENTRAL **178**

Lennon drawings. "I just adore these," says Cindy about the drawings. ■ Back downstairs it was time to get cooking. The kitchen is small in relation to the rest of the house, but "Bill wasn't thinking like a cook when he planned the house," laughs Cindy. ■ Cindy had invited several friends to share the results of our cooking efforts. She loves to cook and entertain, and is also a dedicated mother. Cindy is funny and warm and we immediately became friends. About to tour with the stage play of *Grease*, she has mixed emotions about going back to work. "I love to work. I really do. I have had some of the best jobs an actress can aspire to. But now it is really hard to be on the road and working long hours. I'd rather be home with Bill and the kids!" she says. And who could blame her for that!

PARTY CENTRAL

Jazzy Cheddar SPREAD

Mix together all the ingredients except the almonds and canola oil. Sauté the almonds in the canola oil until toasted. Cool and place in food processer and pulse until ground. Stir into cheese mixture. Makes 2 generous cups.

Serve with pumpernickel toasts or any party crackers.

SERVES 8 TO 12 AS A DIP

INGREDIENTS

- 1½ cups finely shredded cheddar cheese (you can purchase pre-shredded and packaged)
- ½ cup pimento-stuffed olives, minced
- ¼ cup chopped pimentos
- 1 tablespoon fresh cracked pepper
- 1 tablespoon catsup
- ¾ cup mayonnaise
- ½ cup sliced almonds
- 1 tablespoon canola oil

Three CHEESE PÂTÉ with Toasted Leek

INGREDIENTS

- 2 tablespoons extra virgin olive oil
- 1 tablespoon minced fresh garlic
- 2 large leeks, rinsed, trimmed, and shredded
- 1 teaspoon soy sauce
- 2 tablespoons dry vermouth
- 12 ounces Brie cheese
- 8 ounces Bleu, Roquefort, or Gorgonzola cheese
- 8 ounces Neufchatel cheese
- 1 tablespoon cracked black pepper
- Belgian endive leaves for serving

Heat oil in a heavy sauté pan over medium-high heat and stir in garlic and leek. Sauté until golden brown. Stir in soy sauce and dry vermouth and sauté until liquid is absorbed and evaporated. Cool.

Allow cheese to come to room temperature and cut into pieces. Place in food processor bowl fitted with the steel blade. Add leek mixture and pepper and pulse until combined. Place in pastry tube fitted with large opening tip and pipe into endive leaves. Makes about 36 leaves.

SERVES 16 TO 24 AS AN APPETIZER

Peachy SALAD in POPPY SEED VINAIGRETTE

Heat oil and nuts in small saucepan over medium-high heat and stir in garlic.

Sauté until nuts begin to toast. Turn off heat and stir in vinegar, lemon juice, sugar, and poppy seeds. Season with salt and pepper. Cool to room temperature. Just before serving, slice peaches and toss with rinsed basil leaves, greens, and dressing.

SERVES 8 OR MORE AS PART OF A BUFFET

INGREDIENTS

- ½ cup extra virgin olive oil
- 1 cup walnut pieces
- 1 teaspoon minced fresh garlic
- ½ cup balsamic vinegar
- Juice from 1 lemon
- 1½ tablespoons granulated sugar
- ⅓ cup poppy seeds
- Salt and pepper to taste
- 3-4 medium peaches, firm but ripe
- 1 cup fresh basil leaves
- 8-10 ounces baby Italian greens or greens of choice

Purple ASPARAGUS SALAD

Bring a gallon of water to a boil. Pour over trimmed asparagus placed in a strainer in the sink. Slice the asparagus into 1-inch pieces, cutting at an angle. Mix together the oil, vinegar, garlic, sugar or honey, mustard, and oregano. Season with salt and pepper. Arrange asparagus over baby greens. Top with the egg, then the basil and the Gorgonzola. Pour dressing over and serve.

SERVES 8 OR MORE AT A BUFFET

[*If purple asparagus is not available, you may substitute regular fresh baby asparagus.*]

INGREDIENTS

- 1½ pounds fresh small purple asparagus
- ⅓ cup extra virgin olive oil
- ⅓ cup balsamic vinegar
- 1 teaspoon minced fresh garlic
- 1 teaspoon sugar or honey
- 1 tablespoon Dijon mustard
- 1 teaspoon dried crushed oregano leaves, or 1 tablespoon minced fresh
- Salt and pepper to taste
- Fresh baby greens
- 1 cup chopped hard boiled egg
- 1 cup chopped fresh basil
- ½ cup crumbled Gorgonzola cheese

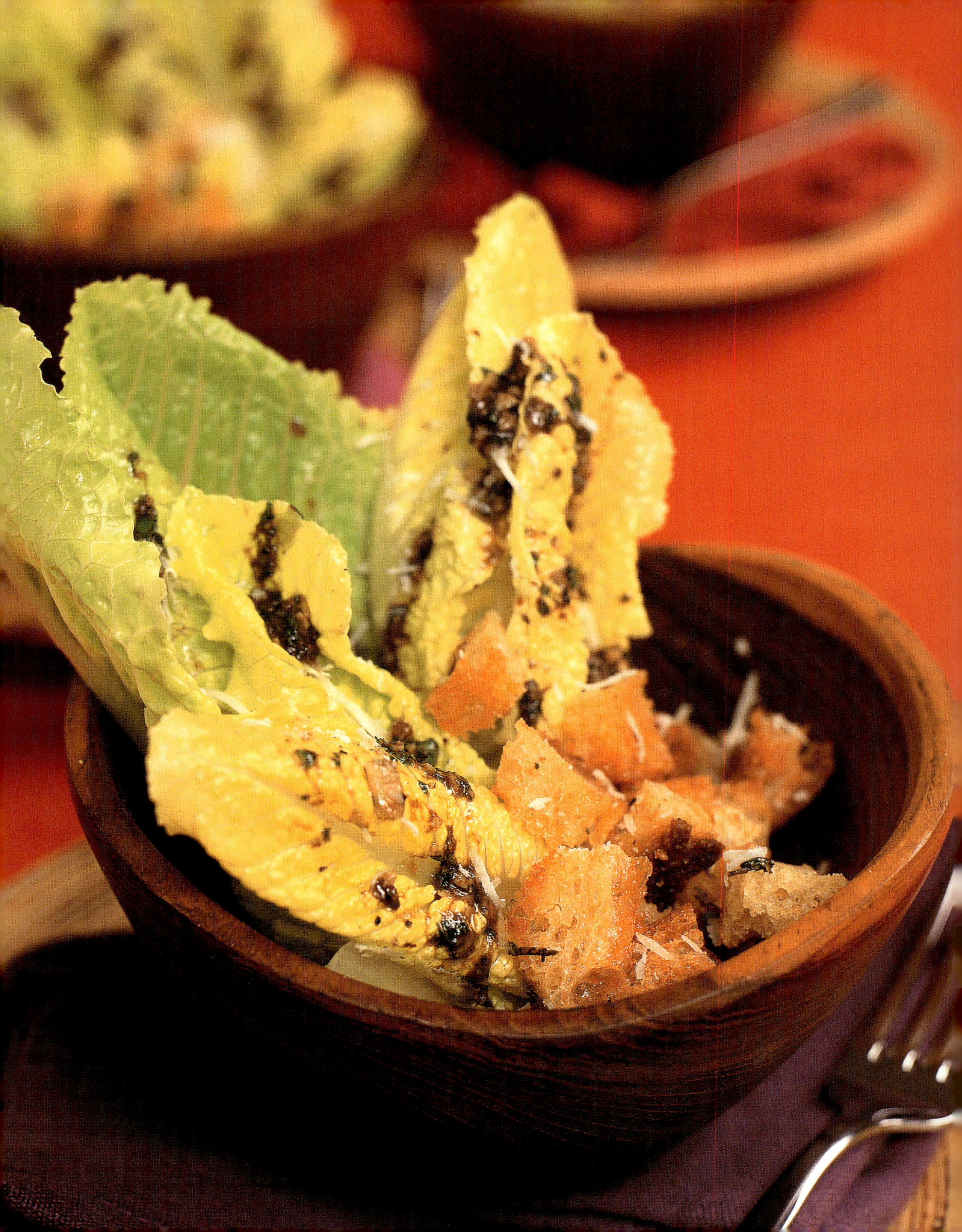

CAESAR SALAD with Rosemary Croutons

The Dressing

Place all ingredients except olive oil in the bowl of food processor fitted with steel blade. Pulse until contents are uniformly ground. Scrape down sides of the bowl. Turn food processor to 'on', and slowly pour in olive oil in a thin stream until dressing emulsifies. Process until mixture is thick and homogeneous.

Toss with romaine, croutons, and shaved Parmesan.

Makes about 2 cups dressing, enough for 12 to 16 servings of salad.

The Croutons

Preheat oven to 350°

Slice the rosemary bread into 1/3-inch thick slices. Arrange on oiled baking or cookie sheets. Heat the olive oil and garlic in a small pan over medium high heat until the garlic begins to sizzle. Remove from heat and "paint" bread slices with garlic oil using a pastry brush.

Bake in preheated 350° oven for 20 minutes. Reduce heat to 225° and bake until crisp, about 1 hour more. (They may be baked all night on lowest heat as an alternative).

Cool and store in an airtight container. Break into small pieces before tossing into salad. Makes enough for 12 to 16 servings of salad.

KITCHEN KLIPS

Always remember to plan a party menu with things that can be made ahead of time. After all, you want to be a guest at your own party, don't you?

INGREDIENTS

THE SALAD

2 heads romaine lettuce, rinsed, drained and torn into pieces

Rosemary croutons (see below)

1/3 cup shaved Parmesan cheese or to taste

THE DRESSING

8 anchovy fillets, patted dry with paper towel

1 tablespoon minced fresh garlic

1/4 cup fresh parsley

1 teaspoon Worcestershire sauce

Juice from 3 fresh lemons

2 tablespoons freshly cracked pepper

1 cup grated Parmesan cheese

1 cup olive oil

THE CROUTONS

1 loaf rosemary bread

1/3 cup extra virgin olive oil

1 teaspoon fresh minced garlic

Blue Cheese **WHEAT TART** with Caramelized Onions

The Crust

Place ingredients into bowl of food processor fitted with steel blade and pulse until texture of soft meal. Press into sides and bottom of 10 inch false-bottomed tart pan.

The Filling

Heat butter in a large, heavy, nonsick sauté pan over medium to high heat and stir in onions. Sauté until onions begin to soften and are reduced to about half of their initial volume. Stir in soy sauce and vermouth.

Cook over low heat, stirring frequently, until onions turn dark brown in color and are completely soft, about 90 minutes They should be reduced to no more than 2 cups. Remove from heat and set aside.

Whisk together the eggs and cream.

To Assemble and Bake

Preheat oven to 350°. Place the caramelized onions in an even layer over the bottom of the crust. Pour the egg/cream mixture over the onions. Sprinkle the cheese and parsley over mixture. Press cheese and parsley into custard gently with the back of a fork. Sprinkle pepper over the top. Line pan with foil and bake in preheated 350° oven until tart is set and browned on top, about 40 minutes. Serve hot, warm, or at room temperature.

SERVES 8 TO 12

INGREDIENTS

THE CRUST

6 large shredded wheat puffs

4 tablespoons butter, cut into pieces

1 teaspoon garlic

½ teaspoon salt

½ teaspoon ground black pepper

THE FILLING

3 sticks unsalted butter

6 large white onions, trimmed and sliced thinly

1 tablespoon soy sauce

½ cup extra dry vermouth

4 eggs

1 cup heavy whipping cream

1 cup bleu cheese

¼ cup chopped fresh parsley leaves

1 teaspoon cracked black pepper

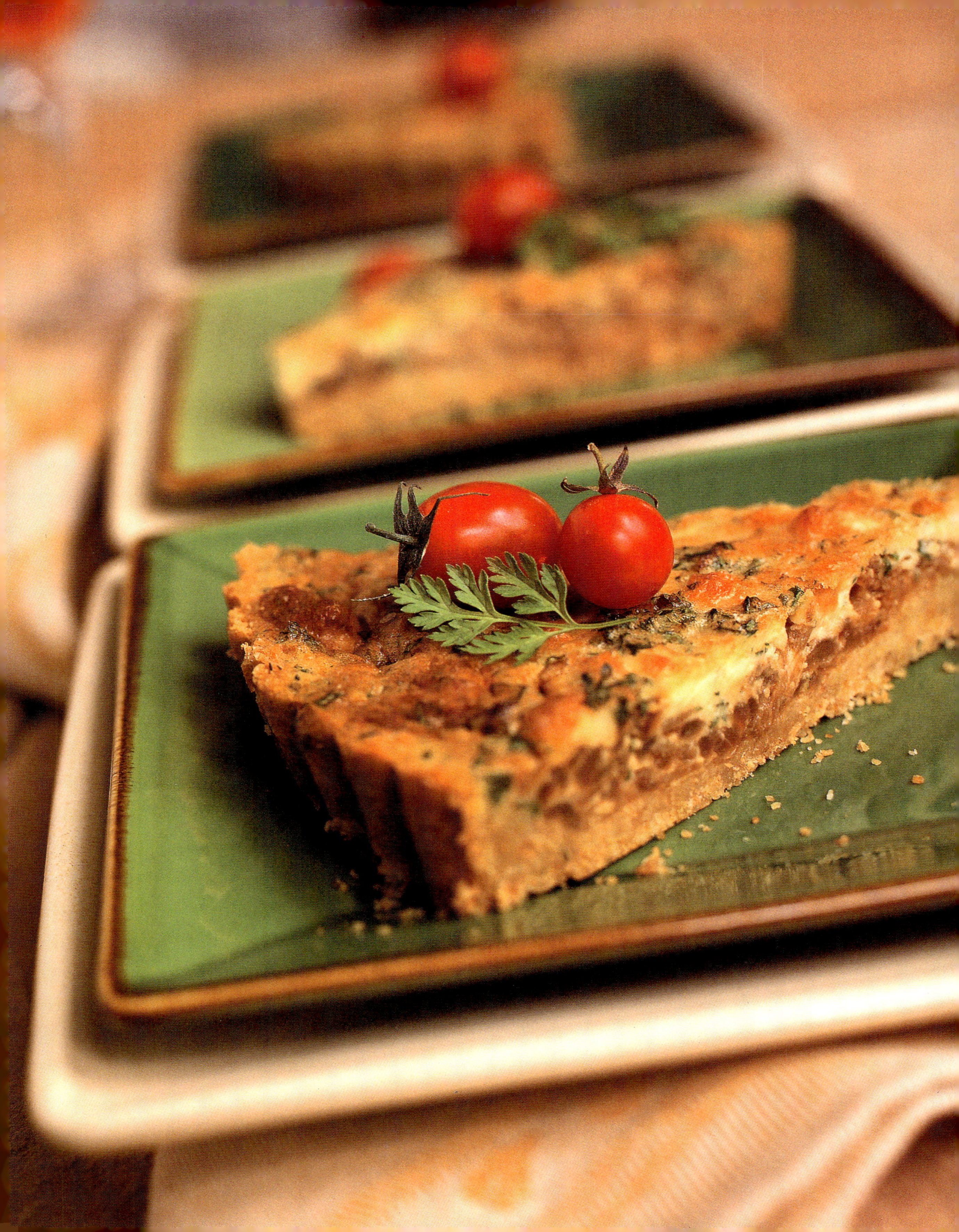

Shrimp TOASTS

Pulse together all of the ingredients in food processor. Spread a generous portion of mixture onto ¼-inch slices of Sourdough baguette. Heat a thin layer of oil on medium-high griddle or in large sauté pan over medium-high heat. Brown breads on both sides, about 3 minutes per side, and keep warm until all breads are browned and serve. Makes 24 toasts.

SERVES 8 TO 12

INGREDIENTS

1 pound cooked cocktail shrimp

1 tablespoon ground ginger

2 tablespoons minced fresh garlic

3 tablespoons toasted sesame seeds

2 eggs

1 Sourdough baguette, sliced into 24 thin slices

BRIE Topped with Peaches in PHYLLO PASTRY

Heat preserves in saucepan over medium heat. Stir in peaches and simmer 1 minute. Cool to room temperature.

Preheat oven to 350°. Place first sheet of phyllo on buttered baking tray and paint with butter. Sprinkle with sesame seeds. Place another sheet on top, paint with butter and sprinkle with sesame seeds and so on until 6 sheets are used. Place Brie in center of phyllo. Drop preserves/peach mixture over top of Brie and sprinkle almonds over Brie. Lay out another sheet of phyllo, paint with melted butter and sprinkle with sesame seeds. Repeat for a total of 6 sheets and place on top of Brie.

Gather pastry and decoratively enclose the Brie, pressing together to seal. Paint entire bundle with butter and bake in preheated 350° oven until pastry is brown and flaky, about 35 minutes.

SERVES 8 TO 12

INGREDIENTS

1 cup apricot preserves

1 cup peach slices, drained if canned

12 sheets phyllo pastry, handled according to directions on box

½ cup melted butter

½ cup toasted sesame seeds

1 whole 2½ pound round Brie

1 cup slivered or sliced almonds

When working with phyllo pastry, keep sheets covered with a damp towel to keep soft. Make sure frozen phyllo has not been stored too long by checking expiration date.

Roasted Pepper LASAGNA

The Sauce

Heat the oil in a large, heavy saucepan over medium high-heat and stir in the onions and garlic. Sauté until golden brown and reduce heat to medium. Stir in basil and oregano and cook for 1 minute. Stir in tomatoes and sugar.

Reduce heat to simmer sauce for 30 minutes. Season with salt and pepper.

MAKES 8 CUPS

The Lasagna

Preheat oven to 325°.

In an ungreased 9 x 13 deep lasagna pan, place about 2 cups of the sauce in the bottom. Place a layer of 3 noodles over sauce. Mix 2 cups of sauce with the ricotta cheese and spoon half of the ricotta cheese mixture over the noodles and spread into an even layer. Sprinkle half of the peppers over this layer and then half of the Parmesan.

Spoon 1 more cup of sauce over that. Place another 3 noodles in an even layer over the previous one and repeat steps to create a second identical layer. Finish with a layer of the last three noodles. Spoon the balance of the sauce over the top.

Sprinkle the mozzarella over top and bake in preheated 325° oven until bubbly and brown, about 50 minutes. Allow to sit 5 minutes before cutting.

SERVES 8 TO 10

INGREDIENTS

THE SAUCE

- 1 tablespoon extra virgin olive oil
- 1 cup chopped fresh onion
- 2 tablespoons minced fresh garlic
- 1 tablespoon dried basil, or 3 tablespoons minced fresh
- 1 teaspoon dried oregano, or 1 tablespoon minced fresh
- 64 ounces pureed or strained tomatoes
- 1 tablespoon granulated sugar
- Salt and pepper, to taste

THE LASAGNA

- 9 cooked 4 X 12 lasagna noodles (you may use the no precooking required kind, too)
- 2 cups ricotta cheese, seasoned with salt and pepper to taste
- 2 cups chopped roasted bell peppers (either homemade or from a jar)
- 2 cups shredded Parmesan
- 2 cups shredded mozzarella cheese

Scalloped POTATOES with PORK Sausage

Peel the potatoes and slice thinly. Poach in lightly salted boiling water until tender. Drain and place in buttered baking dish that accommodates them comfortably.

Heat butter in a saucepan over medium heat and sprinkle the flour over the butter. Stir and cook mixture for 2 minutes. Slowly add milk while stirring. Continue to stir and bring to a simmer. Simmer until thickened. Add sour cream.

Preheat oven to 325°. Pour liquid over potatoes and shake dish gently to allow sauce to run between slices. Slice sausages and place in a ring around the potatoes. Bake casserole in preheated 325° oven until brown on top and bubbly, about 40 minutes.

SERVES 12 TO 16 OR MORE AT A BUFFET

INGREDIENTS

- 6 medium baking potatoes
- 2 sticks unsalted butter
- 1/4 cup unbleached all purpose flour
- 3 cups whole milk
- 1 cup sour cream
- 1 pound sweet pork sausages, grilled to well done and cooled

Don't forget to tell your guests that you plan to serve a meal of appetizers. That way they know not to eat beforehand!

Maple Barbecued PORK

In a large Dutch oven over medium-high heat, melt butter and stir in onions. Sauté 5 minutes. Add pork and brown on all sides. Sprinkle with salt and pepper, and add garlic and beer to the pan. Cover and reduce heat; simmer for 3 hours. Check to make sure pork is cooked well and very tender.

Remove pork from pan. Cool and trim away any remaining fat. Cut in half and grill over medium-hot coals until exterior of pork is charred. Cool. Shred meat by slicing very thinly.

The Barbecue Sauce

In a heavy saucepan, heat oil over medium-high heat and sauté the onion and garlic until golden. Reduce the heat to low and stir in the vinegar. Stir in the tomato puree, brown sugar, maple syrup, and Worcestershire sauce. Bring to simmer and simmer 40 minutes, stirring frequently. Season with salt and hot pepper sauce as desired.

To Serve

Warm meat with barbecue sauce and serve in chaffing dish with a basket of small, soft rolls for mini sandwiches.

SERVES 18 TO 24 AS PART OF A BUFFET

INGREDIENTS

4 tablespoons butter

4 medium onions, thinly sliced

1 4 pound center-loin pork roast

1 teaspoon salt

1 teaspoon pepper

1 garlic clove, minced

3 cups beer

THE SAUCE

1 tablespoon vegetable oil

1 cup minced onion

2 tablespoons minced garlic

$2/3$ cup red wine vinegar

2 cups tomato puree

1 cup brown sugar

$1/2$ cup maple syrup

2 tablespoons Worcestershire sauce

Salt to taste

Hot pepper sauce (such as Tabasco) to taste

KITCHEN KLIPS

Always make sure pork is well done. Use a meat thermometer when in doubt. Rare pork can be dangerous!

Seasoned CHICKEN Strips

Cut each chicken beast in half into 3 long strips. Mix together egg whites and sherry. Marinate chicken in sherry and egg white mixture for 30 minutes, or up to 8 hours.

Mix breadcrumbs with herbs and salt and pepper. Heat $1/2$-inch layer of olive oil in heavy sauté pan over medium-high heat, and stir in half the garlic. Coat chicken strips with seasoned breadcrumbs and place half of them in oil until golden brown and cooked. Drain on paper towel, and reserve in oven on tray while frying remaining chicken. Add remaining garlic to pan and additional oil, if needed, before frying.

SERVES 6 TO 8

INGREDIENTS

- 3 skinless, boneless chicken breasts, split into 6 halves
- 3 egg whites, slightly beaten
- 1/4 cup sherry
- 2 cups breadcrumbs
- 2 tablespoons dried Italian herb blend
- 1 tablespoon salt
- Cracked pepper, to taste
- 1/2 cup of extra virgin olive oil for frying
- 2 tablespoons minced fresh garlic

KITCHEN KLIPS

Marinating chicken in sherry and egg white, with the addition of a little cornstarch, is called velvetizing. The sherry tenderizes the chicken and the egg white and cornstarch cause a coating that seals in the juices for a "velvety" texture.

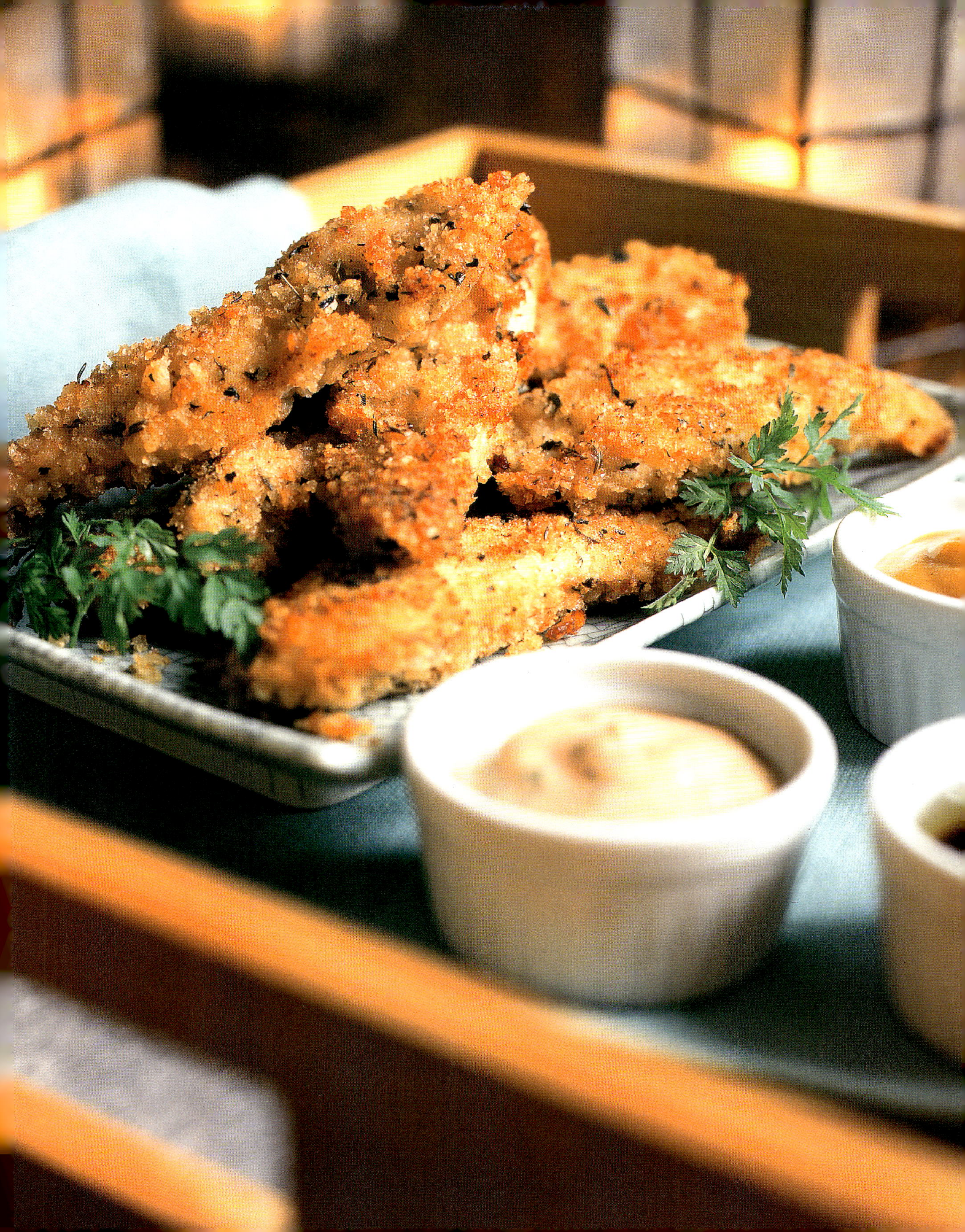

Party PEANUT BRITTLE

Spread peanuts in an even layer on a buttered jelly roll pan. Stir together sugar, syrup, and water in large, heavy saucepan or Dutch oven over medium-high heat to combine, and allow contents to boil softly. Reduce heat to maintain boil and cook to very golden brown (hard crack on candy thermometer) about 25 minutes or so.

Turn off heat and stir in butter and baking soda. Caution: When the baking soda is stirred in, the mixture foams up quickly and settles down. Pour over nuts and allow to cool and harden. Break into pieces to serve.

SERVES UP TO 24 FOR A BUFFET

INGREDIENTS

- 1½ pounds unsalted peanuts
- 4 cups granulated sugar
- 1 cup light Karo syrup
- 1 cup water
- 4 tablespoons butter, cut into bits
- 2 teaspoons baking soda

La Bohème MERINGUES

Using an electric beater, beat egg whites with cream of tartar and slowly add the sugar, one tablespoon at a time, until soft peaks form. Beat in vanilla and continue to beat until glossy and stiff peaks form. Quickly place meringue in pastry bag fitted with fluted tip.

Preheat oven to 275°. Pipe 2-inch rounds with a pointed top onto a parchment paper-lined cookie sheet. Bake in preheated 275° oven for 20 minutes. Reduce heat to 225° and bake another hour or until crisp. Store in airtight container until ready to serve.

To serve, melt chocolate chips and dip bottom of meringues into chocolate and then into the chopped walnuts. Place on waxed paper and, when finished with all meringues, drizzle remaining chocolate over the tops in a decorative fashion. Chill briefly to harden chocolate and serve immediately.

SERVES 14

INGREDIENTS

- 5 egg whites
- 1 teaspoon cream of tartar
- ⅔ cup granulated sugar
- ½ teaspoon vanilla extract
- 8 ounces chocolate chips
- 4 ounces chopped walnuts

A SPECIAL THANK YOU TO

ALTON ENTERTAINMENT:
ABBEY LEVINE, RICK RODGERS, ALEX KELEDJIAN
CHRIS SNYDER, GREG BERG, LINDA JAMES, KEN MARANGELL,
and DIANE DESTEFANO

MIAMI ALTON FRIENDS:
LARRY, JOHN, and JEANIE

LOCATION PRODUCTION CREW:
GARY SKYLES, Producer, Director, Writer
ISAAC RODRIGUEZ, Camera
RAUL MARTIN, Camera
ISAK BEN AMIR, Audio
EDDIE GARCIA, Still Photographer
GREG SACHS, My good friend and the best trainer in the Universe

WEDU, TAMPA:
HEATHER MUDRICK
PAUL GROVE

KCBS, LOS ANGELES:
especially PHYLLIS COBLENTZ, BARBARA ANN CHACONE,
and JOHN SEVERINO

COPLEY NEWS SERVICE, especially GLENDA WINDERS, editor and friend

ANTOINETTE, CAROL LEE, MATT, KATIE, AL, ANN,
and the whole cast and crew at NBC'S *TODAY SHOW*

GREATDAYAMERICA.COM

AMERIWARE COOKWARE
(for direct sales call 1-800-764-2005)

GE.COM

SUR LA TABLE for all the photo props!

THE KITCHEN CONNECTION, Los Angeles

INDEX

A

Alderwood Smoked Salmon Salad 162
Almond:
   Danish, Orange 175
   Orange Loaf, Apple 173
Antipasto, Grilled Artichoke 38
Appetizers:
   Alderwood Smoked Salmon Salad 162
   Bordeaux Olive Pâté and Herb Toasts 119
   Brooklyn Potato Latkes 141
   Cajun Dipped Shrimp 59
   Chicken Sesame Lettuce Wraps 20
   Chopped Herring 163
   Crab Firecrackers 101
   Curried New Potatoes with Caviar 122
   Dungeness Crab Summer Rolls 121
   Gingered Crab Puffs 18
   Grilled Artichoke Antipasto 38
   Loaded Potato Skins 142
   Marinated Artichoke Bruschetta 39
   Oysters Florentine with White Truffles 60
   Poached Scallop Seviche 59
   Queso Fundido 103
   Quick and Cheesy Jalapeño Roll-Ups 100
   Shiitake Mushroom Boxes 21
   Sicilian Eggplant Bruschetta 40
   Shooter Shrimp 101
   Shrimp Toasts 186
   Thrice Cooked Artichokes 78
   Toasted Tofu and Friends 86
Apple:
   Baked, Ginger 90
   Orange Loaf, Almond 173
   Salad, Cabbage, and Onion 167
Apricot Chutney 47
Artichoke:
   Antipasto, Grilled 38
   Bruschetta, Marinated 39
   Thrice Cooked 78
Asparagus, Salad, Purple 181

B

Balsamic Grilled Veggies 84
Barbecue:
   Maple Barbecued Pork 189
   Red Currant Barbecued Ribs 62
Barry's Irish Coffee 156
Basil Cheese Stuffed Manicotti 46
Basil Shrimp Scampi 45
Bayou Greens and Dijon Vinaigrette 56
Beans:
   and Black-Eyed Peas 69
   Green, French, Quick Pickled 150
   Refried, Jumping 110
Beef:
   Corned Beef and Cabbage Reuben 126
   Grilled Pepper Steak 143
   Lemongrass Beef 24
   Shredded Beef and Brie Tostadas 104
   Sweet and Sour Swedish Meatball Stew 169
Beets, Salad of Pickled 167
Benevenuto Swordfish and Brown Rice 45
Bergen Shellfish Soup 162
Berry Peach Crumble 154
Beverages:
   Barry's Irish Coffee 156
   Chef Harry's Frozen Margaritas 113
   Date Granola Shake 91
   Spiced Citrus Cider 157
   Venetian Coffees 51
Black Bottomed Lemon Meringue Pie 153
Black-Eyed Peas and Beans 69
Blue Cheese Wheat Tart with Caramelized Onions 184
Blue Grass Pasta 68
Bordeaux Olive Pâté and Herb Toasts 119
Brandied Coffee 51
Brie:
   Topped with Peaches in Phyllo Pastry 186
   Tostadas, Shredded Beef 104
Bread:
   Grandma's Corn Bread Dressing 147
   Marinated Artichoke Bruschetta 39
   Sicilian Eggplant Bruschetta 40
   Tuscan Bread Salad 39
Brooklyn Potato Latkes 141
Brown Rice:
   and Benevenuto Swordfish 45
   Cashew 88
   Custard 156
   Latin Style 110
   Rickshaw Duck Fried Rice 28
   Shellfish Gumbo 63
Brownies, Cream Cheese and Raspberry Sauce 88
Brunch Dishes, see Lunch dishes
Bruschetta:
   Marinated Artichoke 39
   Sicilian Eggplant 40
Brussels Sprouts, Caramelized 87
Burger, Easy Soy 83
Buttermilk dressing, in Chopped Cobb Salad 123

C

Cabbage:
   Corned Beef and Cabbage Reuben 126
   Salad, Apple and Onion Salad 167
Caesar Salad with Rosemary Croutons 183
Cajun Dipped Shrimp 59
Cake(s):
   Angel, Mandarin Orange, Pudding with Caramel Sauce 32
   Grapefruit, with Pineapple Frosting 133
   Lemon, with Strawberry Sauce 49
   Pineapple Yam 31
   Salmon, Smoked, with Caviar Cucumber Chutney 124
Candy:
   Party Peanut Brittle 192
Caramel:
   Sauce, Quick Warm 91
Caramelized:
   Brussel Sprouts 87
   Greens and Onions 67
Carrot, Cha-Cha Mango Salad 105
Cashew Brown Rice 88
Catfish, in Fjord's Fish and Chips with Dilled Tartar Sauce 168
Caviar:
   Curried New Potatoes with 122
   Salmon Cakes with Caviar Cucumber Chutney 124
Cha-Cha Carrot Mango Salad 105
Cheese:
   Blue, Wheat Tart with Caramelized Onions 184
   Farmer's Cottage Cheese 140
   Flan, Chocolate 111
   Jalapeño Roll-Ups 100
   Jazzy Cheddar Spread 180
   Soufflé in a Pan 150
   Stuffed Manicotti, Basil 46
   Three Cheese Pâté with Toasted Leek 180
Chef Harry's Frozen Margaritas:
   Plain, Watermelon, Raspberry 113
Chicken:
   Coolio's Special Satay 23
   Cutlets, Tennessee Whiskey 61
   Potato Pie, Roasted 149
   Roasted, Rosemary 149
   Salad, Elegant 127
   Sesame Lettuce Wraps 20
   Strips, Seasoned 190
   Southern Comfort Chicken 66
   with Rice Noodles and Spicy Peanut Sauce, smoked 27
Chilaquiles 109
Chocolate:
   Café Chocolate, Venetian Coffees 51
   Cheese Flan 111
   Patricia's Chocolate Ecstasy 112
Chopped Cobb Salad 123
Chopped Herring 163
Chutney:
   Apricot, Garlic Crusted Pork Chops with 47
   Caviar Cucumber, Smoked Salmon Cakes with 124
   Ginger Garlic, Poached Salmon with 132
   Lentil and Corn 79
Cinnamon red hots, in Spiced Citrus Cider 157
Citrus Scallop Salad 125
Citrus Sorbet 50
Cobb Salad, Chopped 123
Coconut:
   Crusted Snapper 26
   Custard Pie 71
   Dipping Sauce, Peanut 23
Coffee:
   Barry's Irish Coffee 156
   Venetian Coffees, 51
Coolio's Special Satay 23
Corn:
   Chutney, and Lentil 79
   Grandma's Corn Bread Dressing 147
Corned Beef and Cabbage Reuben 126
Cottage Cheese, Farmer's 140
Country Meatloaf in Sour Cream Pastry 170
Crab:
   Cakes, Southern Style 60
   Firecrackers 101
   Puffs, Gingered 18
   Summer Rolls, Dungeness 121
Cranberry Citrus Relish 147
Crawfish and Wild Rice Salad 163
Cream Cheese Brownies and Raspberry Sauce 88
Croutons:
   Rosemary, Caesar Salad with 183
   Sourdough 123
Cucumber:
   Caviar Chutney, Salmon Cakes with 124
   Salad, Japanese 31
Curried New Potatoes with Caviar 122

D

Danish Pancakes 173
Danish, Orange Almond 175
Date Granola Shake 91
Desserts:
   Apple Almond Orange Loaf 173
   Berry Peach Crumble 154
   Black Bottomed Lemon Meringue Pie 153
   Brown Rice Custard 156
   Citrus Sorbet 50
   Chocolate Cheese Flan 111
   Coconut Custard Pie 71
   Danish Pancakes 173
   Fruit Confit 174
   Fruits over Vanilla Bean Ice Cream 32
   Ginger Baked Apples 90
   Ginger Lemon Tarts 134
   Grapefruit Cake with Pineapple Frosting 133
   La Bohème Meringues 192
   Lemon Cake with Strawberry Sauce 49
   Mandarin Orange Angel Cake Pudding with Caramel Sauce 32
   Orange Almond Danish 175
   Orange Sesame Yam Pudding 69
   Party Peanut Brittle 192
   Patricia's Chocolate Ecstasy 112
   Peach Ginger Muffins 174
   Quick Ginger Pecan Pie Crust 70
   Quick Warm Caramel Sauce 91
   Sweet Potato Pie 71

Tequila Drenched Fruit 90
Dijon Vinaigrette, Bayou Greens and 56
Dips:
   Muy Picante Salsa 98
   Papaya Salsa 99
   Peanut Coconut Dipping Sauce 23
   Tomatillo Salsa 99
   Tzatziki 26
   Yatze Schmear 140
   Yellow Tomato Salsa 98
Dressing, Grandma's Corn Bread 147
Dressing, Salad:
   Buttermilk dressing 123
   Thousand Island 126
   Warm Pecan, Salad Medley with 56
Drinks, see Beverages
Duck:
   Oyster Mushroom Duck with Jasmine Tea Pancakes 25
   Rickshaw Duck Fried Rice 28
Dungeness Crab Summer Rolls 121

E

Easy Soy Burger 83
Egg:
   Cheese Soufflé 150
   Foo Young, Vegetable 81
   Omelet, White, Veggie 148
   Salad "90265" 129
Eggplant:
   Balsamic Grilled Veggies 84
   Bruschetta, Sicilian 40
   Grilled 86
   Pasta à la Melanzane 84

F

Farmer's Cottage Cheese 140
Fettuccine:
   Pasta Carbonalfredo 44
   with Roasted Vegetables 128
   with Toasted Walnut Sauce 83
   50s Meatloaf and Toasted Scallion Mashed Potatoes 144
Fish:
   and Chips with Dilled Tartar Sauce 168
   Grouper, Hazelnut 65
   Herring, Chopped 163
   Salmon Cakes, Smoked, with Caviar Cucumber Chutney 124
   Salmon, Poached, with Ginger Garlic Chutney 132
   Salmon Salad, Smoked 162
   Snapper, Coconut Crusted 26
   Swordfish and Brown Rice 45
   Trout, Garlic Crusted 44
Fjord's Fish and Chips with Dilled Tartar Sauce 168
Flan, Chocolate Cheese 111
French Green Beans, Quick Pickled 150
Fried Rice, Rickshaw Duck 28
Fruit:
   Citrus Sorbet 50
   Confit 174

Lemon Cake with Strawberry Sauce 49
Mandarin Orange Angel Cake Pudding with Caramel Sauce 32 over Vanilla Bean Ice Cream 32
Tequila Drenched 90
Frosting:
   Pineapple, Grapefruit Cake with 133

G

Garlic:
   and Chive Mashed Potatoes 146
   Pork Chops, Crusted, with Apricot Chutney 47
   Trout, Crusted Trout 44
   Spinach Sauté, Pecan 152
Ginger:
   Baked Apples 90
   Crab Puffs 18
   Garlic Chutney 132
   Lemon Tarts 134
   Muffins, Peach 174
   Pecan Pie Crust, Quick 70
Goat cheese:
   Blue Grass Pasta 68
   Chopped Cobb Salad 123
   Crab Firecrackers 101
   Tzatziki 26
Grandma's Corn Bread Dressing 147
Granola, Date Shake 91
Grapefruit:
   Cake with Pineapple Frosting 133
   Citrus Sorbet 50
Green Beans, Quick Pickled French 150
Greens:
   Bayou, and Dijon Vinaigrette 56
   Caramelized Greens and Onions 67
Grilled:
   Artichoke Antipasto 38
   Balsamic Grilled Veggies 84
   Eggplant 86
   Lamb Chops, Rosemary, with Mediterranean Salsa 42
   Pepper Steak 143
Gumbo, Shellfish 63
Grouper, Hazelnut 65

H

Hazelnut, Grouper 65
Herb Toasts, Bordeaux Olive Pâté and 119
Herring, Chopped 163
Hominy, in South-of-the-Border Posole 108

I

Ice Cream, Fruits over Vanilla Bean 32
Irish Coffee, Barry's 156

J

Jalapeños, Quick and Cheesy Roll-Ups, 100

Japanese Cucumber Salad 31
Jasmine Tea Pancakes, Oyster Mushroom Duck with 25
Jazzy Cheddar Spread 180
Jesse James Soup 118
Jumping Refried Beans 110

K

Kasha, Mom's 87

L

La Bohème Meringues 192
Lamb Chops, with Mediterranean Salsa, Rosemary Grilled 42
Langosta, Baked Stuffed 107
Lasagna:
   Roasted Pepper 187
   Quick Tofu 80
Latkes, Brooklyn Potato 141
Leek, Three Cheese Pâté with Toasted 180
Lemon:
   Cake with Strawberry Sauce 49
   Citrus Sorbet 50
   Meringue Pie, Black Bottomed 153
   Spiced Citrus Cider 157
   Tarts, Ginger 134
Lemongrass Beef 24
Lentil and Corn Chutney 79
Lime:
   Citrus Sorbet 50
   Spiced Citrus Cider 157
Loaded Potato Skins 142
Loaf, Apple Almond Orange 173
Lobster:
   Baked Stuffed Langosta 107
   Bergen Shellfish Soup 162
Lunch Dishes:
   Bordeaux Olive Pâté and Herb Toasts 119
   Chopped Cobb Salad 123
   Citrus Scallop Salad 125
   Corned Beef and Cabbage Reuben 126
   Curried New Potatoes with Caviar 122
   Dungeness Crab Summer Rolls 121
   Egg Salad "90265" 129
   Elegant Chicken Salad 127
   Fettuccine with Roasted Vegetables 128
   Ginger Lemon Tarts 134
   Grapefruit Cake with Pineapple Frosting 133
   Jesse James Soup 118
   Poached Salmon with Ginger Garlic Chutney 132
   Red and White New Potato Salad 131
   Smoked Salmon Cakes with Caviar Cucumber Chutney 124

M

Mandarin Orange:
   Angel Cake Pudding with Caramel

Sauce 32
Citrus Scallop Salad 125
Mango:
   Cha-Cha Carrot Salad 105
   Fruits over Vanilla Bean Ice Cream 32
Manicotti, Basil Cheese Stuffed 46
Maple Barbecued Pork 189
Margaritas, Chef Harry's Frozen:
   Plain, Watermelon, Raspberry 113
Marinated Artichoke Bruschetta 39
Mashed Potatoes:
   Garlic and Chive 146
   Toasted Scallion, 50's Meatloaf and 144
Meat, see Beef, Lamb, Pork, Veal
Meatball Stew, Sweet and Sour Swedish 169
Meatloaf:
   and Toasted Scallion Mashed Potatoes, 50's 144
   in Sour Cream Pastry, Country 170
Meringue:
   Black Bottomed Lemon Pie 153
   La Bohème Meringues 192
Mexican cheese:
   Queso Fundido 103
Miso, Quick Soup 18
Mom's Kasha 87
Mozzarella:
   Basil Cheese Stuffed Manicotti 46
   Quick Tofu Lasagna 80
   Roasted Pepper Lasagna 187
   Salad Medley with Warm Pecan Dressing 56
Muffins, Peach Ginger 174
Mushrooms:
   Oyster, Duck with Jasmine Tea Pancakes 25
   Shiitake, Boxes 21
Mussel, Portuguese Pot 40
Muy Picante Salsa 98

N

New Potatoes:
   Jesse James Soup 118
   Salad, Red and White 131
   with Caviar, Curried 122
Noodles, Smoked Chicken with Rice and Spicy Peanut Sauce 27

O

Oatmeal, in Berry Peach Crumble 154
Olives:
   Bordeaux, Pâté and Herb Toasts 119
   in Chopped Cobb Salad 123
   in Marinated Artichoke Bruschetta 39
   in Quick and Cheesy Jalapeño Roll-Ups 100
Omelet, Veggie, Egg White 148
Onions:
   Carmelized, Blue Cheese Wheat Tart with 184
   Caramelized Greens and 67

INDEX **197**

Salad, Cabbage, Apple, and 167
Orange:
   Almond Danish 175
   Angel Cake, Mandarin Pudding with Caramel Sauce 32
   Citrus Sorbet 50
   Loaf, Apple Almond 173
   Sesame Yam Pudding 69
   Spiced Citrus Cider 157
Oyster:
   Florentine with White Truffles 60
   Mushroom Duck with Jasmine Tea Pancakes 25

P

Pancakes:
   Danish 173
   Jasmine Tea, Oyster Mushroom Duck with 25
Papaya Salsa 99
Parmesan cheese:
   Caesar Salad with Rosemary Croutons 183
   Cheese Soufflé in a Pan 150
   Fettuccine with Roasted Vegetables 128
   Pasta à la Melanzane 84
   Pasta Carbonalfredo 44
   Roasted Pepper Lasagna 187
Party Dishes:
   Blue Cheese Wheat Tart with Caramelized Onions 184
   Brie Topped with Peaches in Phyllo Pastry 186
   Caesar Salad with Rosemary Croutons 183
   Jazzy Cheddar Spread 180
   La Bohème Meringues 192
   Maple Barbecued Pork 189
   Party Peanut Brittle 192
   Peachy Salad in Poppy Seed Vinaigrette 181
   Purple Asparagus Salad 181
   Roasted Pepper Lasagna 187
   Scalloped Potatoes with Pork Sausage 188
   Seasoned Chicken Strips 190
   Shrimp Toasts 186
   Three Cheese Pâté with Toasted Leek 180
Party Peanut Brittle 192
Pasta:
   à la Melanzane 84
   Basil Cheese Stuffed Manicotti 46
   Blue Grass 68
   Carbonalfredo 44
   Fettuccine with Roasted Vegetables 128
   Fettuccine with Toasted Walnut Sauce 83
   Quick Tofu Lasagna 80
   Roasted Pepper Lasagna 187
   Smoked Chicken with Rice Noodles and Spicy Peanut Sauce 27
Pastry:
   Brie Topped with Peaches in Phyllo 186
   Shiitake Mushroom Boxes 21

Sour Cream, Country Meatloaf in 170
Pâté:
   Bordeaux Olive, and Herb Toasts 119
   Three Cheese, with Toasted Leek 180
Patricia's Chocolate Ecstasy 112
Peach(es):
   Berry Crumble 154
   Ginger Muffins 174
   Peachy Salad in Poppy Seed Vinaigrette 181
   Topped with, Brie, in Phyllo Pastry 186
Peanut:
   Brittle, Party 192
   Dipping Sauce, Coconut 23
   Sauce, Smoked Chicken with Rice Noodles and 27
Pea(s):
   Black-Eyed, and Beans 69
   Roasted Chicken Potato Pie 149
   Soup, Potato 164
Pecan:
   Dressing, Warm, Salad Medley with 56
   Garlic Spinach Sauté 152
   Pie Crust, Quick Ginger 70
Pepper(s):
   Dusted Shrimp Tempura 30
   Lasagna, Roasted 187
   Steak, Grilled 143
Pickled:
   Beets, Salad of 167
   Chopped Herring 163
   French Green Beans, Quick 150
Pie:
   Chicken Potato, Roasted 149
   Coconut Custard 71
   Crust, Ginger Pecan, Quick 70
   Lemon Meringue, Black Bottomed 153
   Sweet Potato 71
Pie Crust, Quick Ginger Pecan 70
Pineapple:
   Frosting, Grapefruit Cake with 133
   Fruits over Vanilla Bean Ice Cream 32
   Glazed Spareribs 29
   Rickshaw Duck Fried Rice 28
   Yam Cakes 31
Poached:
   Citrus Scallop Salad 125
   Salmon with Ginger Garlic Chutney 132
   Scallop Seviche 59
Pork:
   Barbecued, Maple 189
   Chops, Garlic Crusted, with Apricot Chutney 47
   Country Meatloaf in Sour Cream Pastry 170
   50s Meatloaf and Toasted Scallion Mashed Potatoes 144
   Sausage, Scalloped Potatoes with 188
   Queso Fundido 103

Portuguese Mussel Pot 40
Posole, South-of-the-Border 108
Potatoe(s):
   Fjord's Fish and Chips with Dilled Tartar Sauce 168
   Latkes, Brooklyn 141
   Mashed, Garlic and Chive 146
   Mashed, Toasted Scallion, 50s Meatloaf and 144
   New, Curried, with Caviar 122
   Pie, Chicken, Roasted 149
   Salad, New, Red and White 131
   Scalloped, with Pork Sausage 188
   Skins, Loaded 142
   Soup, and Pea Soup 164
Poultry, see chicken and turkey
Pudding:
   Mandarin Orange Angel Cake, with Caramel Sauce 32
   Orange Sesame Yam 69
Puffs, Gingered Crab 18
Pumpkin, Soup in Pumpkin Bowls 76
Purple Asparagus Salad 181

Q

Queso Fundido 103
Quick and Cheesy Jalapeño Roll-Ups 100
Quick Ginger Pecan Pie Crust 70
Quick Miso Soup 18
Quick Pickled French Green Beans 150
Quick Tofu Lasagna 80
Quick Warm Caramel Sauce 91

R

Radicchio:
   Balsamic Grilled Veggies 84
   Salad Medley with Warm Pecan Dressing 56
Radish, Salad, White 77
Raspberry(ies):
   Chef Harry's Frozen Margaritas 113
   Sauce, Cream Cheese Brownies and 88
   Tequila Drenched Fruit 90
Red and White New Potato Salad 131
Red Currant Barbecued Ribs 62
Refried Beans, Jumping 110
Relish, Cranberry Citrus 147
Reuben, Corned Beef and Cabbage 126
Ribs:
   Barbecued, Red Currant 62
   Pineapple Glazed Spareribs 29
Rice:
   Brown, Benevenuto Swordfish and 45
   Brown, Latin Style 110
   Cashew, Brown 88
   Custard, Brown 156
   Fried, Rickshaw Duck, 28
   Noodles, and Spicy Peanut Sauce, Smoked Chicken with 27

Salad, Wild, Crawfish and 163
Rickshaw Duck Fried Rice 28
Ricotta:
   Basil Cheese Stuffed Manicotti 46
   Quick Tofu Lasagna 80
Roasted:
   Chicken Potato Pie 149
   Vegetables, Fettuccine with 128
   Vegetables, Winter, Rosemary Roasted 80
Rolls, Dungeness Crab Summer 121
Roll-Ups, Quick and Cheesy Jalapeño 100
Rosemary:
   Croutons, Caesar Salad with 183
   Lamb Chops, Grilled, with Mediterranean Salsa 42

S

Salad:
   Alderwood Smoked Salmon 162
   Bayou Greens and Dijon Vinaigrette 56
   Cabbage, Apple, and Onion 167
   Caesar, with Rosemary Croutons 183
   Cha-Cha Carrot Mango 105
   Chopped Cobb 123
   Citrus Scallop 125
   Crawfish and Wild Rice 163
   Egg, "90265" 129
   Elegant Chicken 127
   in Poppy Seed Vinaigrette, Peachy 181
   Japanese Cucumber 31
   Medley with Warm Pecan Dressing 56
   of Pickled Beets 167
   Purple Asparagus 181
   Red and White New Potato 131
   Tuscan Bread 39
   White Radish 77
Salmon:
   Cakes with Caviar Cucumber Chutney 124
   Curried New Potatoes with Caviar 122
   Poached, with Ginger Garlic Chutney 132
   Salad, Smoked, Alderwood 162
Salsa:
   Mediterranean, Rosemary Grilled Lamb Chops with 42
   Muy Picante 98
   Papaya 99
   Tomatillo 99
   Yellow Tomato 98
Sandwiches:
   Corned Beef and Cabbage Reuben 126
Sauce(s):
   Caramel, Mandarin Orange Angel Cake Pudding with 32
   Caramel, Quick Warm 91
   Peanut Coconut Dipping 23
   Raspberry, Cream Cheese Brownies and 88
   Sesame Scallion 30

Tartar, Dilled, Fjord's Fish and Chips with 168
Walnut, Toasted, Fettuccine with 83
Sausage, Scalloped Potatoes with Pork 188
Sauté, Pecan Garlic Spinach 152
Scallions, 50s Meatloaf and Toasted Mashed Potatoes 144
Scalloped Potatoes with Pork Sausage 188
Scallops:
   Bergen Shellfish Soup 162
   Poached, Seviche 59
   Salad, Citrus Scallop 125
   Shellfish Gumbo 63
Scampi, Basil Shrimp 45
Schmear, Yatze 140
Seafood, see fish; shellfish
Seasoned Chicken Strips 190
Sesame:
   Lettuce Wraps, Chicken 20
   Scallion Sauce 30
   Yam Pudding, Orange 69
Seviche, Poached Scallop 59
Shake, Date Granola 91
Shellfish:
   Baked Stuffed Langosta 107
   Basil Shrimp Scampi 45
   Bergen Shellfish Soup 162
   Cajun Dipped Shrimp 59
   Citrus Scallop Salad 125
   Crab Firecrackers 101
   Crawfish and Wild Rice Salad 163
   Dungeness Crab Summer Rolls 121
   Gingered Crab Puffs 18
   Gumbo 63
   Oysters Florentine with White Truffles 60
   Pepper Dusted Shrimp Tempura 30
   Poached Scallop Seviche 59
   Portuguese Mussel Pot 40
   Shooter Shrimp 101
   Shrimp Toasts 186
Shiitake Mushroom Boxes 21
Shredded Beef and Brie Tostados 104
Shrimp:
   Basil Shrimp Scampi 45
   Bergen Shellfish Soup 162
   Cajun Dipped 59
   Shellfish Gumbo 63
   Shooter 101
   Tempura, Pepper Dusted 30
   Toasts 186
Sicilian Eggplant Bruschetta 40
Skins, Loaded Potato 142
Smoked Chicken with Rice Noodles and Spicy Peanut Sauce 27
Snapper, Coconut Crusted 26
Sorbet, Citrus 50
Soufflé, Cheese in a Pan 150
Soup:
   Bergen Shellfish 162

Jesse James 118
Potato Pea 164
Pumpkin, in Pumpkin Bowls 76
Quick Miso 18
Tortilla 96
Winter Squash 76
Sour Cream, Country Meatloaf in Pastry 170
Southern Comfort Chicken 66
Southern Style Crab Cakes 60
South-of-the-Border Posole 108
Soy, Easy Burger 83
Spareribs, Pineapple Glazed 29
Spiced Citrus Cider 157
Spinach:
   Oysters Florentine with White Truffles 60
   Pecan Garlic Sauté 152
Squash:
   Pumpkin Soup in Pumpkin Bowls 76
   Soup, Winter 76
Steak, Grilled Pepper 143
Stew, Sweet and Sour Swedish Meatball 169
Strawberry(ies):
   Berry Peach Crumble 154
   Sauce, Lemon Cake with 49
   Tequila Drenched Fruit 90
Sweet and Sour Swedish Meatball Stew 169
Sweet Potato Pie 71
Swordfish, Benevenuto and Brown Rice 45

T

Tart(s):
   Blue Cheese Wheat with Caramelized Onions 184
   Ginger Lemon 134
Tartar Sauce, Dilled 168
Tempura, Pepper Dusted Shrimp 30
Tennessee Whiskey Chicken Cutlets 61
Tequila:
   Chef Harry's Frozen Margaritas 113
   Chocolate Cheese Flan 111
   Drenched Fruit 90
   Shooter Shrimp 101
Thousand Island Dressing 126
Three Cheese Pâté with Toasted Leek 180
Thrice Cooked Artichokes 78
Toasted Leek, Three Cheese Pâté with 180
Toasts:
   Herb, Bordeaux Olive Pâté and 119
   Shrimp 186
Tofu:
   Lasagna, Quick 80
   Toasted, and Friends 86
Tomatillo:
   Salsa 99
   Tortilla Soup 96
Tomato:
   Basil Cheese Stuffed Manicotti 46

Benevenuto Swordfish and Brown Rice 45
Bergen Shellfish Soup 162
Chopped Cobb Salad 123
Crawfish and Wild Rice Salad 163
Egg Salad "90265" 129
Farmer's Cottage Cheese 140
Fettuccine with Roasted Vegetables 128
Jesse James Soup 118
Loaded Potato Skins 142
Maple Barbecued Pork 189
Marinated Artichoke Bruschetta 39
Poached Scallop Seviche 59
Portuguese Mussel Pot 40
Red and White New Potato Salad 131
Roasted Pepper Lasagna 187
Rosemary Grilled Lamb Chops with Mediterranean Salsa 42
Shellfish Gumbo 63
Shooter Shrimp 101
Sicilian Eggplant Bruschetta 40
Tomatillo Salsa 99
Tortilla Soup 96
Tuscan Bread Salad 39
White Radish Salad 77
Yellow Tomato Salsa 98
Tortilla Soup 96
Tostadas, Shredded Beef and Brie 104
Trout, Garlic Crusted 44
Truffles, Oysters Florentine with White 60
Turkey, Traditional 146
Tuscan Bread Salad 39
Tzatziki 26

V

Vanilla Bean Ice Cream, Fruits over 32
Veal:
   50s Meatloaf and Toasted Scallion Mashed Potatoes 144
Vegetable(s):
   Egg Foo Young 81
   Grilled, Balsamic 84
   Roasted, Fettuccine with 128
   Roasted, Winter, Rosemary 80
   Veggie Egg White Omelet 148
Vegetarian foods:
   Balsamic Grilled Veggies 84
   Caramelized Brussels Sprouts 87
   Cashew Brown Rice 88
   Cream Cheese Brownies and Raspberry Sauce 88
   Date Granola Shake 91
   Easy Soy Burger 83
   Fettuccine with Toasted Walnut Sauce 83
   Ginger Baked Apples 90
   Grilled Eggplant 86
   Lentil and Corn Chutney 79
   Mom's Kasha 87
   Pasta à la Melanzane 84
   Pumpkin Soup in Pumpkin Bowls 76

Quick Tofu Lasagna 80
Quick Warm Caramel Sauce 91
Rosemary Roasted Winter Vegetables 80
Tequila Drenched Fruit 90
Thrice Cooked Artichokes 78
Toasted Tofu and Friends 86
Vegetable Egg Foo Young 81
White Radish Salad 77
Winter Squash Soup 76
Venetian Coffees:
   Brandied Coffee 51
   Café Chocolate 51
Vinaigrette:
   Citrus 125
   Dijon, Bayou Greens and 56
   Poppy Seed, Peachy Salad in 181

W

Walnut:
   Elegant Chicken Salad 127
   Sauce, Toasted, Fettuccine with 83
Wheat Tart, Blue Cheese with Caramelized Onions 184
White Radish Salad 77
Wild Rice, Crawfish and Salad 163
Winter Squash Soup 76
Wraps, Chicken Sesame Lettuce 20

Y

Yam:
   Cakes, Pineapple 31
   Pudding, Orange Sesame 69
   Rosemary Roasted Winter Vegetables 80
Yatze Schmear 140
Yellow Tomato Salsa 98
Yogurt:
   Curried New Potatoes with Caviar 122
   Date Granola Shake 91
   Fjord's Fish and Chips with Dilled Tartar Sauce 168
   Tzatziki 26

Z

Zucchini:
   Balsamic Grilled Veggies 84
   Fettuccine with Roasted Vegetables 128

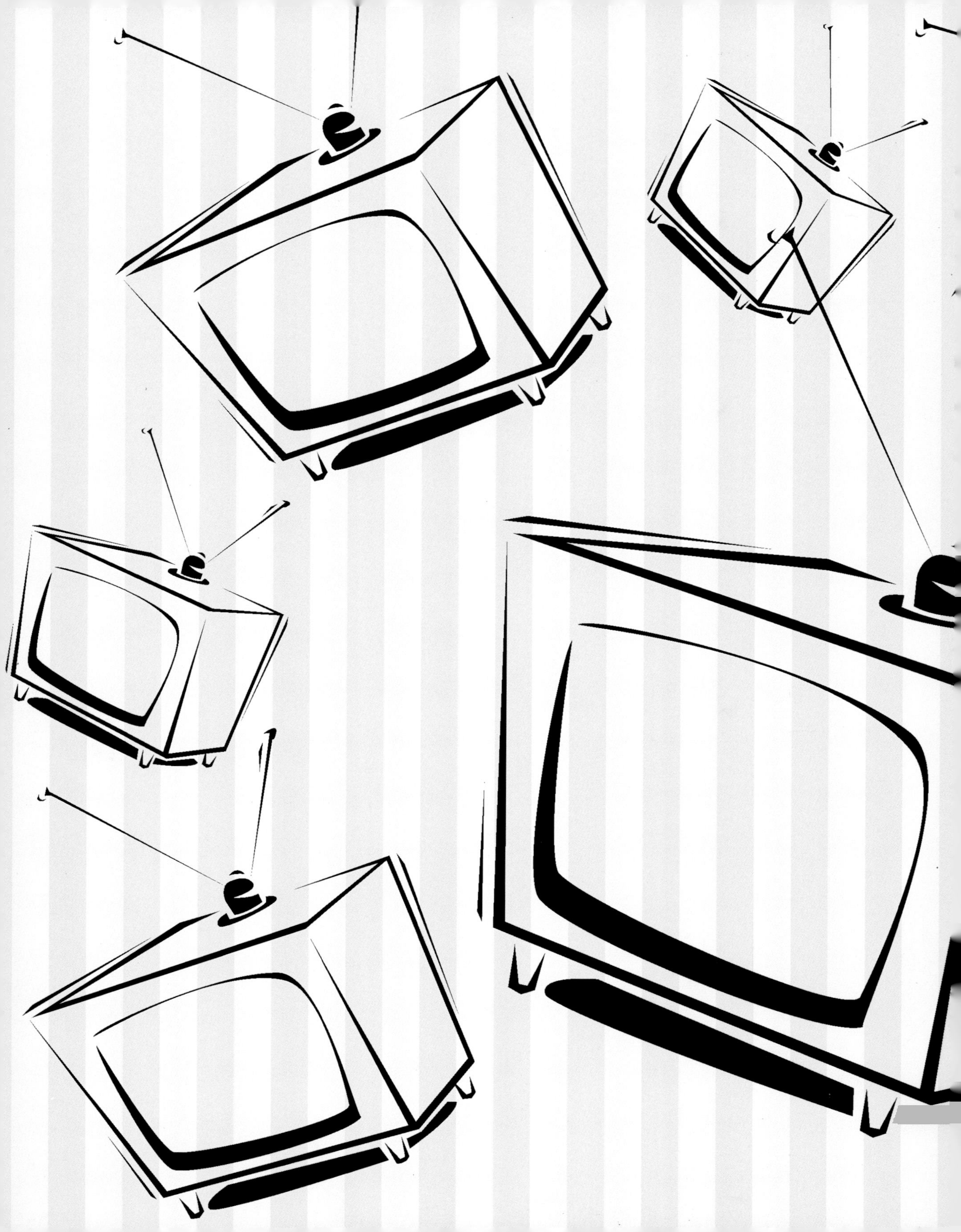